COACHING FOOTBALL'S
46 DEFENSE

Rex Ryan
Jeff Walker

Coaches Choice
www.coacheschoice.com

©1999 Coaches Choice. All rights reserved. Printed in the United States.

No part of this book may be reproduced, stored in a retrieval system, or transmitted, in any form or by any means, electronic, mechanical, photocopying, recording, or otherwise, without the prior permission of Coaches Choice.

ISBN: 1-58518-234-6
Library of Congress Catalog Card Number: 99-60462

Cover design and book layout: Paul Lewis
Front and back cover photos: Courtesy of the Baltimore Ravens

Coaches Choice
P.O. Box 1828
Monterey, CA 93942
www.coacheschoice.com

DEDICATION

I would like to dedicate this book to my two sons, Payton and Seth.

—R.R.

Dedicated to Dayson Nugent, Eagle Scout, Pacific war veteran, father and grandfather. And to Aileen Nugent, actress, playwright, master educator, mother and grandmother. Thanks for giving me a beautiful wife and providing Gabriel with a wonderful mother.

—J.W.

ACKNOWLEDGMENTS

During the course of writing this book on the "46," one individual worked tirelessly to get this book done. This book could not have become a reality without the effort and dedication of Jeff Walker. I would also like to thank my wife, Michelle, who has supported me throughout my career. Thanks to my dad for teaching me everything I know about defense.

—R.R.

Thanks to the following individuals: Terry Siddall, the best friend I never met, for his invaluable expertise, support, and input into the writing of this book; Rick Gohlke for his unerring friendship and brotherhood; Johnny Cryer for his longtime loyalty; Peter Parker for his amazing abilities; Greg Marquardt for helping me to understand the concept of working for the common good; and brother, Lonnie Sewell, for his unwavering support.

Further acknowledgment goes to the staff of St. Elizabeth Foundation in Baton Rouge, Louisiana, for their devotion to families and their part in answered prayers. And thanks to one tough football player, Jimmy Pace, and his Johnson City classmates for being the students that every teacher dreams of teaching.

—J.W.

CONTENTS

Dedication 3

Acknowledgments 4

Preface 7

Chapter

1 Background of the 46 Defense 9

2 The 46 Pressure Philosophy 14

3 Characteristics of the 46 Bear Defense 19

4 Principles of Defensive Line Play 21

5 Defensive Line Play versus the Run 29

6 Pass Rush Techniques 55

7 Linebacker and Strong Safety Play 61

8 Defending the Option 67

9 Secondary 87

10 46 Stunts and Blitzes 159

About the Authors 178

PREFACE

In January of 1986, the Chicago Bears' defense, "the Monsters of the Midway," held the New England Patriots to a mere 10 points in Super Bow XX. The "46" defense utilized by the Bears held their opponent to six yards rushing. This 46-10 victory followed a record-setting season. A season which included an 18-1 record, back-to-back play-off shutouts, and 72 quarterback sacks, leading many to call this defense the greatest in NFL history. The architect of that defense is my father, Buddy Ryan. The "46" was not designed in 1985 as some people believe. The "46" had its beginnings in the early 1980s as a way to put pressure on the passer. The following year, this system was redesigned into the system seen today. Buddy played this aggressive style every down and was just as successful stopping the run as he was the pass.

Since that time, his system has been implemented by several professional teams and some college teams. In the eight years I have coordinated this system, my defenses have ranked nationally five years. In his first year as defensive coordinator at Oklahoma State University, my brother Rob turned a poor defensive unit into a nationally ranked defense. It has also been successfully integrated into the high school level. Kevin Carty, head football coach at Sommerville High School in New Jersey, took over an 0-10 program, introduced the "46" and took them to the state championship in one season.

My father says the "46" puts pressure on everybody on offense—not just the quarterback. This system will make good players great, average players good.

—R.R.

CHAPTER 1

BACKGROUND OF THE 46 DEFENSE

Without question the most dominating defensive scheme in the history of the National Football League, the 46 Defense applies pressure to every offensive flank and debilitates every phase of the hand-off running game. Unlike the popular 4-3 slide front and other "pass-conscious" 7-man front schemes, the 46 is a fundamental defensive structure of the attacking 8-man front family. A "stop-the-run-first" defense, the 46 presents a formidable defense for run-based offenses at all levels of play.

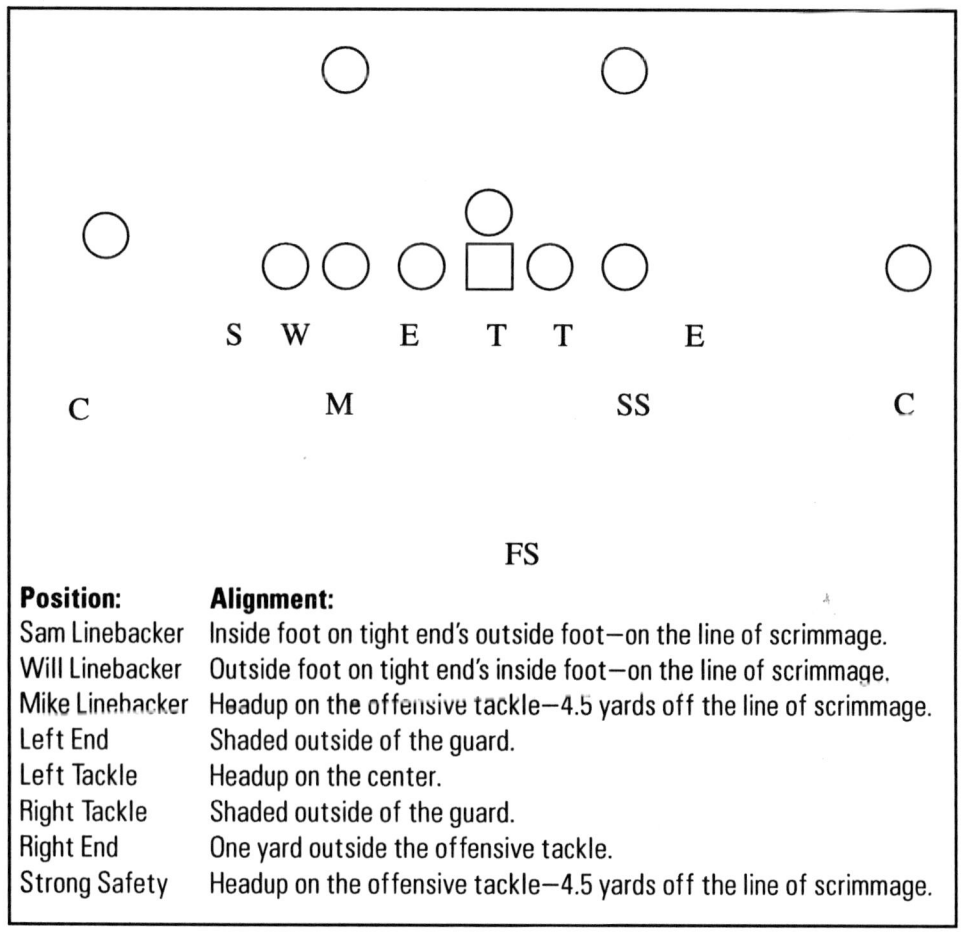

Position:	Alignment:
Sam Linebacker	Inside foot on tight end's outside foot—on the line of scrimmage.
Will Linebacker	Outside foot on tight end's inside foot—on the line of scrimmage.
Mike Linebacker	Headup on the offensive tackle—4.5 yards off the line of scrimmage.
Left End	Shaded outside of the guard.
Left Tackle	Headup on the center.
Right Tackle	Shaded outside of the guard.
Right End	One yard outside the offensive tackle.
Strong Safety	Headup on the offensive tackle—4.5 yards off the line of scrimmage.

Diagram 1-1: The traditional 46 alignment versus a pro-right formation.

The 46 defense is closely related to the dominant defensive scheme of professional football in the 1940s and early-to mid-1950s. During this period, run-based attacks were the predominant systems of choice in offensive football. The solid run-stopping double eagle scheme credited to Earle "Greasy" Neale of the Philadelphia Eagles was a popular front structure of defensive football during this time frame in modern football history. In the post-World War II era, the double eagle front was a dominant force in professional football.

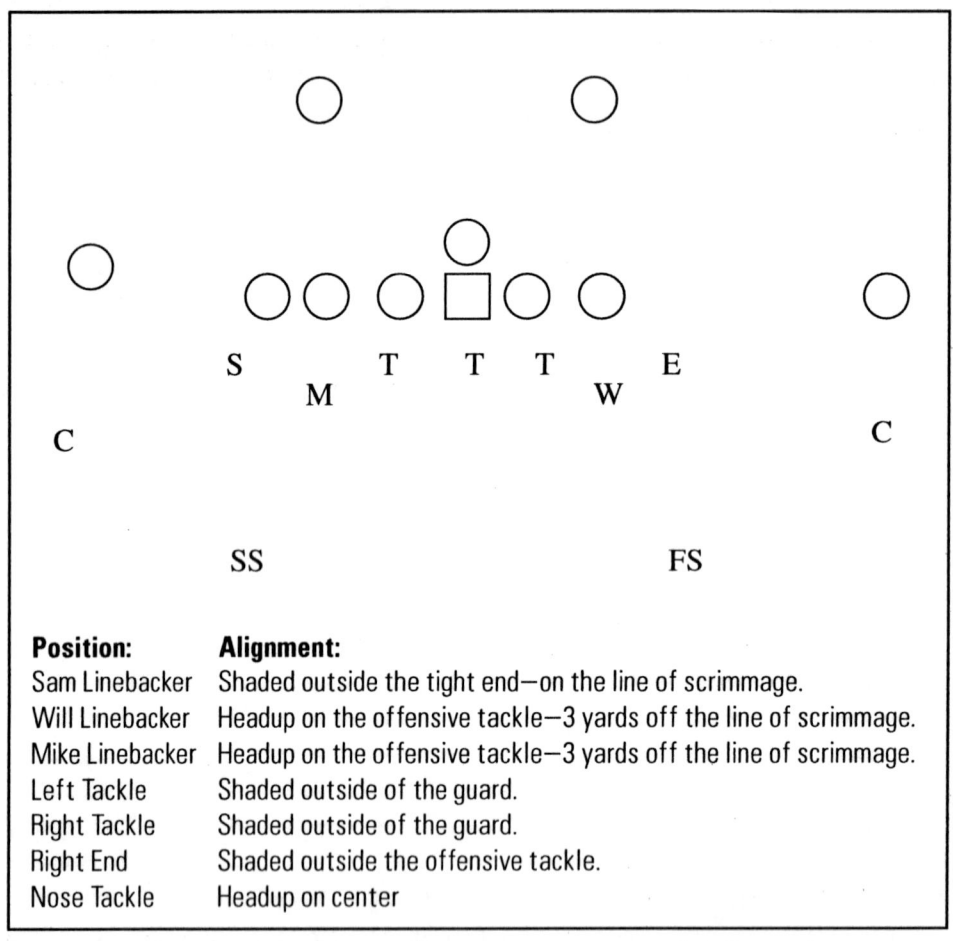

Position:	Alignment:
Sam Linebacker	Shaded outside the tight end—on the line of scrimmage.
Will Linebacker	Headup on the offensive tackle—3 yards off the line of scrimmage.
Mike Linebacker	Headup on the offensive tackle—3 yards off the line of scrimmage.
Left Tackle	Shaded outside of the guard.
Right Tackle	Shaded outside of the guard.
Right End	Shaded outside the offensive tackle.
Nose Tackle	Headup on center

Diagram 1-2: Double eagle defense alignment versus a pro-right formation.

Football historians recognize the dominance of the double eagle defensive scheme up until the time the offensive genius of the legendary Paul Brown began to find ways to exploit its inherent inflexibility. A recently merged member of the NFL, the Cleveland Browns used a wide-open offensive attack which utilized the tight ends and backs in pass patterns. Although the cause-effect relationship of the Paul Brown offensive philosophy to the declining popularity of the familiar double eagle is oversimplified in this discussion, the emergence of Brown's offensive philosophy did cause a major advancement in defensive philosophy. The end result of this revolutionary style of offensive football would quickly lead to a transition of defensive football from the double eagle scheme to the umbrella look of Steve Owens' 6-1 alignment.

The consequent evolution of the 6-1 Umbrella gave football Tom Landry's flexible 4-3—a less rigid defensive descendant of Owens' 6-1 Umbrella. Finally, Landry's pro 4-3 defense underwent its own recent evolutionary change as defensive coordinators searched for a front that allows for even more flexible coverage rules versus the one-back and no-back attacks. It is the trend toward this flexibility of defensive thought that has resulted in the current swing to the coverage-friendly 4-3 Slide (i.e., Miami 4-3 front).

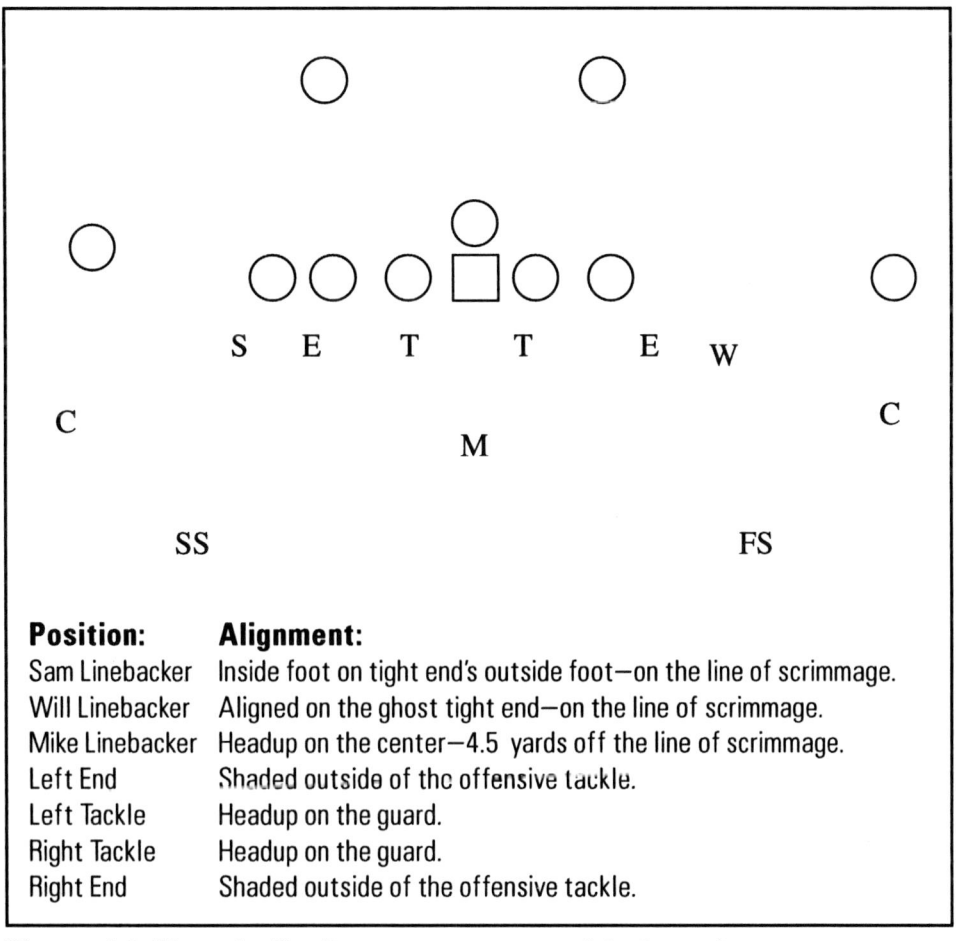

Position:	Alignment:
Sam Linebacker	Inside foot on tight end's outside foot—on the line of scrimmage.
Will Linebacker	Aligned on the ghost tight end—on the line of scrimmage.
Mike Linebacker	Headup on the center—4.5 yards off the line of scrimmage.
Left End	Shaded outside of the offensive tackle.
Left Tackle	Headup on the guard.
Right Tackle	Headup on the guard.
Right End	Shaded outside of the offensive tackle.

Diagram 1-3: The umbrella alignment versus a pro-right formation.

For nearly 30 years, the pattern in the defensive evolutionary process was toward more flexibility and a better capacity to react to offensive attacks and cover the passing zones. While the 4-3 Slide was still winning over coaches to the "cover-all" bend-but-don't-break style of play, a select few of the defensive elite of the game saw the need for defense to again assume its role as the supreme dictator of game flow. One such visionary was Buddy Ryan. Coach Ryan incorporated a more sophisticated second level of support for the old double eagle in developing his 46 scheme as a return to basics, where defense—not offense—dictated the flow of the

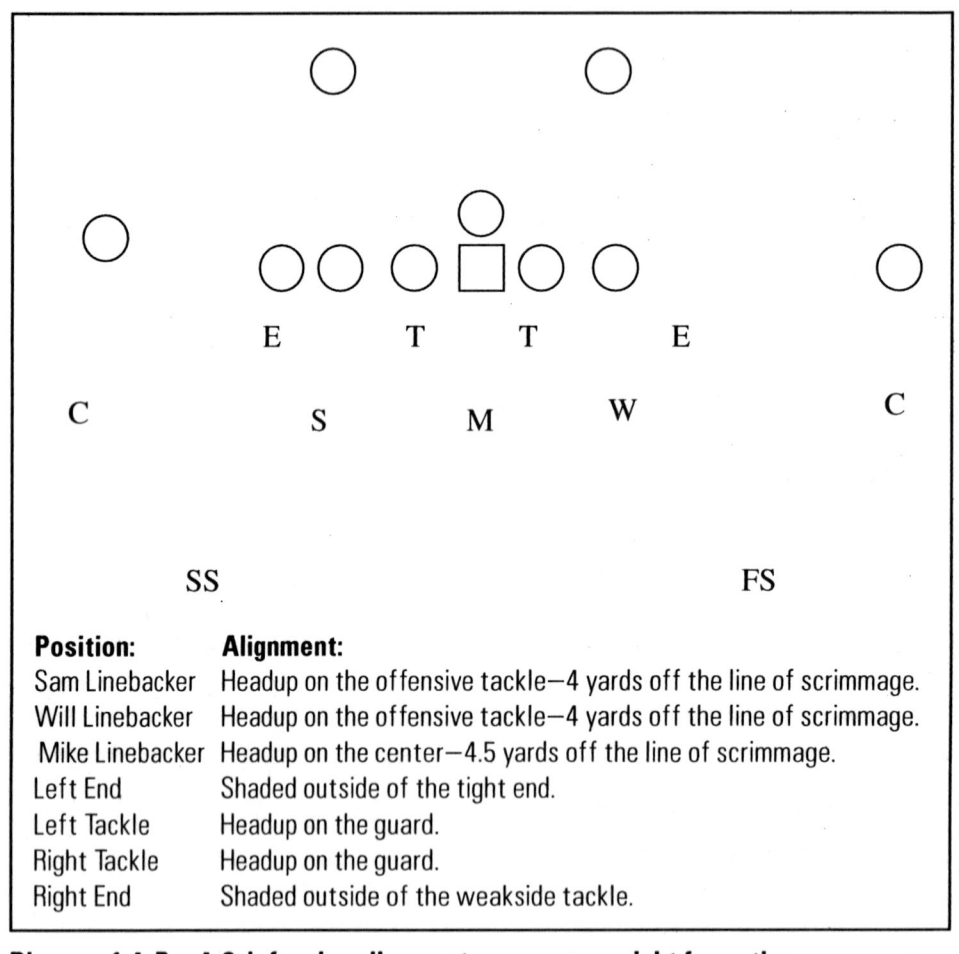

Position:	Alignment:
Sam Linebacker	Headup on the offensive tackle—4 yards off the line of scrimmage.
Will Linebacker	Headup on the offensive tackle—4 yards off the line of scrimmage.
Mike Linebacker	Headup on the center—4.5 yards off the line of scrimmage.
Left End	Shaded outside of the tight end.
Left Tackle	Headup on the guard.
Right Tackle	Headup on the guard.
Right End	Shaded outside of the weakside tackle.

Diagram 1-4: Pro 4-3 defensive alignment versus a pro-right formation.

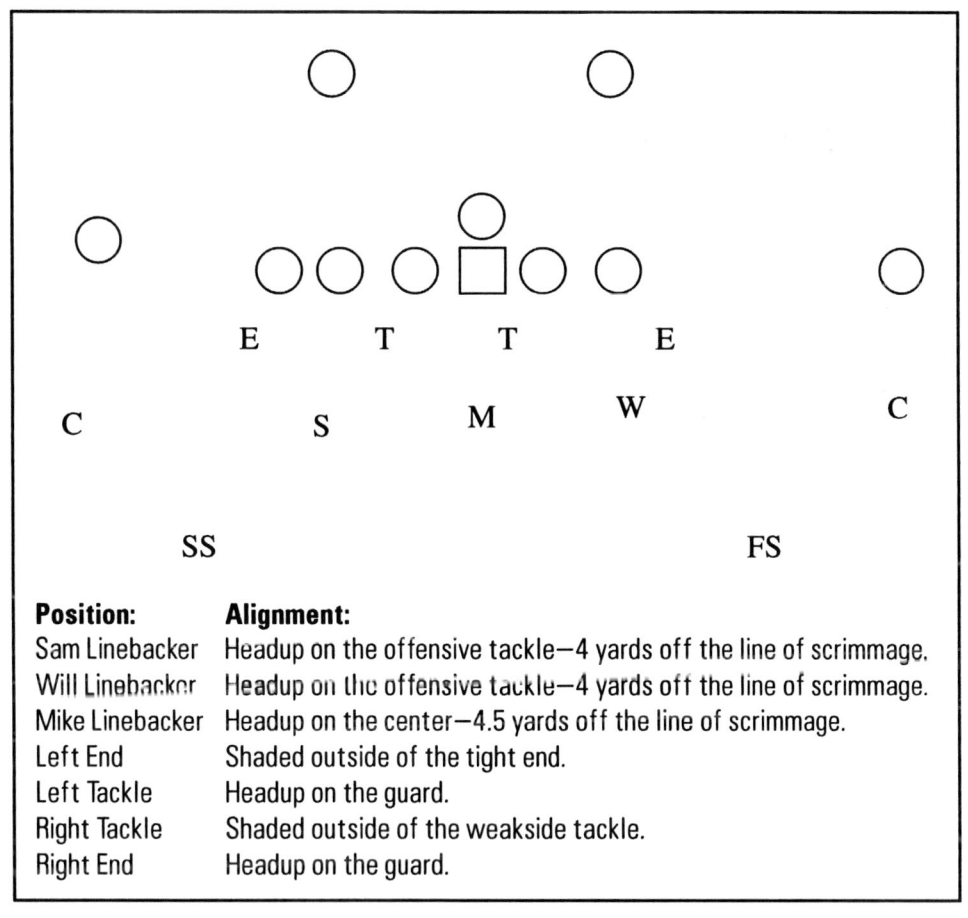

Position:	**Alignment:**
Sam Linebacker	Headup on the offensive tackle—4 yards off the line of scrimmage.
Will Linebacker	Headup on the offensive tackle—4 yards off the line of scrimmage.
Mike Linebacker	Headup on the center—4.5 yards off the line of scrimmage.
Left End	Shaded outside of the tight end.
Left Tackle	Headup on the guard.
Right Tackle	Shaded outside of the weakside tackle.
Right End	Headup on the guard.

Diagram 1-5: Slide 4-3 alignment versus a pro-right formation.

game. It was only a natural progression of the nature of strategic defensive football for Buddy Ryan's 46 Defense to gain prominence as the single most desired defensive scheme in football after Chicago's 1985 World Championship season. The dominance of the Chicago Bears' scheme under Ryan's coordination was so complete that the 46 defense soon became immortalized with a nickname, Bear. More than any one scheme, the Bear has revived programs which have suffered from the reputation of having revolving doors at the coaching offices. With the proper installation and coaching of the 46 defense, the endless cycle of toothless defense against the run is broken and the revolving door becomes an entry into dominance and coaching success.

CHAPTER 2

THE 46 PRESSURE PHILOSOPHY

The 46 philosophy is designed around a simple concept: Pressure wins games. To win, we will do everything we can do within the rules. Understandably, we realize that we can only control what happens on the defensive side of the ball. It is the acceptance of this understanding of our limitations that makes us work even harder to develop and hone a winning defensive game plan. Any winning defensive game plan has five major points of emphasis. These points include the defensive responsibility to accomplish the following:

- *Score on defense.*
- *Create turnovers.*
- *Play exceptional possession-down defense.*
- *Control field position.*
- *Stop the opponent in short-yardage and goal-line situations.*

In order to play pressure defense, you must set forth certain principles and expectations from your players. During our preseason meetings, we establish our expectations and communicate these desires to our coaching staff and players. We feel that in order to meet our defensive responsibilities, we must make a commitment to the following principles:

- *No opponent will out-hustle our defensive unit.*

    Big offensive plays are usually the result of a missed tackle coupled with a breakdown of defensive pursuit. Conversely, big defensive plays are usually the result of relentless pursuit and gang-tackling.

- *Great defense is the offspring of individual commitment.*

    Each player must carry out his personal assignment. To effectively perform his assignment, he must be mentally alert during the game-planning and practice. The cause of a defensive breakdown can always be traced back to the failure of an individual to carry out his personal assignment.

- *Defensive excellence comes from a high level of conditioning.*

    Desire means nothing on game day if a player has not pushed himself to a level of high conditioning. You must sell your players on the necessity of being in shape if they are to meet their individual responsibility to the team.

Even though pressure is a constant in the 46 package, every successful defensive coach realizes that different situations require different tactics. In fact, the definition of the term—*pressure*—requires a liberal boundary in the world of even the 46 coach. Pressure defense means different things at different times. Too often, coaches and fans think *pressure* means a sold-out approach to stacking up on the line of scrimmage and a full-scale blitz on the quarterback, when in fact *pressure* means applying the proper strategy for the situation in order to maximize your defensive force. To maximize the defensive force in all situations and apply pressure, you need to consider the following situations of defensive play:

- *Normal situations*

    Normal situations are linked closely to the clock and circumstances of the game. The primary objective in normal situations is to force the opponent to work for every yard and not give up the long pass or run. Generally speaking, defenses selected for normal situations are delaying tactics designed to optimize pursuit and provide gang-tackling opportunities. Normal situations call for a defensive orientation toward containment.

- *Penetrating situations*

    Penetrating situations are circumstances when either you are enjoying the upperhand or looking for a turn of the tide. Defenses used in the penetrating situations require an ability to read on the run. Extra effort is required to fill the proper pursuit angles, but the payoff is the high incidence of offensive mistakes and turnovers forced by the attacking style of play. The attacking type of defense used in the penetrating situations is the backbone of the 46 package. The physical makeup of the defensive unit is usually tailored for applying pressure in penetrating situations. It is this defensive scheme designed for the penetrating situations that coaches and fans equate with the traditional 46 Bear pressure known for its past success.

- *Prevent situations*

    The prevent situation calls for implementing our nickel prevent package. We use this look when it is late in the half or game and we are ahead. Our primary purpose in the prevent situation is to delay the offensive team's progress, preventing the long gainer or successful trick play. The prevent package is also used in long-yardage situations after the pressure package used in the penetrating situation has garnered a big sack or other type of loss. It can be used anytime the offense is facing an unusually long-yardage situation on a possession down.

What is pressure defense? It is probably easier to explain what pressure defense isn't. Pressure defense is not a rigid concept. It is a sound and flexible concept with specific rules established to guarantee its integrity in all possible situations. Some of the rules that are needed for implementation of a sound and forceful defensive scheme include the players' responsibility in:

- *Being alert to the down and distance.*
- *Being alert to the offensive personnel groupings and strategy.*
- *Knowing the defensive game plan components (e.g., possession, short yardage, long yardage, etc.).*
- *Maintaining poise during the critical game situations (e.g., before the half, near the end of the fourth quarter, two-minute drill, etc.).*

Considered by many coaches to be an unconventional defense, the 46 attack package is unconventional in only the matter of never allowing your opponent any breathing room. Unlike many contain-based packages, the structure of the penetrating 46 attack package provides the defensive coordinator with certain advantages, some of which are the following:

- *Outnumber the tackle-to-tackle blocking schemes at the point of attack.*

    The solid look faced by the guard-center-guard along with the inside-eye, outside-eye shades on the tight end present special considerations for any type of traditional two-back attack.

- *Pressure the quarterback relentlessly on every pass play.*

    Man protection schemes are severely tested by the 1-on-1 match-ups presented by the solid alignment over the guard-center-guard. Because the offensive line is overmatched in the interior area, the running backs must be included in the protection scheme.

- *Force major adjustments in run and pass blocking schemes.*

    Spy reads (i.e., reads which provide for one of two defenders to cover a running back attempting to slip out into a route) take away the possibility of hot read dump-offs to the running back. The dual alignment of both inside and outside shades on the tight end present a significant problem to the strongside pass protection and run-blocking scheme.

- *Force offensive schemes to use unfamiliar alternatives to their base philosophy of attack.*

    Offensive attacks such as the wing-T must make adjustments to their flank attack because of the inability to pull both guards without allowing penetration by one of the outside-eye shades aligned on the guard. Option offenses are limited because of the inability to scoop block to the next level with a "jump through" technique. Other two-back formations are stressed by the downhill play of the linebackers shielded by the solid front of the 46 alignment. Veer blocking attacks such as the flexbone face difficulty attacking off-tackle versus the double 3 technique shades. One-back and no-back offensive schemes such as the run-and-shoot become a chuck-and-duck under the intense pressure of simply being outnumbered in the box.

- *Blitz at will without substitutional changes.*

    Multiple blitzes are available due to the constant "8 in the box" feature of the 46. Because the 46 is a pressure front, substitutions are not needed to "shore up" the box as with many 7-man front packages.

- *Cover all possible pass patterns while continuing to pressure the quarterback.*

    Pattern reading is the primary feature of a multiple secondary supported by fierce pressure inside. A built-in ability of the linebackers to blitz on pass flow coupled with a spy coverage technique of the defensive ends put the protection schemes in jeopardy of a breakdown on every dropback pass.

- *Dictate the flow of the game.*

    Other defensive packages are built for reacting to an offensive threat. With the 46 defense, the offense is the one phase that is threatened. The 46 is built around the premise of "taking." It takes away what the opponent does best and forces it to compromise. In this manner, the 46 defense dictates, rather than reacts to, the flow of the game.

- *Free the second level (i.e., linebackers and strong safety) to run to the football.*

The base 6-man line structured in accordance with the legacy of the tenacious double eagle front of the 1950s has one primary function—to free the linebackers so that they may play downhill to the football.

In summary, the practictioner of pressure must not only demand a high standard from his players, he must demand a high standard from himself. The following chapters in this book detail the blueprint of the 46 pressure scheme. The heart and commitment of every coach and athlete determine if that blueprint builds a winning defense.

CHAPTER 3

CHARACTERISTICS OF THE 46 BEAR DEFENSE

The structure of the 46 (Bear) defense exhibits several unique characteristics not normally found in the realm of defensive football strategy. Several of the characteristics exhibited by the 46 defense are related to its "pressure" alignment versus all types of offensive formations. Factors of the Bear alignment include the following:

- *The strong safety traditionally aligns on the side of the formation opposite the tight end.*

This feature is the hallmark of the 46 defense. In fact, the name of the defensive concept—46—was taken from the "unusual" alignment of the adjuster, Doug Plank. Plank, the starting strong safety for the World Champion Chicago Bears, was consequently immortalized during the Chicago Bears' dominance in the mid-1980s and wore number 46.

- *Against most formations, the traditional strong safety normally aligns within close proximity of the line of scrimmage.*

The strong safety's primary responsibility is that of a tackler—a linebacker. He doesn't need to possess premier coverage skills. His role is to function as the hub of the defense, connecting the pressure front characteristics of the 46 to the aggressive route-reading coverage system of the Bear secondary. The strong safety has numerous duties, including but not limited to supplying support to the strength of a formation, acting as the force on the nub of a formation, and covering from a removed position versus a multiple receiver set.

- *The nose tackle is isolated on the center.*

    As pointed out in chapter two, no other base defensive alignment in the game guarantees isolation of the nose tackle technique on a center. The two impossible-to-hook 3 techniques playing with outside leverage on the guards force the guards to work hard at reversing the natural defensive leverage angles. The tight alignment of a defensive lineman to the ball gives the offensive blocking schemes little latitude in attempting to combo inside or double-team the nose tackle. The end result is one-on-one trench warfare from guard-to-guard. A substantial defensive advantage within the interior line is enjoyed by the Bear defensive line coach.

- *The strongside linebacker aligns on the primary tight end and is read-responsible for countering the various options of the tight end.*

    He must be able to cover the tight end—or a short zone—on an outside release by the tight end. Similarly, he is responsible for jamming the tight end and preventing an easy release off the line of scrimmage. Versus a run blocking read, the strongside linebacker must physically whip the tight end and "turn the edge" to force a long edge for the running back. By forcing a long edge, the linebacker prevents the running back from running around a collapsed short edge; the running back is made to run a bowed path in an attempt to get around the defensive flank.

While the aforementioned characteristics are descriptive of the traditional 46 defense designed by Buddy Ryan, the following chapters describing the tactics, techniques, and schemes of the 46 defense relate to a slightly different structure of the 46 defense. As you will see, the 46 defense can be based from various standard defensive structures. For example, you can base the 46 alignment from a standard 4-4 package, or a 4-3 package which is identical to Buddy Ryan's philosophy. While the structure of the 46 scheme described in the following chapters is based from a 4-3, the particular dynamics of the 46 structure described did slightly different than Buddy Ryan's original 46 alignment. In the 46 concept described in later chapters, the strong safety aligns on the tight end side in a 9 technique. He replaces one of the outside linebackers in Buddy Ryan's scheme. We have generally referred to this outside linebacker position as the Jack linebacker. Consequently, the other major difference between the scheme described in this book and Buddy Ryan's original concept is Will linebacker's alignment as the weakside 40 technique linebacker position. In Buddy's package, this alignment was well known as the strong safety's base alignment. It is important to note that only the names are different. The position player aligned at the particular spot observes most of the same rules and techniques regardless of whether it is the traditional Buddy Ryan alignment or not. For example, in Buddy's system, the strong safety aligned in the linebacker position is the adjuster. In the system described in the following chapter, the Will linebacker—who aligns in the same position as Buddy's strong safety—is the adjuster. Only the names are different.

CHAPTER 4

PRINCIPLES OF DEFENSIVE LINE PLAY

The defensive lineman of the 46 scheme enjoys a leading role in the defense. With this role comes a greater responsibility and a higher level of difficulty than in most other defensive schemes. More than any other defense, the defensive lineman in the 46 package must be a dependable player, capable of dominating his opponent and maintaining the integrity of the defensive front. As a coach of the 46 pressure defense, you should search for a particular type of athlete to play on your defensive line. The ideal defensive lineman for the 46 package demonstrates the following characteristics:

- *Quickness.*

    The defensive lineman must demonstrate quickness in his ability to move in all directions. He should demonstrate an above-average reactive ability for his size.

- *Fluidity.*

    The defensive lineman must demonstrate fluid movement as he reacts and changes direction on the field.

- *Flexibility.*

    A defensive lineman must demonstrate extraordinary flexibility for his size. Flexibility is a requirement for maintaining the proper leverage as he defeats the blockers.

- *Power.*

    The defensive lineman must be able to strike a blow with power. He should have a knack for delivering an explosive blow to the opponent. He cannot be a "leaner." He must be able to quickly shed the blocker.

- *Recognition skills.*

    The defensive lineman should be able to make the proper adjustments and adapt to changing situations. He has to be able to recognize offensive blocking patterns quickly and respond with an immediate physical reaction.

- *Consistency.*

    The defensive lineman must demonstrate reliability and consistency under pressure. He should respond to his reads properly at all times. He should demonstrate a football IQ in that he is able to relate to down and distance tendencies, field position tendencies, clock factors (i.e., time remaining), formation tendencies, etc.

The exceptional defensive lineman is involved in the leadership process of the unit. He not only rises to the occasion, he leads through his body and mind. Some of the things that the involved defensive lineman does for his team include:

- *Checking the yard markers and reminding teammates of the offensive tendencies.*
- *Helping his teammates be alert for the opponent's special plays (e.g., draw, screen, fake punt, etc).*
- *Anticipating "checks" and other such defensive audibles.*
- *Understanding the relationship of the secondary perimeter support call to the front scheme.*
- *Appreciating the impact of the field position (e.g., red zone, green zone, four-down territory, etc.).*
- *Understanding the relevance of the weather on the style of play.*

The five essentials:

It is our belief that productive defensive line play consists of five essential elements.

- *Stance.*

    You should not overemphasize the stance parameters of the defensive lineman. What is important is that the stance allow the defensive lineman to take a somewhat neutral position. He should be able to move in either direction with an explosive power-step.

- *Attack.*

    We do not teach the big first step coaching point that many coaches edify in their desire to gain penetration. We feel that the big first step puts the defensive lineman at a disadvantage against every type of block, save one. The only blocking scheme against which the big first step technique is effective is the high-hat read (i.e., pass protection block). Against all other blocks, the big first step puts the defensive lineman on the edge or in a position of imbalance against a blocker using short power strides. In order for a player to contact the blocker in a fundamentally sound body position, it is extremely important that the player utilize short, powerful steps while maintaining a good base.

- *Neutralize.*

The effective defensive lineman must neutralize the blocker's impact and stabilize the line of scrimmage. The aim of the 46 scheme's defensive lineman is not to create a new line of scrimmage, but to maintain the integrity of the front line and allow the linebackers to scrape downhill to the ball carrier. Neutralizing a blocker or a combination blocking scheme involves several reactions: Getting an upfield push on a pass protector, spilling a trap blocker, disrupting a combo block, etc. In order to consistently neutralize a blocker or blocking scheme, the productive defensive lineman must be able to move quickly and efficiently in eight different directions. See Diagram 4-1:

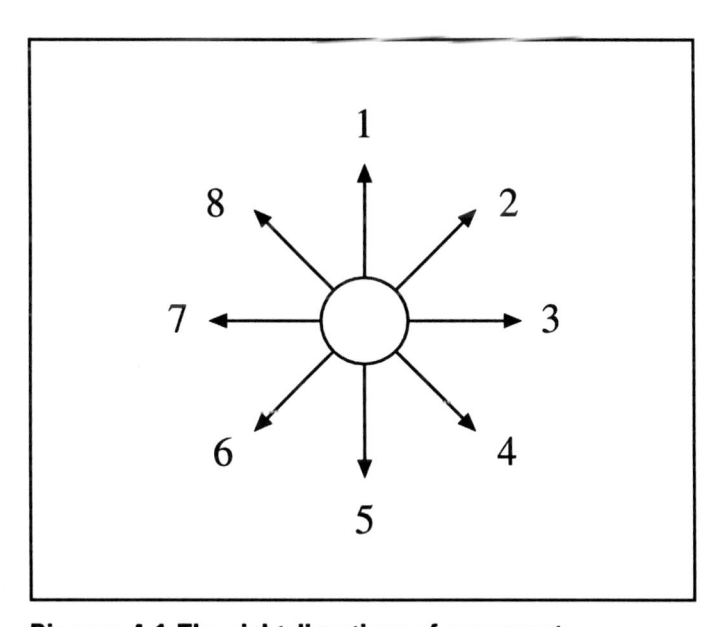

Diagram 4-1: The eight directions of movement.

- *Escape.*

This is where the kinship of defensive line play and wrestling is strongest. A primary characteristic of an effective defensive player is his ability to quickly and violently shed a blocker. Against the run, escaping predominantly entails lateral movement ability. Against the pass, the defender may have to throw the blocker aside with a club move in order to clear the pass rushing lane. Good technique and leverage is simply not enough. The escape factor is a critical component to defensive line play—and it should be practiced on a daily basis with specific drills which hone the player's technique in escaping from contact with the blocker.

- *Pursuit.*

    An effective escape puts the defensive lineman into position to effective pursuit. In Chapter one, we stated that no one can out-hustle our defense. It is a principle of the 46 pressure scheme. In addition to out-hustling our opponent, our players (through the use of the proper escape technique) will pursue the ball carrier according to the proper angle and leverage. Hustle and angle are the two components of effective individual pursuit.

The two teaching styles:

Two teaching styles are used to instruct the defensive lineman in the proper technique of defensive line play. The first style is a comprehensive style of teaching the defensive lineman. The second teaching style provides generic coaching of a limited number of skills needed to defeat a myriad of blocking schemes.

In our choice of using the generic coaching style, we use the two-rule philosophy of coaching defensive linemen. The general standard of play under the generic coaching play allows for a simpler and more effective style of coaching. The two rules of defensive line play are:

- *Don't get reached.*
- *Don't allow the jump-through.*

While we prefer the generic two-rule style of coaching, many expert coaches remain devoted to the comprehensive style of coaching. For example, Buddy Ryan practiced a comprehensive style of defensive line coaching. Because both philosophies can be effective, the choice is basically up to you. For this reason, we present the details and coaching points of each philosophy in the following paragraphs. Naturally, it is our hope that we convince you of the merits of using our favored style, the generic coaching.

The comprehensive philosophy:

In the comprehensive style, the defensive lineman is taught to recognize and defeat each type of block he may face during a season. For years, this coaching method has been the preferred choice among defensive line coaches. In fact, for much of the history of modern football, the comprehensive teaching style was the only choice available to defensive line coaches. In order to be a defensive line coach at the highest levels of play, you had to be a competent teacher and drill master at instructing defensive linemen of all ability levels (mental and physical) to perform a rote reaction to a specific blocking scheme. These blocking combinations could also be one of many forms of one-man schemes, two-man schemes, trap schemes, backfield inclusive schemes, or pass protection schemes. Additionally, within these categories of blocking combinations there are several unique variations. For example, the one-man scheme category includes the zone block, the jump-through (i.e., the scoop), the turn-out, the reach, and the drive block. In the comprehensive style of coaching defensive line, each individual defensive technique would have a set response to an individual block, and each response would have to be taught and drilled in a sequential manner.

The drawbacks of the comprehensive style were at first inconsequential. During the early days of modern football, blocking schemes were less numerous and less sophisticated. The run-based attacks of an earlier time used a predominance of angle blocks, drive blocks, pull blocks, and double-team blocks.

Just to name one example—the combo block was little used prior to the 1960s. Before the combo block, if two blockers fired off the ball and contacted the defender the block was a double team—a block designed to effect a vertical push off the lineman in order create a gaping hole and cut off the linebacker from pursuit. If two blockers made contact with an outside shaded defensive lineman, the defensive lineman was trained to drop to the ground. He was trained to drop to the ground because the defensive line coach knew that the single objective of two blockers contacting a down lineman was to drive him backward and flip him on his back; thus cutting off the pursuit of the second-level pursuit. Therefore, if a defensive lineman successfully read a double team, he was to drop to the ground and simply make a pile to prevent both blockers from knocking him off the ball. The development of the combo block made this defensive strategy obsolete. In a combo block, the objective of the lead blocker (i.e., outside man of the tandem) is to chip off the down lineman and move to the next level so that he may cut off the linebacker. The traditional defensive reaction of getting the outside hip to the ground on recognition of the double team actually facilitates the goals of the combo block. In a combo block, the primary blocker's objective is to take over control of the down lineman while the lead blocker chips to the next level. As you can visualize, the defensive lineman who drops to the ground is allowing the primary blocker to block him one-on-one while the lead blocker chips off the fallen defender to cut off the linebacker. And since a combo block starts out identically like a double team, it is impossible for a defensive lineman to read the difference between a double team and a combo block. Naturally, it always has been a sound practice to drop to the ground versus a double team—and it still is. The dilemma is: How does the defensive lineman recognize the difference between a double team and a combo block?

Another equally difficult read is the difference between an inside release and a gap-down type of block (i.e., inside angle block). An inside release can indicate several things. A trapping guard may show from behind the inside release or a blocker may simply be attempting to release up through the next level to cut off a linebacker. For the defensive lineman instructed in the comprehensive style of coaching the defensive line, each of these two scenarios requires a remarkably different defensive reaction. Although the blocks can be correctly interpreted in time and with practice, only the highly skilled defensive lineman will eventually be able to consistently respond to the subtle differences between the many inside blocks. An inexperienced defensive lineman will constantly face the dilemma of when to wrong-shoulder the trapper, or when to squeeze parallel to the line of scrimmage.

While dilemma is the operative word of the comprehensive coaching style, an even more descriptive phrase related to the coaching of the comprehensive style is "read conflict." Read conflict refers to the inability of a defender to interpret a blocker's intentions due to the numerous similar blocks initiated by a common move. For example, when a defender plays in a comprehensive system, he is taught to respond precisely to the individual scheme. In the modern game of football, some 50 different blocking schemes may indeed exist. On any given game a defensive lineman will see a series of blocking patterns. These patterns can most easily be described according to the following categories:

- *one-man blocks*
- *two-man blocks*
- *pull blocks*
- *pass sets*

Within the four previously mentioned categories are found multiple schemes. One example, the two-man blocking category, includes all of the following schemes:

- *double team*
- *combo*
- *fold*
- *tag (i.e., a type of fold)*
- *gut (i.e., a type of fold)*
- *scoop*
- *zone*
- *influence and kick-out*
- *down and kick-out*
- *down and log*
- *down and load*

In the comprehensive system of coaching the defensive lineman, you must provide adequate instruction, practice, refinement and remediation in the proper technique against each individual block. Time becomes a critical preparation factor. And time is not something which a coach has in surplus. For this reason alone, you may consider the comprehensive system prudent only at the professional level. Youth coaches, junior-high and middle school coaches, high school coaches, and college-level coaches are all competing for numerous interests and demands on the athletes' time. For these coaches—as with myself—the time demands of teaching a precise reaction to a specific blocking read is simply not "doable."

The third negative feature of the comprehensive style of coaching relates to the individual considerations of your athletes' physical and mental capacities. In the comprehensive philosophy, the standard for success is extremely rigid. An athlete must be able to accomplish two things in two completely different realms. He must first be cognizant of the proper techniques and reactions to every possible block—the mental realm. Then, he must be able to effectively react and counter the block once he makes that precise read—the physical realm. A tremendous physical specimen with some learning difficulties is a glorified bench sitter in the comprehensive system. He simply can't master the cognitive realm—he can't remember what to do because he has too much to do. And without question, the athlete who is unable to master the physical realm (while being close in performance to the physical specimen) is also unable to make the winning grade. Too often the comprehensive system favors the less physical player who is a better "reader" or diagnostician. And to this statement I add the question, "Who would you rather have on the field as a coach, the physical specimen or the great technician who is the lesser athlete?"

It is a simple question to answer when you think about it. Our job is to get the best athletes on the field and teach them to perform at the optimum level. A system that favors lesser athletes over more talented individuals is a system destined to fail.

Combine the negative points of the comprehensive system and you will quickly begin to search for an alternative coaching style. Read conflicts, time management, and an overemphasis on the athlete's mental talents all point to a need for a better way. In the 46 Bear defensive system, we have the better way. It is most accurately referred to as generic coaching.

Generic coaching:

Generic defensive line coaching refers to teaching the defensive lineman one sound response movement against multiple blocking patterns. This is in contrast with the traditional comprehensive system of defensive line coaching where a tailored defensive movement is demanded for each type of blocking pattern. Besides being a more time-consuming mode of instruction, the comprehensive system can lead the defensive lineman into pitfalls such as read conflicts.

A read conflict occurs when a defensive player incorrectly interprets the actions of a blocker or combination of blockers. Different blocking patterns often share common characteristics during the first moments after the ball is snapped. And since the defensive player must make a nearly instantaneous diagnosis of the blocker's or blockers' intentions, read conflicts are a persistent problem for many defensive players. The fact that so many different blocks can look so similar during the initial charge of the blockers makes the problem of read conflicts a difficult one for the coach to eliminate. The examples shown in Diagrams 4-2 and 4-3 (the double team and combo block) illustrate a pair of blocking patterns which often generate a read conflict for even the most experienced lineman. The previously described read conflict caused by the similarity of the double team and combo block is a common occurrence—and just one piece of philosophical evidence in support of the generic coaching style.

Most coaches study the game in order to learn as much about techniques and training as they possibly can learn. The continuous quest for further knowledge and a deeper understanding of the dynamics of the game are the mark of the good coach. Ironically, it is the coach who knows more but requires less of his players who normally wins championships. In other words, a coach should achieve the status of a lifelong student but only to the extent that he continually seeks new ways to make things simpler and easier for the athlete.

Keeping things simple is sometimes referred to as the KISS philosophy. KISS stands for Keep It Simple Stupid. (Coaches who use the KISS acronym sometimes prefer to define it as Keep It Simple and Sound.) Our philosophy, while simple, is described best by another acronym—KILL. The KILL acronym should not be inferred as a promotion of unnecessary violence, nor as a trivialization of crime. Rather, it refers to the dominant theme of our defensive coaching style—Keep it Likeable and Learnable. The KILL acronym is probably a bit too politically incorrect to use with younger athletes, but it provided an effective framework for communication with our professional athletes—men who were mature enough to understand the mechanism as simply a means of communicating a cornerstone of our teaching.

The "keep-it-likeable-and-learnable" philosophy led us to develop a simple way of categorizing blocks. We knew that if we weren't careful, we would fall into a trap and develop multiple categories of blocking schemes and define appropriate defensive recognitions to each scheme. This would bring us right back to where we started from—a comprehensive system of defensive line play—50 different reactions to 50 different schemes. We knew that was not what we wanted.

CHAPTER 5

DEFENSIVE LINE PLAY VERSUS THE RUN

In order to make sure we stayed within the parameters of our generic *Keep It Likeable and Learnable* philosophy, we identified two categories of blocks. Like the significance of certain numbers to certain religions, the number two is of special significance to our planning. We strongly desire to keep sequences limited to no more than two (e.g., two choices, two rules, or two categories, etc.). Therefore, just as we defined the role of the defensive lineman in accordance with his two rules— don't get reached and don't allow the jump-through—we limited the categories of reaction to two types of blocks:

- *Rule blocks*

  —the reach block

  —the jump-through

  —the double team

- *Reactionary blocks*

  —the fold block

  —the trap block

  —the high-hat read (i.e., dropback pass protection)

The reach block:

The primary rule block is the reach block (i.e., hook block). Defeating the reach block and maintaining outside leverage is the primary goal of the outside-shaded defensive lineman. (In the 46 pressure defense, the outside-shaded defensive lineman on the guard is identified as a 3 technique.)

To defeat the reach block, the 3 technique must react to position his hips in a manner which allows him to maintain playside leverage. In other words, the 3 technique must work to keep his hips outside of the blocker's frame. Note that since the 3 technique aligns in an outside shade on the guard, he need only to maintain a position with his hips in a leverage position. Our 3 technique is trained to maintain outside leverage in a three-yard area outside of the reach blocker.

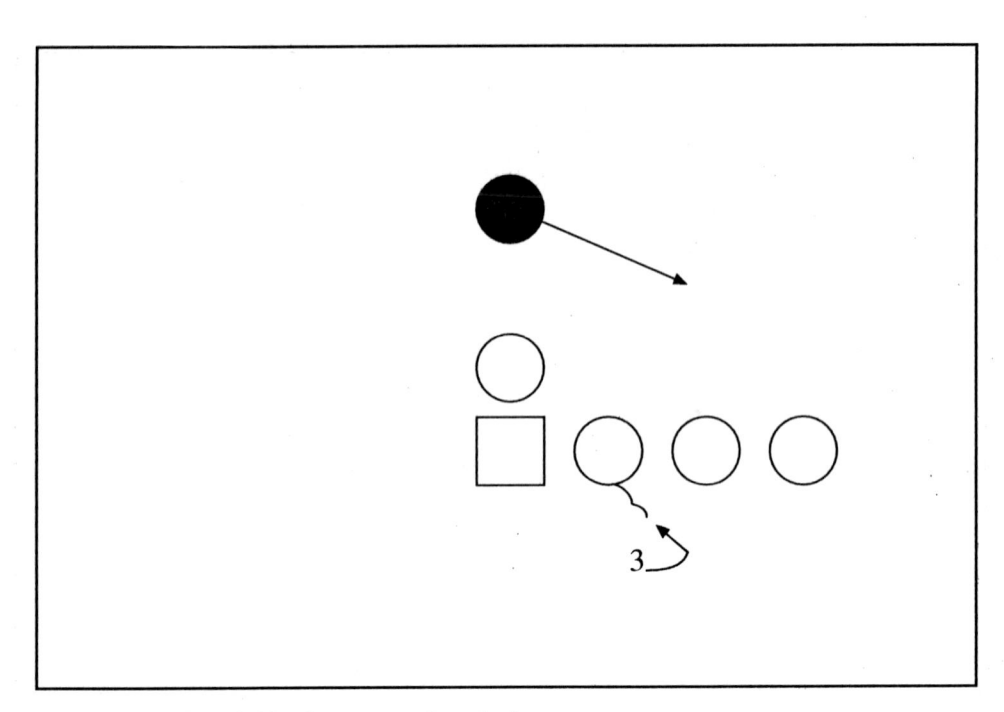

Diagram 5-1: Reach block versus a 3 technique.

Historically, defensive line coaches have taught the 3 technique defender to make sure he is able to get his hat (i.e., headgear) outside of the blocker's headgear. In this style of teaching, the primary goal of the 3 technique defender versus the reach block was to get his hat outside the blocker's hat. We feel this terminology and teaching methodology is flawed.

We prefer to emphasize the positioning of the defender's hips, not his head. If you think about it, a defensive lineman can get his head outside of the reach blocker's head, but still not gain playside leverage. His hips could possibly trail the shoulders and remain in the blocker's framework, even though he gains playside leverage with his head. It is our contention that if the defender's hips don't gain playside leverage, the defender is hooked inside. Consequently, we not only de-emphasize the placement of the head, we totally disregard the historically accepted coaching point of the head placement. Hip placement is the key to beating a reach block, not head placement.

In order to beat a reach block, your 3 technique must get his hips in the hole. We teach our 3 technique to swivel his tail to the outside as he reads the reach block. This action guarantees that he cannot be hooked.

At this point, we should mention a critical coaching point of effective defensive line play in the 46 pressure package. A productive defensive lineman knows that the offensive lineman desires to effect lift through thrust. The offensive lineman wants to snap his hips

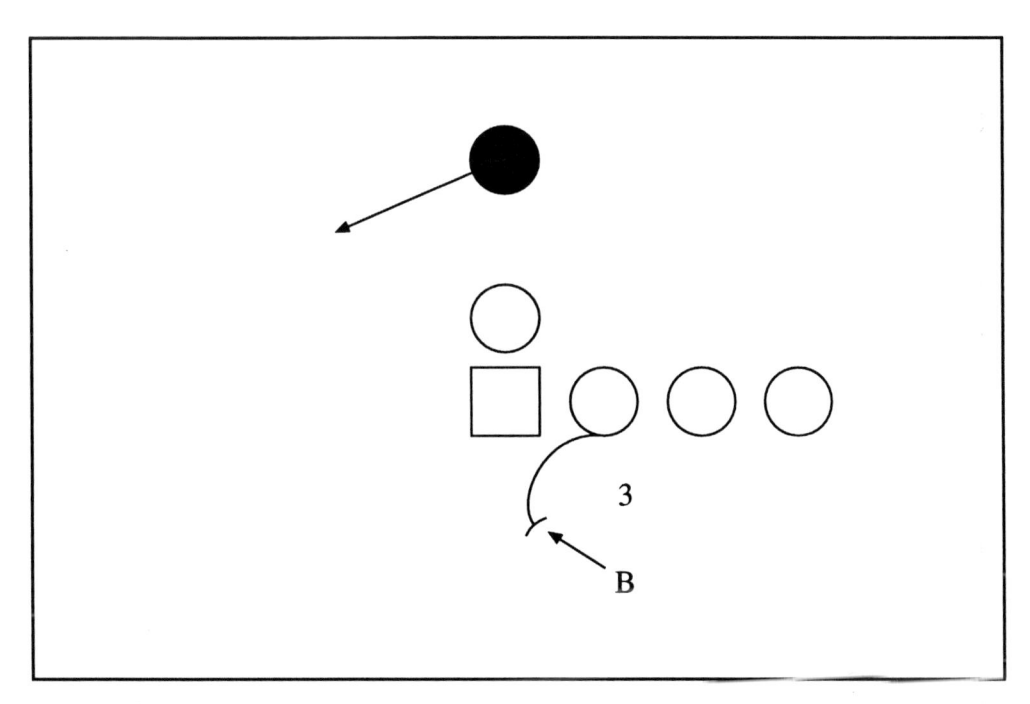

Diagram 5-2: The guard executes a jump-through block.

forward and maximize a belly-to-belly positioning on the defensive lineman. This belly-to-belly positioning lifts the defender's pads, making an upright and easily toppled target. Conversely, the effective defensive lineman maintains a pad-low posture by keeping his hips flexed behind the plane of his shoulders. His hips remain clear of contact as he stabilizes himself and fights against the pressure of the blocker.

By swiveling his buttocks to the playside and maintaining the pad-low posture with flexed hips, the 3 technique is able to stay clear of the offensive guard's leverage angle and get into the pursuit angle. This technique of playing the reach block is a principal feature of the generic style of defensive line play. As you read about the proper technique of playing the double team and combo schemes in the following paragraphs, you will see how this style of defeating the reach block generically applies to the concepts of playing off other blocking schemes that attempt to deny the defender lateral leverage.

The jump-through block:

The second rule block is the jump-through block (i.e., scoop block). You should remember that the second priority of the defensive lineman is to not allow a successful jump-through. The term jump-through identifies the action of the offensive lineman whose assignment is to scoop inside on a J-shaped path to the next level. The primary objective of the jump-through blocker is to intercept the linebacker and cut him off from pursuit. He normally takes a J-shaped path to the inside. His path is facilitated (and thus identified) by the blocker's initial lateral step to the inside. This lateral step allows the blocker to avoid the interference of the defensive lineman—particularly if the defensive lineman is playing according to the "big first step" philosophy. The "big first step" initial move puts the defensive lineman on an upfield path, allowing the offensive lineman to escape unmolested to cut off the linebacker.

Experienced defensive line coaches agree that effective use of the hands is the key to successful defensive line play. To stop a jump-through, the outside-shaded defensive lineman should shoot his hands to a point between the blocker's numbers and belt. By throwing the hands low on the blocker, the defender assures himself that he will make solid contact on the blocker's torso. If the defender doesn't shoot his hands low on the blocker's body, his inside arm and hand could glance over the blocker's shoulders. By making solid contact with the blocker's torso, the defensive lineman can grab cloth and pull.

Grabbing cloth is another critical component of the defensive lineman's technique in stopping the jump-through. Once he shoots his inside hand to the proper position on the blocker's torso, the defensive lineman should grab cloth and pull the blocker toward him. Pulling the blocker toward him accomplishes two things. First, it detours the blocker from his intended path to intercept the linebacker. His path is disrupted as his shoulders are twisted toward the defensive lineman. Secondly, by grabbing the blocker's jersey and jerking, the defender is able to use this transfer of force to catapult himself through the "B" gap and into the perfect angle of pursuit.

A jump-through by a guard is always accompanied by a tackle also scooping to the inside. The primary goal of the scooping offensive tackle is to prevent penetration by the 3 technique defender. While the tackle is not a primary worry of the 3 technique, he counters the scoop block of the offensive tackle in the following manner. As the defensive lineman uses his inside hand to pull the blocker's jersey, he dips his outside shoulder while ripping his outside arm upward in the manner of an uppercut punch. Dipping and ripping decreases the available blocking surface for the offensive tackle and increases the likelihood of clearance past the scooping tackle.

The aforementioned catapult reaction resulting from the 3 technique defensive lineman using his inside hand to pull on the guard's jersey is enhanced by the 3 technique snapping his outside leg across in a crossover type move as he dips and rips the outside shoulder. If the outside hip lags, the outside leg drags. The outside leg drags when the 3 technique fails to snap his outside hip over (snapping the hip over results in a type of crossover stride). Keep in mind that the well-coached offensive tackle is trained to get around on the defender and cut his inside leg. And while the defensive tackle's primary objective versus the jump-through is to divert the guard and not allow him through to the next level. It is also extremely important for the defensive lineman to avoid being cut off by the offensive tackle.

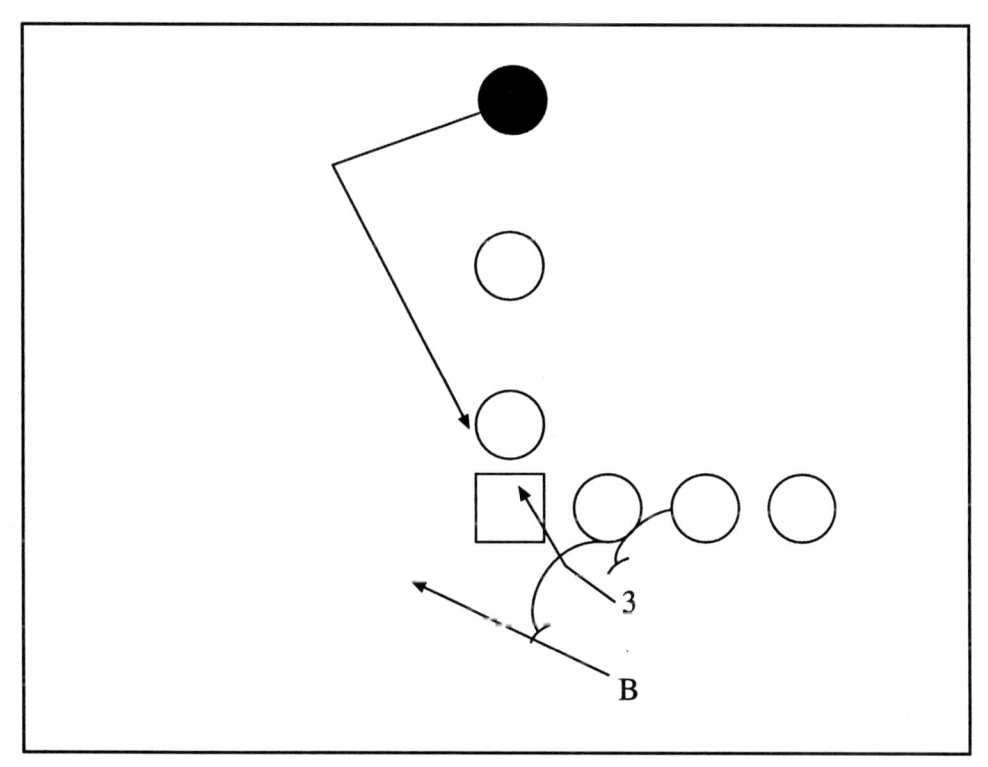

Diagram 5-3: The 3 technique responds to a jump-through and plays the cutback.

If the 3 technique is cut off by the offensive tackle, he cannot get into the pursuit angle. And by not getting into the pursuit angle down the line of scrimmage, the defensive tackle forces the linebacker to compensate. Granted, the linebacker can replace the defensive lineman in the cutback pursuit lane. The unfortunate tradeoff occurs when a linebacker is asked to fly to the football consistently. A linebacker can rarely be a big first-hitter if he is also given the added duty of compensating and assuming cutback responsibility. Whenever a linebacker has to cover a breakdown along the defensive line, the defensive front is much more susceptible to the "big play"—something any defensive scheme must prevent.

The double-team block:

The third rule block is the double team. Once the player masters the double-team technique, we feel he has developed the necessary skills for defensive line play. Fortunately for our players and our coaching staff, our generic system of coaching allows for the skills required for playing the reach block to transfer into playing the double team. In other words, if a player learns to play the reach block effectively, he need learn only one additional coaching point to play the double team effectively.

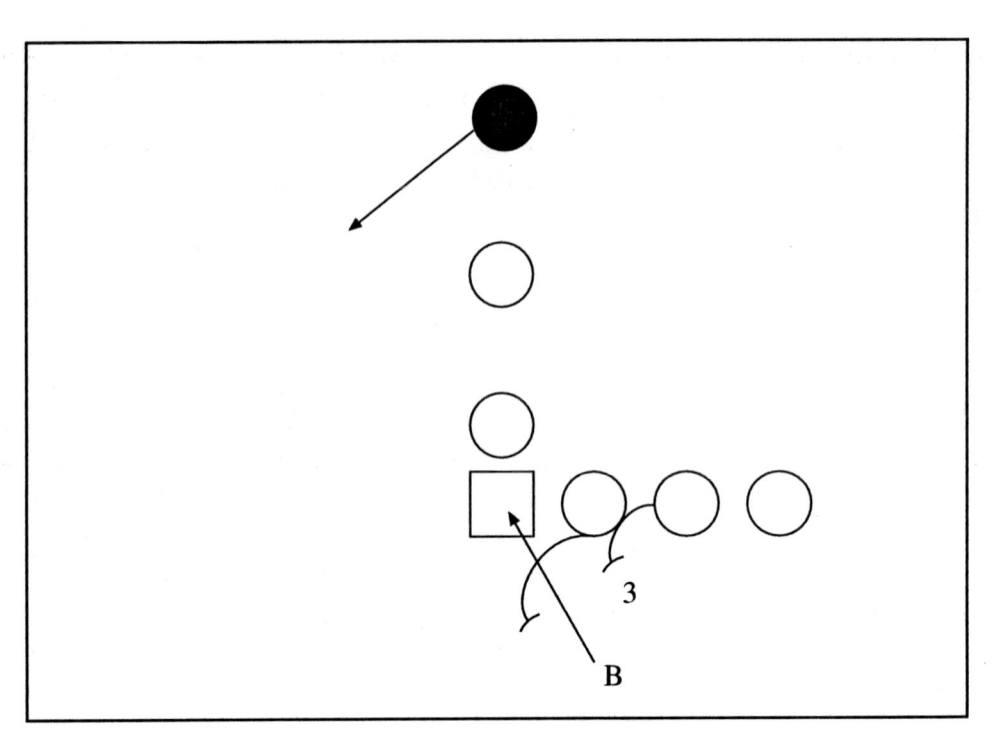

Diagram 5-4: The 3 technique is cut off by the tackle, and the linebacker is forced to compensate.

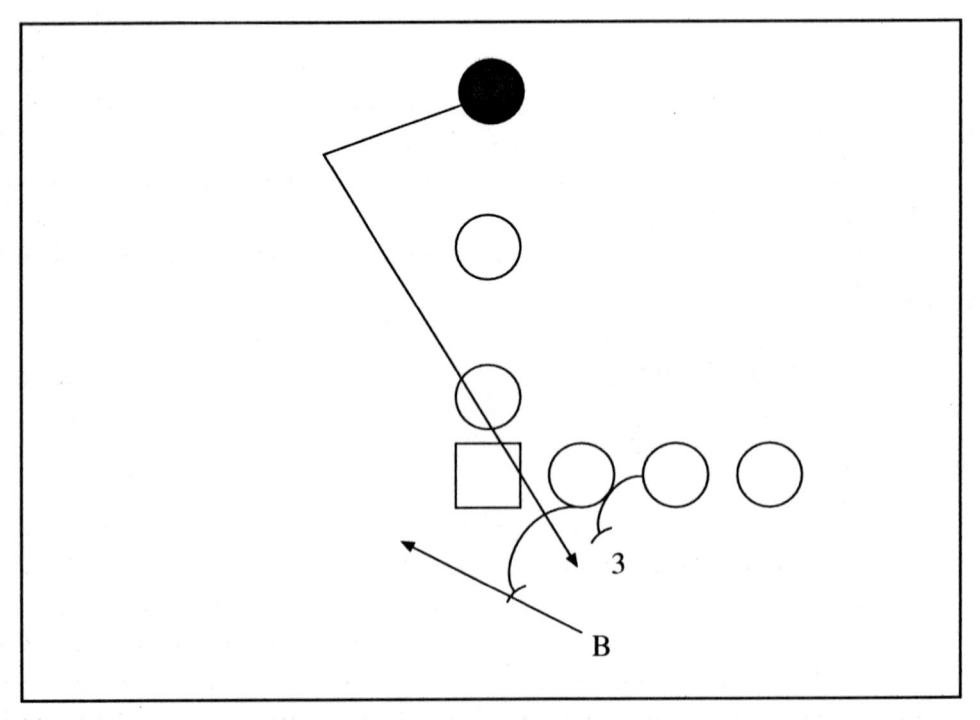

Diagram 5-5: The ball carrier cuts back if the linebacker fails to compensate for the 3 technique's failure to beat the tackle's block.

To emphasize a point: *In our system of coaching, the double team is played just like the reach block.* The only difference between playing a reach block and a double team is the defensive lineman's exaggerated hip swivel when playing the double team. To defeat the reach block, the defensive lineman must swivel his hips to the outside. Likewise, to defeat the double team, the defensive lineman must swivel his hips to the outside. Remember, it isn't the position of the head that matters, it is the position of the hips. You can get your head into the outside leverage position, but you can't be assured of keeping outside leverage unless your hips are outside of the reach blocker's hips.

The outside-shaded defender must play with a heightened consciousness of his "B" gap (i.e., guard-tackle gap) responsibility. Since he can never be reached, the outside-shaded defender must play the reach block and double team with a hair trigger. Through instant recognition of the double team, the 3 technique defensive lineman can throw his outside hip and buttocks into the offensive tackle and create a pile. Throwing his outside hip and buttocks into the offensive tackle also prevents the offensive tackle from converting his blocking technique from a pure double team to a combo block. By keeping his tail back and throwing his outside hip into the offensive tackle, the tackle prevents the blocker from getting a clean shot on our backside linebacker.

Nearly all combo blocks begin as a pure double team. On a pure double team against a 3 technique, the offensive tackle pushes off his outside foot and glides inside with a slightly angular step upfield to the blocking landmark. He attempts to keep his shoulders square and drive through the outside portion of the defender. As he drives through the outside portion of the defender, he uses his inside arm to punch and rip through the defender's outside shoulder. This action turns the defender's shoulders and provides the maximum blocking surface for the guard. If the guard is presented with the maximum blocking surface, he should be able to work around on the defender and gain outside leverage. Once the guard obtains outside leverage, he is able to finish the defender with a solo reach blocking technique. The offensive tackle drives upfield and intersects the path of the linebacker, cutting him off.

In the previous paragraph, the double team turned into a combo block. The conversion of the double team into a combo block occurred when the offensive tackle drove through the outside portion of the defender and turned the defender's shoulders so that the guard could take over.

You can see how the traditional method of playing the double team with the shoulders staying square to the line of scrimmage actually facilitates the double team-combo block conversion. Our method of playing the double team eliminates the tackle from the combo block formula. By swinging his hips into the offensive tackle, our 3 technique prevents the tackle from converting his double-team technique into a chip technique to the linebacker. Therefore, by rule, we eliminate the combo block. Because we eliminate the offensive tackle's option to chip to the next level on the combo block, we always force the offensive blocking scheme to waste two blockers on our 3 technique.

Once the defensive tackle swings his hips into the lead blocker (i.e., outside blocker of a double-team tandem), the defensive tackle uses his leverage and upper-body strength to get into the pursuit. While we don't expect the double-teamed defensive tackle to make tackles or even get into the defensive pursuit, we do expect him to waste the lead blocker and secure the "B" gap. If he accomplishes this objective, the linebacker corps will be the focus of numerous highlights.

Reactionary blocks:

The fold block, the trap block, and the high-hat (i.e., pass protection block) are the three reactionary blocks. We designate these three blocks as reactionary because we feel that in playing these blocks, no "wrong way" exists. The defensive lineman is trained to react to these blocks using one or more defensive techniques. Because the proper defensive reaction actually varies with the offensive technique used by the blockers, the defensive technique of playing off these blocks is categorized as a reactionary technique.

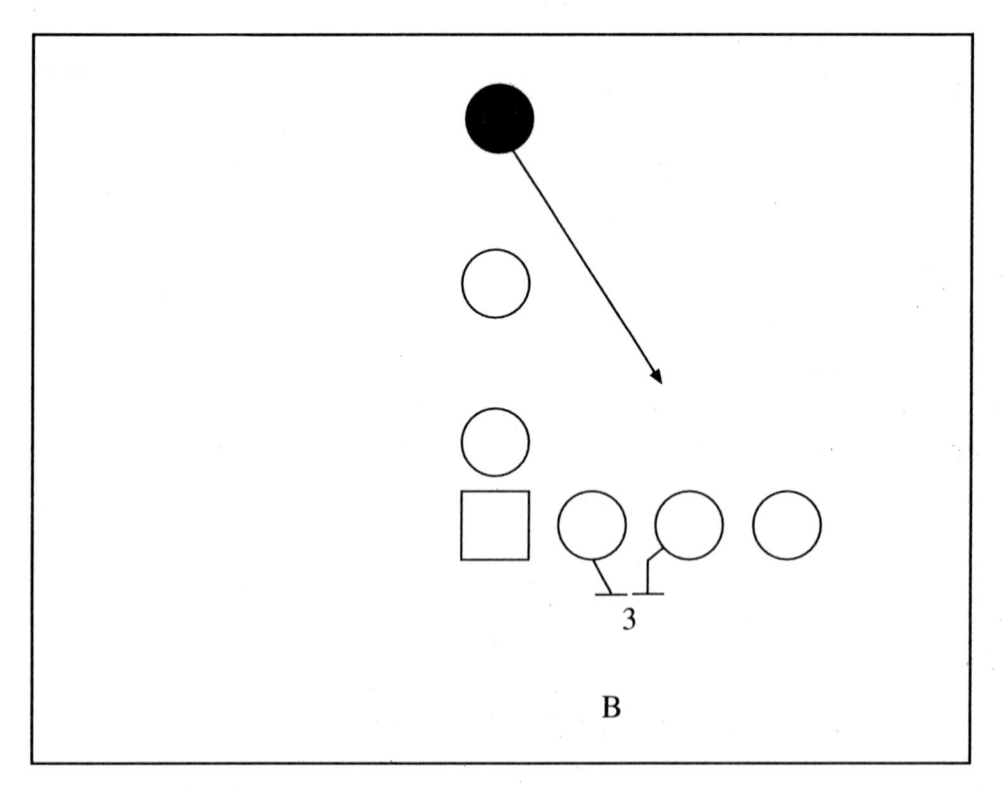

Diagram 5-6: The double team.

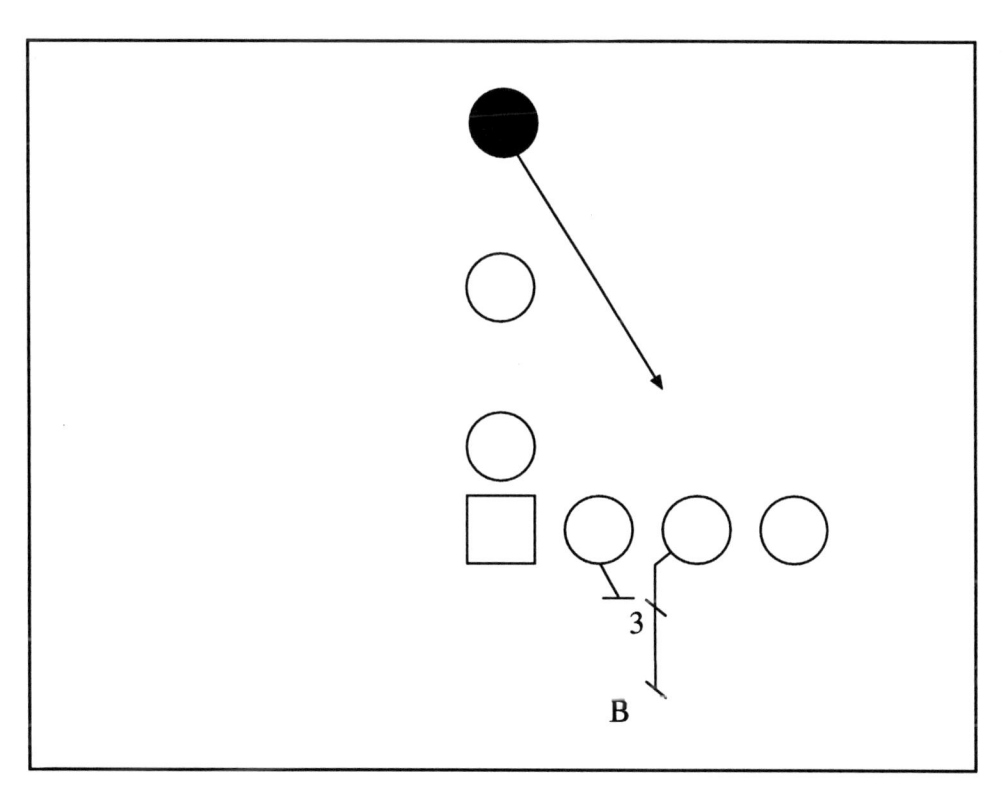

Diagram 5-7: The combo block.

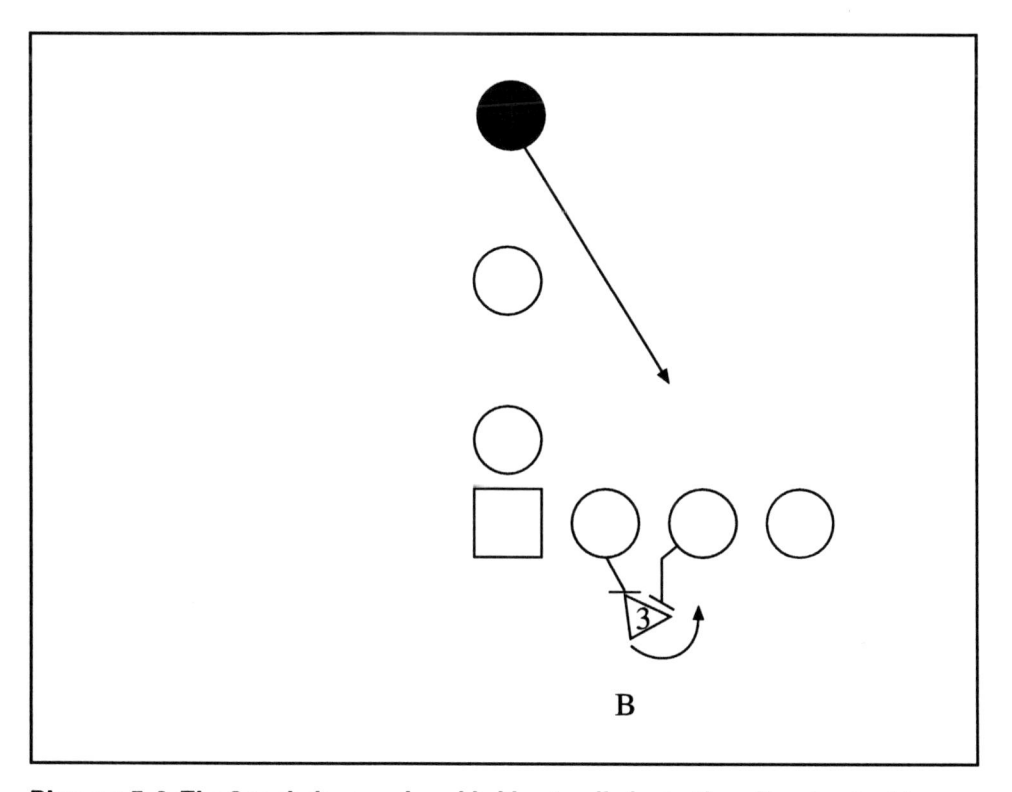

Diagram 5-8: The 3 technique swings his hips to eliminate the offensive tackle.

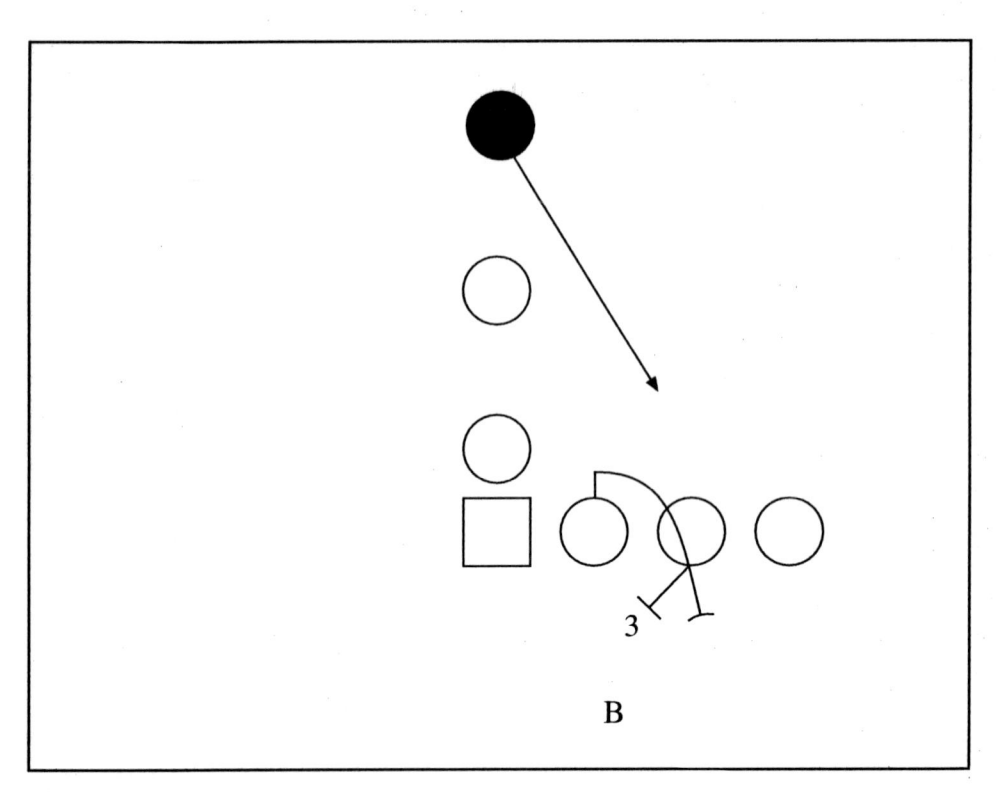

Diagram 5-9: The outside fold block.

The fold block:

The fold block is a combination of two blocking techniques performed by side-by-side linemen. The two components of a fold block are an angle block and a short pull. If the angle block is executed by the outermost lineman of the tandem, the fold block is designated as an outside fold block. Conversely, if the angle block is executed by the innermost lineman of the tandem, the fold block is designated as an inside fold block.

The outside fold block is a common combination scheme employed against the outside-shaded defensive lineman. In fact, the outside fold block combination is the first scheme to which the opponent will turn when his combo scheme is defeated by our 3 technique's rule block reaction. The execution of the combo blocking scheme is disrupted by the defensive lineman swiveling his hips toward the lead blocker. Knowing this fact and being comfortable with their level of training in defeating the combo block, our defensive linemen realize that the opponent will try the outside fold block combination as an alternate means of sealing the 3 technique inside while getting a blocker into position to cutoff the linebacker. Our linemen understand that the outside fold block is simply another way to accomplish the goal of the combo blocking scheme.

Inside fold blocks are used most commonly against an inside-shaded defensive lineman but are also seen occasionally by the outside-shaded defensive lineman. Both the outside

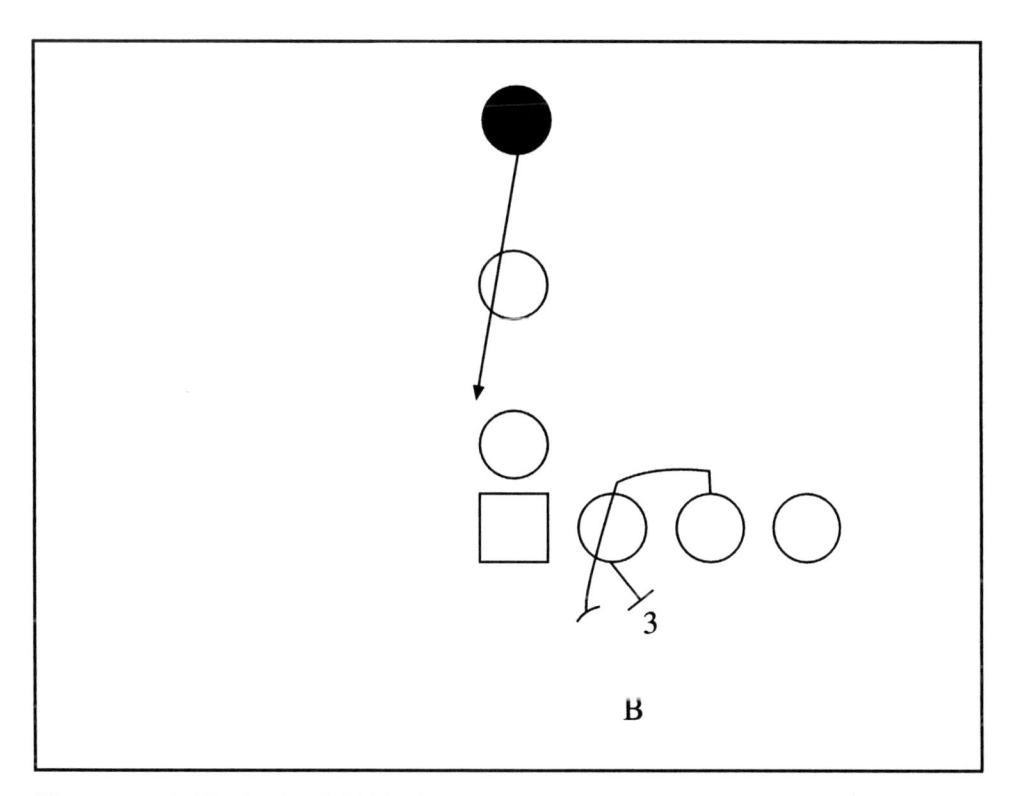

Diagram 5-10: The inside fold block.

fold block and the inside fold block are defeated with a quick defensive reaction. The proper defensive reaction to the outside fold block is essentially the mirror image of the proper defensive reaction to the inside fold block. Detailed in the following paragraphs are the options available to the 3 technique defensive tackle in his attempt to defeat an outside fold scheme.

Two reactionary options are available to the 3 technique who is attacked by the fold scheme. The first option is the run-around reaction. The second option is the cross-the-face reaction. The third option is the club-push reaction.

On an outside fold, the angle block is a down block executed by the offensive tackle. The run-around reaction is a reaction in which the 3 technique runs behind the down block of the offensive tackle. Again, we do not take the "big first step" on the snap of the football. Our read step technique—a short, power step on the snap of the football—allows our defensive lineman to read the outside pull of the guard and exercise one of the two reactionary options. A "big first step" on the snap of the football puts the defensive lineman in a position to exercise only one option—the run-around reaction. You can easily see how being limited to only one option versus a nearly unstoppable blocking scheme gives the offense a tremendous advantage.

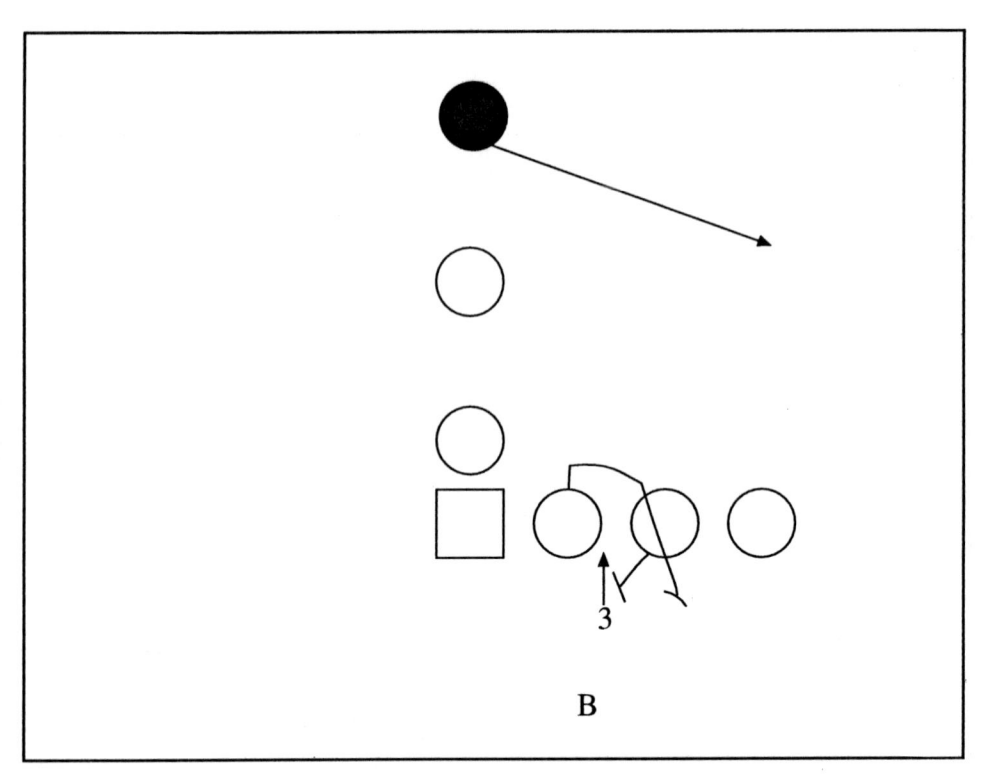

Diagram 5-11: The big first step puts the 3 technique out of position against the fold block.

By using the short power read step, the 3 technique tackle can read the down block offensive tackle. In reading the down block, the 3 technique makes an immediate diagnosis of the nature of the down blocker's angle. Is he too flat? Is his angle too far upfield?

If the 3 technique "feels" the tackle's angle to be too far upfield (i.e., toward the defender's hips), the 3 technique makes a quick decision to get into the hip pocket of the guard and run-around. He dips his outside shoulder and twists his upper body (exactly opposite of his technique used to avoid the tackle's scoop block on a jump-through combination) as he flattens his path outside to pass just behind the tackle's buttocks. This action allows him to clear the down blocking tackle and disrupt the guard's short pull technique.

It is important for the 3 technique to use his outside arm in a manner to facilitate his clearance behind the tackle's down block. The 3 technique should use his outside arm in the manner of an uppercut punch, throwing a violent flexed-arm punch as he makes his initial move behind the tackle. Throwing the punch provides added momentum and snaps the 3 technique's hips forward in an explosive forward thrust. This forward thrust behind the tackle's buttocks often is the critical factor in executing the run-around.

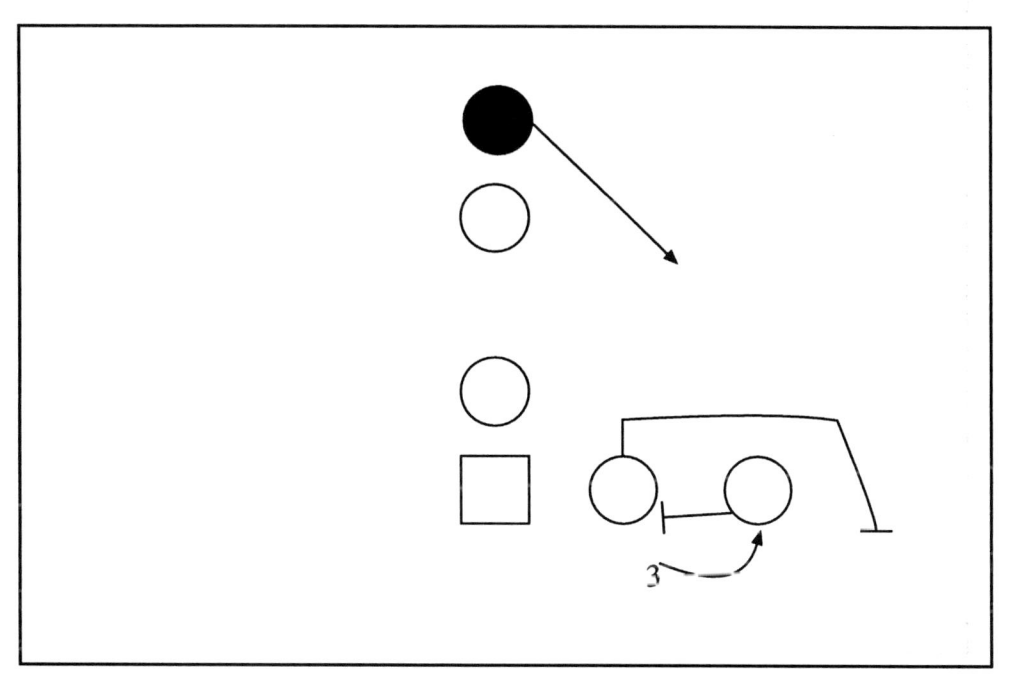

Diagram 5-12: The tackle's angle is too flat.

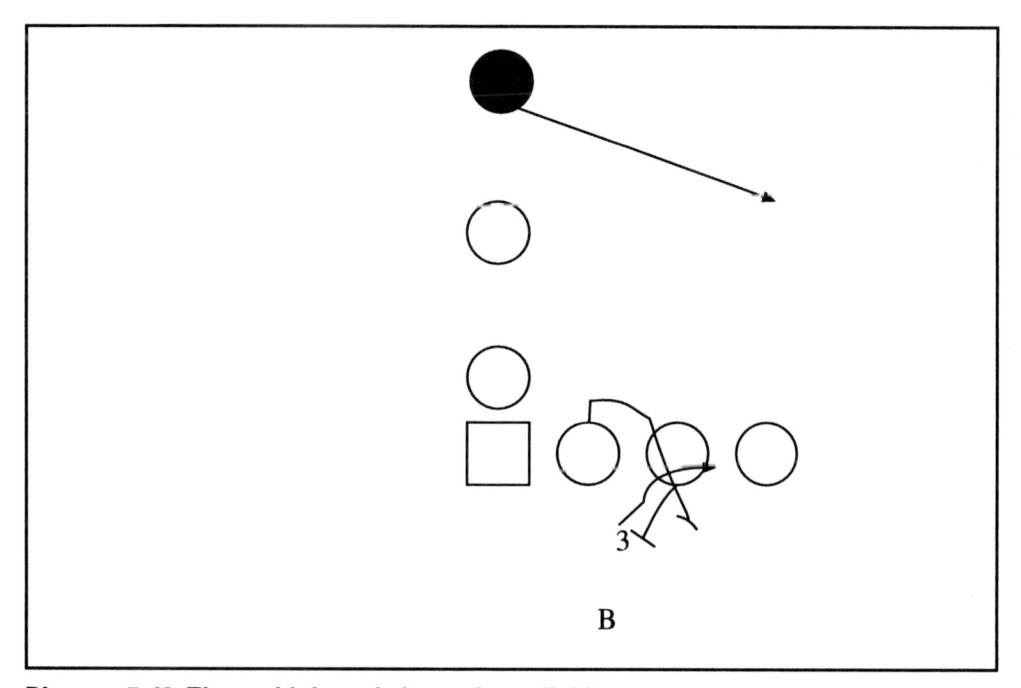

Diagram 5-13: The tackle's angle is too far upfield.

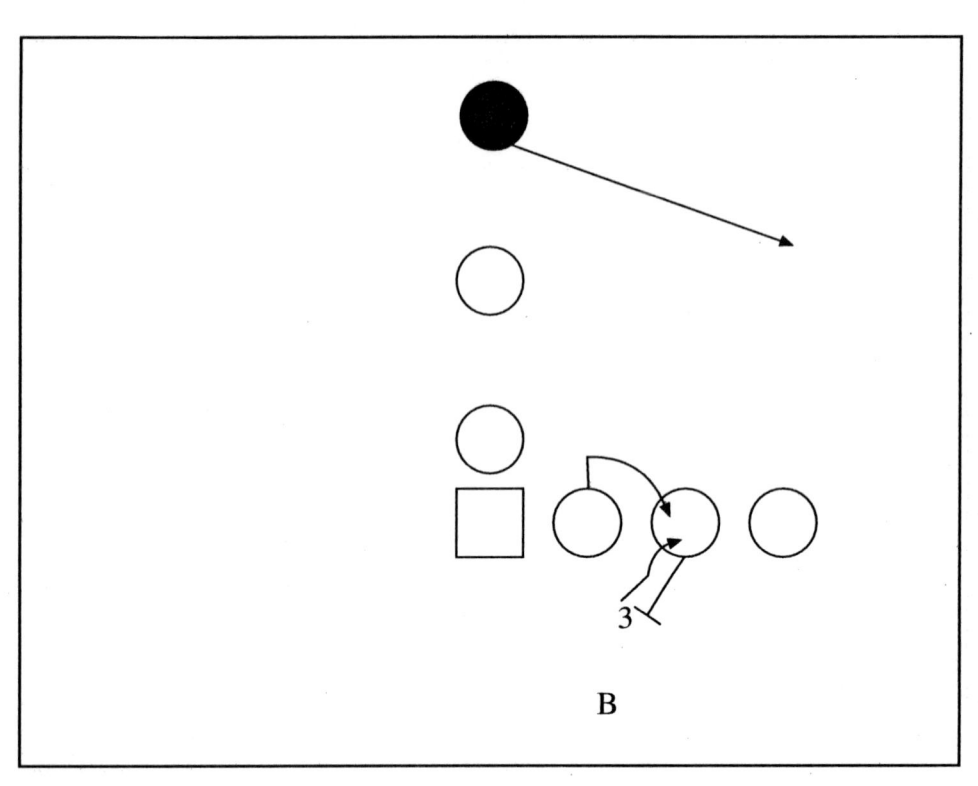

Diagram 5-14: The 3 technique executes the run-around technique and disrupts the scheme.

If the 3 technique "feels" the tackle's angle to be too flat, the 3 technique should exercise the across-the-face reactionary option. One coaching point to consider: The across-the-face option is generally successful only when the 3 technique knows the tackle's down block is coming. The 3 technique can recognize the impending down block through one of several ways, including:

- *scouting report of down-and-distance tendencies.*
- *scouting report of formation tendencies.*
- *unusually tight line split between the tackle and guard.*
- *a staggered guard-tackle alignment.*

Of the four keys to the fold block, the dead key (i.e., key that is highly reliable in tipping off an impending offensive scheme or strategy) to the fold block is the staggered guard-tackle alignment accomplished either through the alignment of the guard at an abnormal depth from the line of scrimmage or by an extremely close alignment of the tackle to the line of scrimmage.

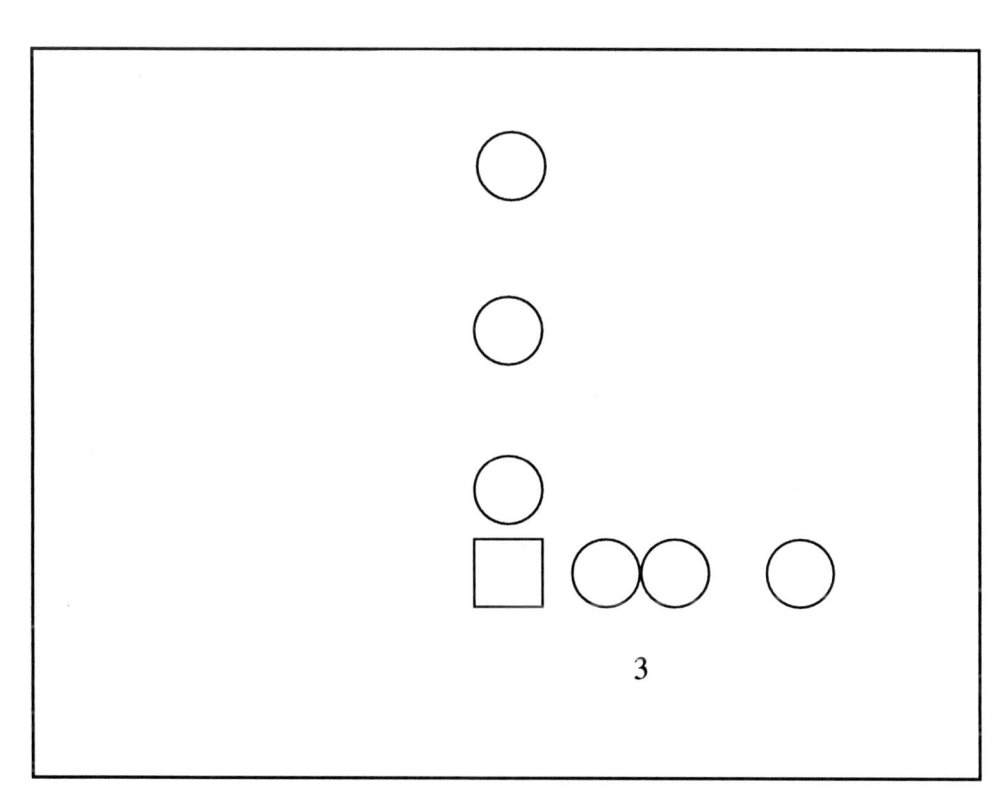

Diagram 5-15: The 3 technique recognizes an unusually tight split between the tackle and guard.

The *across-the-face* reactionary response is the preferred way of playing the fold block, particularly the outside fold block. However, as mentioned previously, the defensive tackle must have some inclination to believe that the fold block will occur if he is to use the *across-the-face* reactionary technique. Playing the angle block across the blocker's face not only wastes the offensive tackle's angle block, it puts the defensive tackle into an excellent pursuit angle and destroys the guard's ability to wrap around the horn of the down block. In fact, a well-coached offensive guard is trained to log the first defender around the horn. Therefore, if the defensive tackle successfully crosses the face of the down blocking tackle, the guard should engage the defensive tackle. Knowing the guard will attempt to log him to the inside, the defensive tackle should be ready to dip and rip his inside pad across the guard, as well as the tackle. Ideally, the defensive tackle will cross the face of the offensive tackle, then dip and rip to cross the face of the short-pulling guard, consequently defeating two blockers. Certainly, just crossing the tackle's face in itself is adequate for the realization of the defensive advantage. By crossing the face of the down blocking tackle, the 3 technique is able to waste one blocker and occupy another, thus freeing the linebacker to scrape downhill.

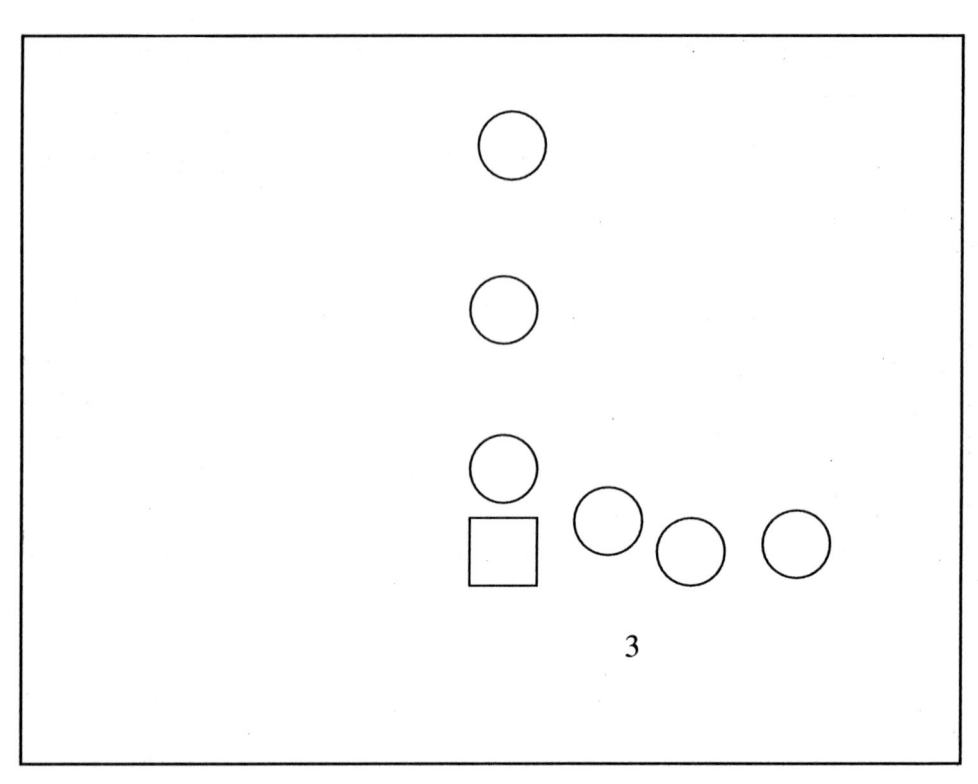

Diagram 5-16: A staggered guard-tackle alignment with the guard aligned deep.

The third reactionary response to a fold block is the push response. Like the across-the-face reactionary response, the push response involves clubbing across the angle blocker. The push is used as an emergency maneuver. Our tackles are trained to club the angle blocker and use their hip leverage to counter the pressure. We use the push whenever the defensive lineman is caught in sort of a no-man's land. This occurs sometimes against a well-coached offensive tackle. If the offensive tackle blocks down on a perfect angle, he can usually capture your defensive lineman in the no-man's land. The push technique is designed to minimize the disadvantage of being caught in no-man's land. To push, the defensive tackle attacks the angle blocker (the offensive tackle on an outside fold). As he attacks the blocker, the defensive tackle presses his hips backward and uses his upper-body strength to separate from the block. While the defensive tackle is most likely eliminated from the pursuit, he can achieve a position which allows him to play the cutback.

The trap block:

Because the trap block involves an inside release of one blocker, the 3 technique uses a similar technique that is similar to his technique against the jump-through. An inside release in the first phase of a trap combination differs only slightly from a jump-through. The inside release and the jump-through are comparable in many ways, including:

- *the objective of the blocker on both the inside release and a jump-through is to get inside to block another defender.*
- *both the jump-through and the inside release are techniques used by a blocker against an outside-shaded technique.*
- *while the angle of the two blocks differs, (the jump-through requires a flatter release) the blocker must get a free release to be successful on either block.*

To defeat the inside release (the first component of the trap scheme), the defensive tackle must use his jump-through technique. If the defensive tackle executes his defensive technique in stopping the jump-through and uses his inside hand and arm to pull the blocker's jersey, he will catapult himself inside to meet the trapping lineman. The catapult of the defender into the trapper's path results in somewhat of a face-to-face relationship of the defender. By more or less "facing up" to the trapper, the defensive lineman is able to use the wrong-shoulder technique.

The wrong-shoulder technique is one of two techniques used to play the trap. The other, less favored, technique is the squeeze or right-shoulder technique. In fact, the

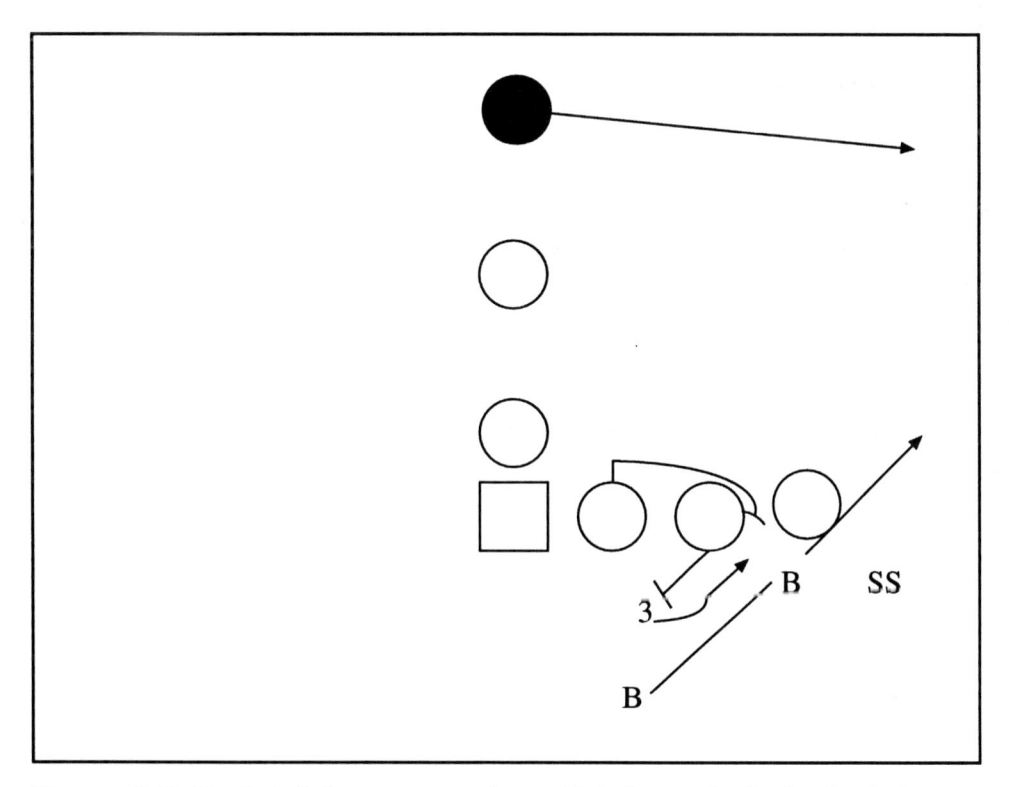

Diagram 5-17: The 3 technique crosses the tackle's face—the linebacker is free.

descriptions of the techniques as "wrong-shoulder" and "right-shoulder" is misleading. The techniques are a matter of choice or coaching philosophy. Neither technique is necessarily the "wrong" or the "right" way to play a trap. Indeed, both techniques are acceptable. It is simply a matter of which technique is most suitable for the defensive scheme. Most defensive coaches prefer the wrong-shoulder technique of playing the trap.

The wrong-shoulder technique results in what most coaches refer to as a spill of the trap. The technique can best be described in the following manner.

If the right defensive tackle gets an inside release out of the guard, he uses his jump-through technique to catapult himself inside. Upon sighting the trapper, the defensive tackle uses his right shoulder to attack the trapper's right shoulder. This attack technique puts the defender in an inside-out position on the trapper and closes off the hole. By closing off the hole in this manner, the defender forces the ball carrier to adjust his path. When the ball carrier adjusts his path to one side of the intended trap hole, the trap is said to be spilled. A successful wrong-shoulder technique spills the trap and forces the ball carrier into the linebacker's pursuit angle.

You can see that the wrong-shoulder technique fits well within our generic teaching system and relates closely to our technique in stopping the jump-through. The right-shoulder technique doesn't result in a spill. The right-shoulder technique requires the right defensive tackle to use his left shoulder to attack the trapper. (A trapper always comes from the inside.) This "outside-shoulder free" technique (i.e., right-shoulder technique) requires the linebacker to fill the trap hole. While our linebackers will be in a position to fill the trap hole, they understand that our defensive linemen will use the wrong-shoulder technique to spill the trap. Should something prevent our defensive lineman from spilling the trap, the linebacker will plug the hole. Should our defensive lineman do his job and spill the trap, the linebacker will fit with the lineman and make the hit on the spilled ball carrier.

The pull-away:

The important thing to remember when coaching the reactionary response to the pull-away is that we never fight across the accompanying fill block. In other words, when the 3 technique recognizes the pull-away, he should play behind the center's attempt to fill for the pulling guard. While we normally prefer the 3 technique to use a rip technique to get around the horn and pursue down the line, we understand that the swim move is another good way for the 3 technique to accomplish the defensive objective.

The rip technique requires the defensive lineman to rip his inside arm upward in the manner of an uppercut punch. The uppercut punch prevents the center from establishing a firm landmark and allows the 3 technique to sweep behind the block.

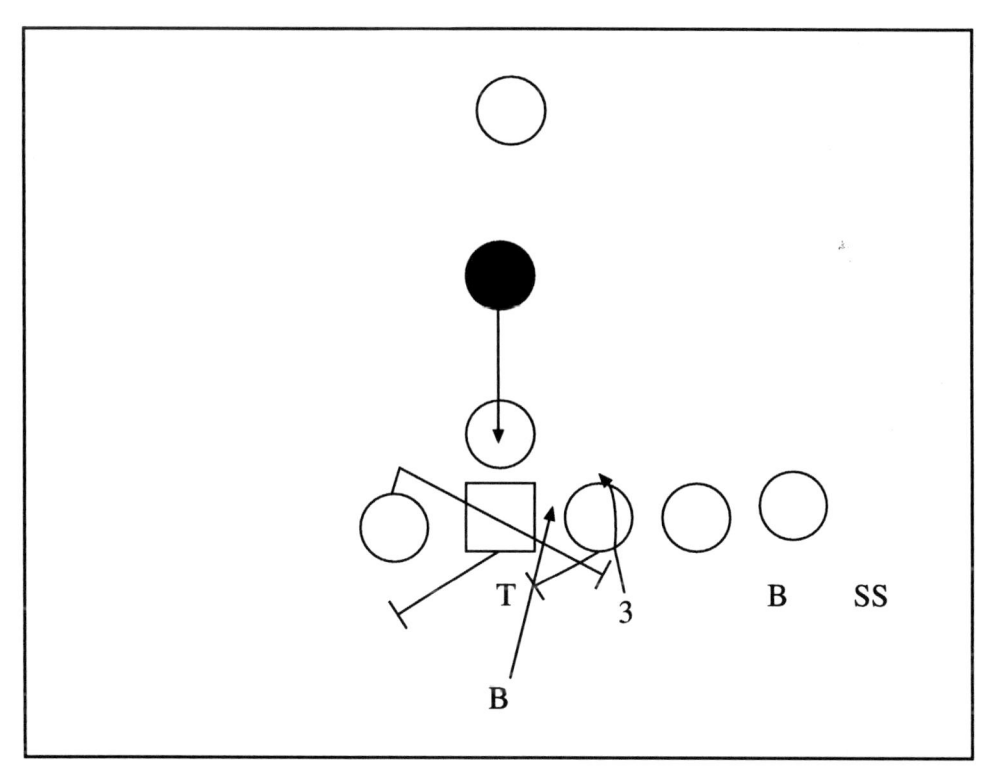

Diagram 5-18: The 3 technique fails to split the trap, and the linebacker plugs the hole.

A swim move can also be a good move versus the center check block (i.e., fill block). The swim move is particularly effective when the center's aiming point is too sharp (i.e., toward the defender's hip).

The high-hat read:

The high-hat is deemed a read, not a block, because it is a preemptive move (i.e., a move leading to the development of a block). The high-hat read can lead to the development of a dropback pass block or an influence trap. Although the high-hat read most commonly is a dropback pass block, the influence block is trickier to read.

The purpose of the influence block is to bait the defensive lineman into rushing the passer. Once the defender commits to rushing the passer, the high-hatted blocker drives outside to block another defender. The pass rushing defensive lineman then realizes he has been baited. However, at that point it is too late. The defensive lineman is easily trapped because he is too far upfield.

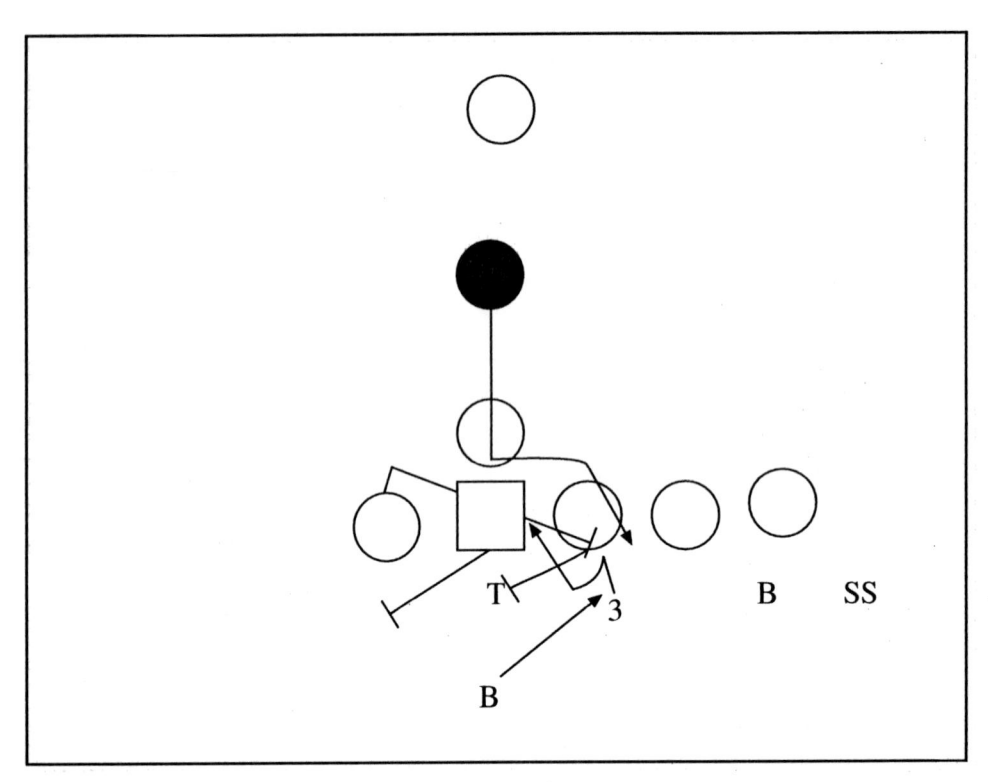

Diagram 5-19: The 3 technique spills the trap. The linebacker fits and makes the hit.

An influence trap is rarely used versus an outside-shaded defender. But it may be used if the outside-shaded lineman is particularly skilled at his jump-through response. Often, the guard will call an influence scheme at the line of scrimmage if he feels he can't get inside cleanly. In this case, an outside-shaded defender would be baited with a high-hat influence.

To play the high-hat influence effectively, the defensive lineman must learn to throw his eyes inside upon recognizing a high-hat. This momentary visual check inside should be a natural reaction to the high-hat. It will allow the defensive lineman to avoid being baited upfield. If he sees the trapper coming, or if he sees a tipoff to the impending trap, the defender can put on the brakes and attack the trapper. Just as he does on the normal trap read, the defender should use the wrong-shoulder technique to attack the trapper.

It is a good idea to practice the high-hatted influence trap on a regular basis. The influence trap is not as effective as the regular trap; it depends on trickery and poor defensive line technique to succeed. A well-coached defensive lineman shouldn't be hurt by the influence trap.

The second high-hat read is the basic pass pro (i.e., protection) technique. The high-hat read is detailed in Chapter 6.

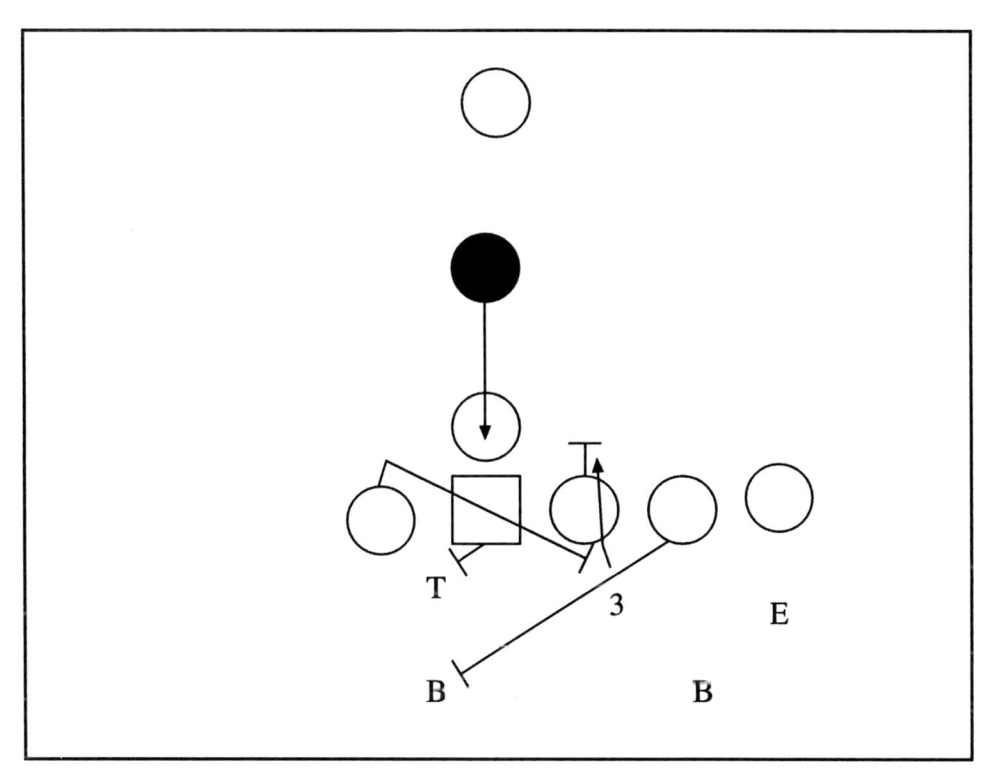

Diagram 5-20: The 3 technique is trapped easily after he is influenced by a high-hat read.

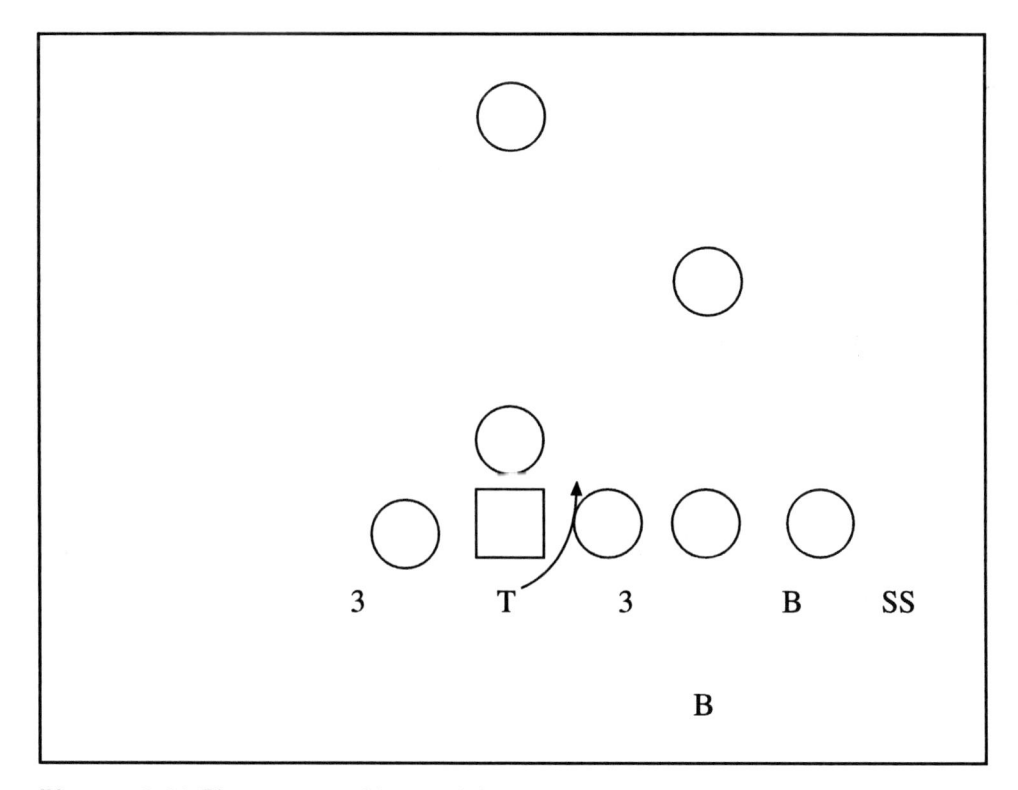

Diagram 5-21: The noseguard jumps right on the center.

The zero technique:

The zero technique aligns in the position traditionally called the noseguard position. Our noseguards normally play from a three-point stance as they align head-up on the center. He has two options available to him: jumping the center, and the 2 gap technique.

Jumping the center is a technique that highlights the quickness of the noseguard. Most noseguards are quick, as well as strong. Our noseguard is normally allowed to jump the center to the side of his choice. He can jump the center to his right or to his left, it doesn't really make any difference to our scheme. If the noseguard does exercise his center-jump option, he must get penetration into the "A" gap. This is a highly effective technique for the quick noseguard.

The 2 gap technique assigns the *playside* "A" gap to the noseguard. Since the determination of which "A" gap is playside cannot be made until the development of the play, the noseguard must read the center's hat to play the 2 gap technique. If the center's headgear moves to the noseguard's right, the noseguard quickly works his hips into the right "A" gap. If the center's headgear moves to the noseguard's left, the noseguard quickly works his hips into the left "A" gap. Remember, as with the 3 technique's technique, the key is getting the hips into the playside "A" gap, not the head.

The defensive end:

Other than the same responsibilities shared by the 3 technique (e.g., anchoring the line, not getting reached, etc.), the defensive end has two additional responsibilities. He must always be the force man and he must be responsible for bootleg, counter, and reverse (B.C.R.).

Being the force man means never getting leveraged by the ball carrier. This responsibility fits well within the defensive end's responsibility of never being reached. To contain the ball and leverage the ball carrier, the defensive end should work to keep his outside foot back in a stagger. This protects his outside leverage and allows him to stay outside the primary blocker.

B.C.R. responsibility entails a three-fold defensive alert to bootleg, counter, and reverse. Bootleg involves the quarterback faking a handoff to the opposite side and then rolling back toward the defensive end to pass or run. The bootleg can be executed with or without an offensive lineman pulling to protect the quarterback. The counter is a play in which the running back breaks back toward the defensive end; it is normally characterized by a pulling lineman acting as a lead blocker. The reverse is usually sprung as a surprise play. Although an inside reverse is an effective ploy, most reverses are outside reverses characterized by the ball being handed or tossed backward to a reversing wide receiver.

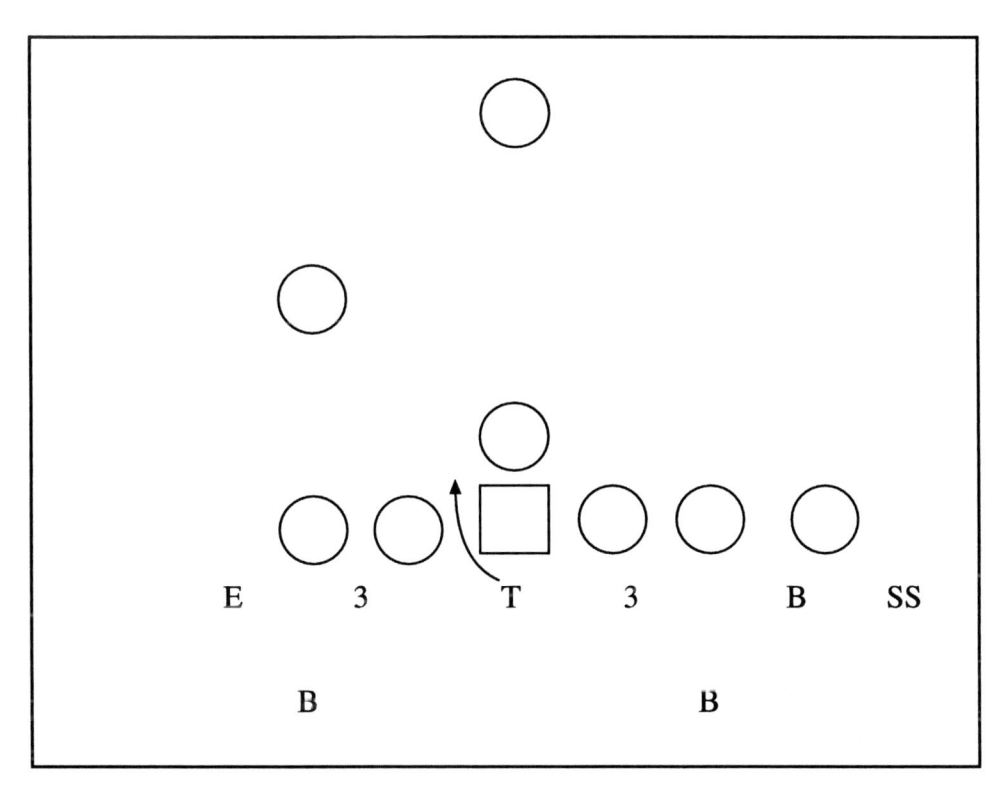

Diagram 5-22: The noseguard jumps left on the center.

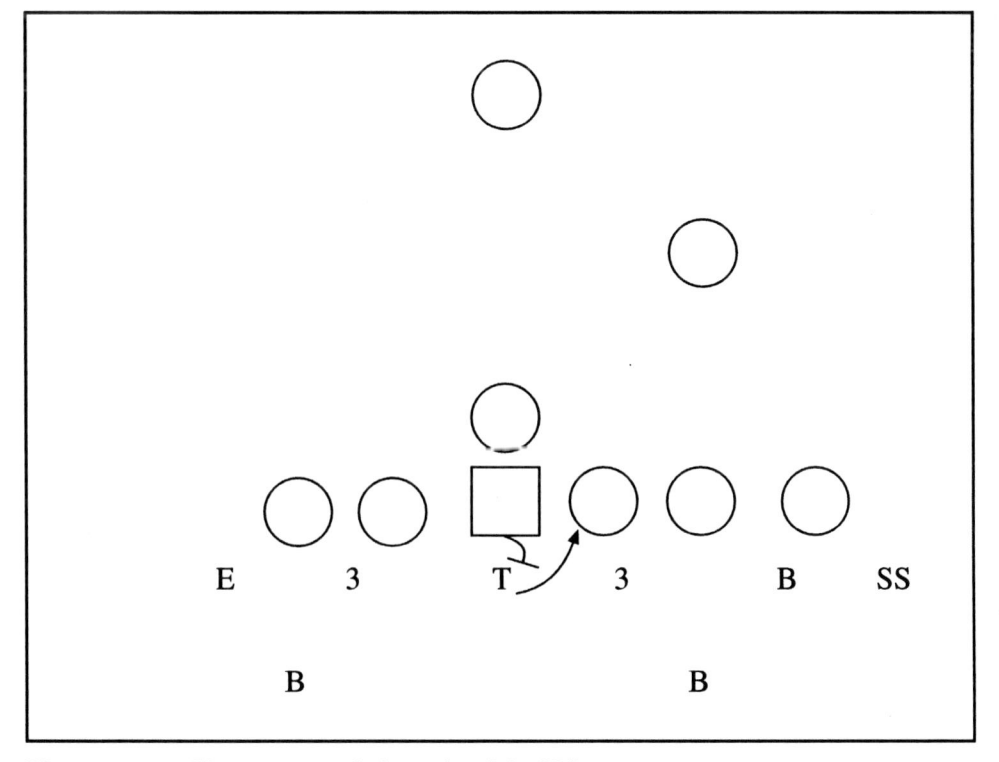

Diagram 5-23: The noseguard plays the right "A" gap.

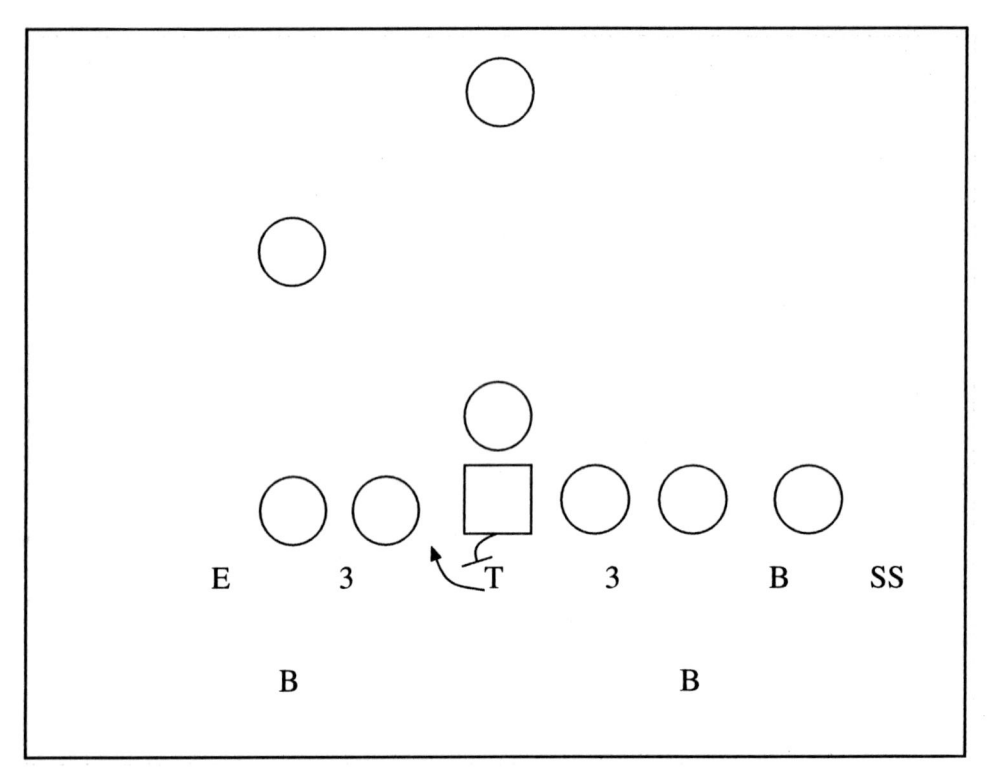

Diagram 5-24: The noseguard plays the left "A" gap.

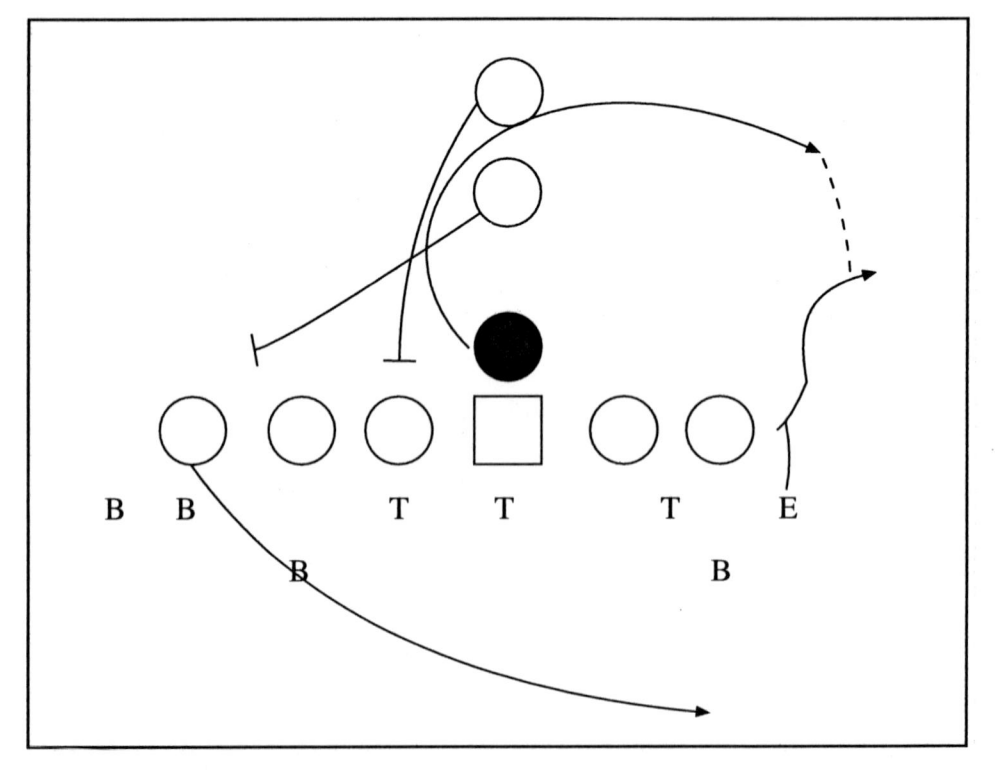

Diagram 5-25: This is the bootleg.

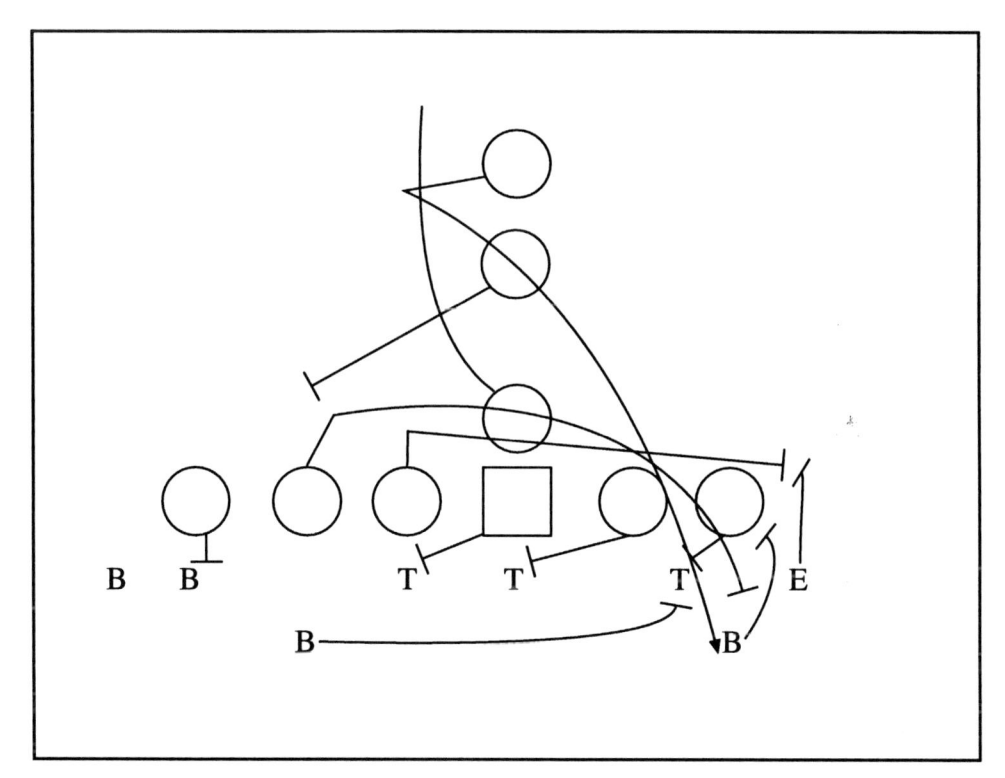

Diagram 5-26: The counter "OT."

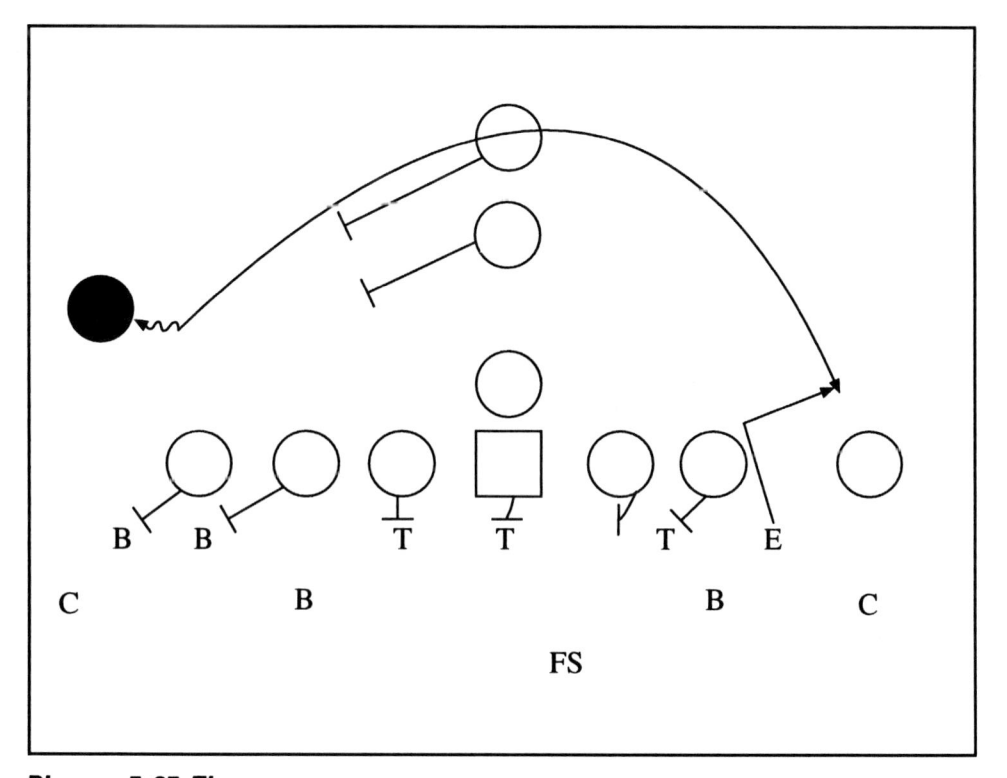

Diagram 5-27: The reverse.

When aligned on the open end (i.e., the side opposite the tight end), the defensive end should have an increased awareness of his B.C.R. responsibility. The bootleg, counter, and reverse are all run off a "flow away" read. In other words, the offensive tackle who is located on the open end will attempt a jump-through or pull-away. The tackle's action on the bootleg, counter, and reverse will cue the defensive end to shuffle inside. When shuffling inside, the defensive end should keep his shoulders square and his outside leg back. Keeping the outside leg back allows the defensive end to quickly drive upfield should an alarm occur. For the defensive end, an alarm occurs when the ball carrier—or other type of key such as a guard—suddenly appears out of the flow away.

An alarm should sound in the defensive end's head on the following situations:

- *The quarterback pops out of the backfield on a bootleg.*

- *A guard pulls opposite the flow—indicating bootleg, counter, or reverse.*

- *A back or receiver is seen passing behind the ball carrier to take a reverse handoff or pitch.*

To respond properly to an alarm, the defensive end should push off his inside foot and drive upfield and outward. Keeping his outside foot back also enhances the defensive end's ability to maintain outside leverage on the ball carrier or blocker. When the outside foot is staggered back, the player's hips are open to the outside. This open-hip position increases the defensive end's ability to recover his position of outside leverage and pressure the flank.

CHAPTER 6

PASS RUSH TECHNIQUES

As mentioned in Chapter 5, the high-hat read can indicate an influence trap or a pass protection (i.e., pass pro) read. Attacking and defeating a pass pro high-hat involves several considerations, some of which are as follows:

- *the depth at which the blocker sets up.*
- *the initial technique the blocker uses to engage the pass rusher.*
- *the depth of the quarterback's drop.*
- *the relative size and height disparity between the blocker and defender.*
- *the pre-snap keys available (e.g., down and distance, blocker leaning backward, formation, etc.).*

The depth at which the blocker sets up is a critical factor in the defender's decision as to which technique to use. Versus a shallow set, the defender should engage the defender and use a two-handed power move. Normally, a shallow set is an indicator of a shallow quarterback drop and a quick pass. Versus a shallow drop, the defensive lineman doesn't have much time to make a move. Often, his best option versus a shallow pass set is the simplest move—the two-handed push (i.e., bull rush).

The bull rusher's primary objective is to elevate the blocker's shoulders and force him on his heels. Once the defensive lineman reads the high hat and becomes a pass rusher, he should use the heel of his hands to strike the blocker. The heel of each hand should be positioned just below the top of the number. Once he stuns the blocker, the defender should violently bench press the blocker backward. The defensive lineman presses the blocker so that the blocker's shoulders rise. Getting the blocker's shoulders to rise is a key factor of success in the bull rush. A rise of the shoulders causes the blocker's weight to shift backward. Once the weight shift is achieved, the defensive lineman has gained the advantage. The bull rushing defender should visualize himself driving the blocker back into the quarterback, using the blocker's body to bother the quarterback.

The second option versus a shallow set is the push-pull move. A complementary technique to the bull rush technique, the push-pull technique requires the rusher to keep a low center of gravity. An effective bull rush technique stuns and lifts the pass protector. After stunning the blocker, the pass rusher finishes the bull rush technique with an explosively strong bench press. Grasping the blocker just below the top of the numbers, the pass rusher quickly jerks the pass protector toward him, then releases his grip, and clears the blocker. When used as a complement to the bull rush, the push-pull complement is a very effective technique in the interior line. It is an especially good technique to use at the lower levels where young offensive linemen often tip their weight forward when pass blocking. The push-pull technique uses the blocker's overextension against himself.

The initial technique of the pass blocker is another factor which determines the most appropriate pass rush technique. If the assigned pass rusher is aligned wide, the offensive tackle will normally gain depth on the snap. His objective is to create a cushion between himself and the pass rusher. This cushion gives him a chance to set up and use his hands to keep the rusher from getting to his body. If the pass protector does take a deep set, the defender has several pass rushing options:

- *Bull rush.*

- *Speed rush outside.*

    When engaging a deep setting pass blocker, the defender has an option to use the outside speed rush. To execute an outside speed rush, the pass rusher should dip his inside shoulder as he powers past the blocker. The speed rush should begin with the defender using his outside hand to pull the blocker's arm forward. This pull should be made in an explosive snatching manner. Reaching across his body to grab and pull the blocker's outside arm allows the rusher to gain upfield leverage on the blocker. As he reaches across his own body to snatch the blocker's outside arm, the pass rusher rips his leverage arm (i.e., arm closest to the blocker) upward in the manner of an uppercut to the blocker's armpit. Actually, the defender attempts to drive his arm upward in the manner of an uppercut punch not directly to the armpit, but to a point outside the plane of the blocker's body. This uppercut punch will force the blocker to turn his shoulders and open the gate to the quarterback. By dipping his inside shoulder, the pass protector offers less of a blocking surface to the blocker. The blocker's inside arm really has no available frontal surface to contact. The blocker is forced to use his inside arm and hand to "hip-steer" the pass rusher. Hip-steering is the last resort of a beaten pass protector. The pass rusher can finish his speed rush and defeat the hip-steer technique if he accelerates and sharpens his angle to the quarterback. If the pass rusher doesn't sharpen his angle to the quarterback, the "hip steering" technique—a technique where the protector puts his off hand on the hip of the speed rusher—can be an effective recovery technique on the edge.

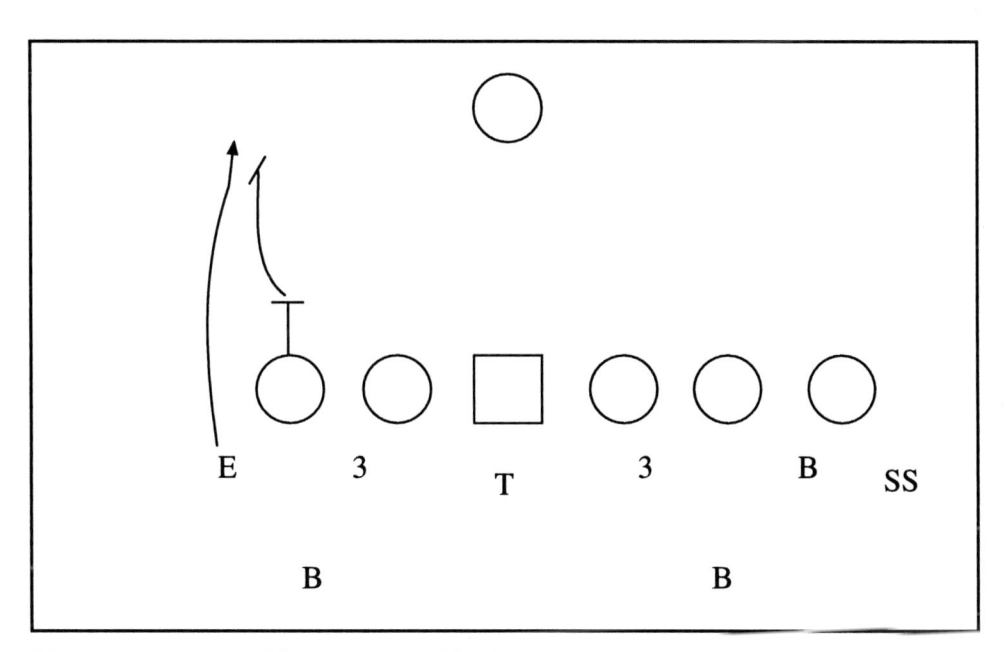

Diagram 6-1: The tackle recovers with a hip-steering technique.

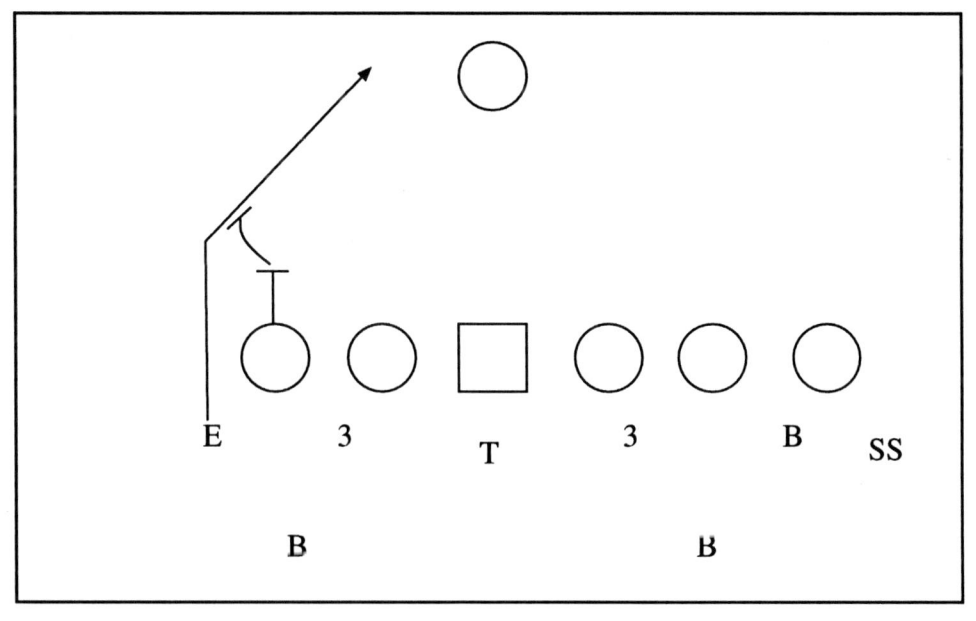

Diagram 6-2: The pass rusher sharpens his path to the quarterback, the hip-steer is ineffective.

While somewhat effective on the edge, hip-steering is normally a totally ineffective technique in the interior line. On a dropback pass, the interior defensive lineman has the advantage of a direct line to the quarterback. The pass rusher need only to push the middle while keeping his offside arm up to distract the quarterback. Once the pass rusher is free of contact with the pass blocker, the interior pass rusher should rush the pocket passer with both arms raised.

- *Club-and-under move (á la Reggie White).*

    One of the more physical pass rushing techniques, the club and under is an excellent technique when it is used by the talented defensive lineman. When executing the club technique, the pass rusher gets a vertical push to one side of the blocker. The blocker will react by shifting his weight to stop the rusher's upfield penetration. The pass rusher should instantaneously drive his inside forearm into the chest and shoulder of the blocker. The pass rusher's club technique forces the blocker toward the direction of his weight shift and uses his own momentum against him. Knocking the blocker off balance with his inside forearm club, the pass rusher then finishes the move by using the outside arm to rip underneath the blocker. Like other techniques, the club technique can be used to beat the blocker to the inside or to the outside. Because he has more area in which he can fake and maneuver, the club and under move is most commonly used by a defensive end.

- *Swim move.*

    The outside swim move begins like the speed rush—with a swift snatch and downward pull of the blocker's outside shoulder using the outside hand (i.e., hand opposite the blocker). The outside hand snatch-and-pull of the swim technique is slightly different from the offside hand snatch-and-pull of the rip technique. The speed rush snatch-and-pull is made in a sideways motion, in the manner of a roundhouse punch. The outside hand snatch-and-grab of the swim technique is made with a more high-to-low motion. When initiating the swim technique, the pass rusher snaps the outside hand downward and grabs the blocker high on the shoulder slightly behind the point of the shoulder. Grabbing the blocker's jersey in this manner enables the pass rusher to jerk the blocker's outside shoulder downward. By using his off-hand to reach across and pull downward on the pass blocker's shoulder, the pass rusher gives himself clearance to punch his inside hand (i.e., hand nearest the blocker) over the depressed shoulder of the pass protector. A key coaching point of this technique is using the word "punch" to describe the action of the on-hand swinging over the top of the pass protector's depressed shoulder. The traditional word to describe this action is "swim"—hence, the name of the technique. Several knowledgeable defensive coaches have examined the use of the word to describe the overhand motion to clear the blocker's shoulder. The word causes most people to visualize a swimmer using a broad, sweeping motion as he reaches to propel himself through the water. Many defensive line coaches believe that a more appropriate word to describe the motion of the swimming hand as a more compact and more violent "punch."

You should teach your player to move his inside hand and inside foot as one body part. Teach the move with the "same hand, same foot rule." As the inside hand punches over the depressed shoulder of the pass protector, the inside foot drives to a point near the heel of the blocker's outside leg. The defender's objective in simultaneously driving the foot to the heel of the blocker is to get the hip past the blocker's hip. Once the pass rusher's hip has cleared the hip of the blocker, the pass protector cannot recover. The pass rusher can add a final touch to the move by using his inside hand to push off the pass protector's back after he punches his inside-hand over and clears the blocker.

The swim move is most productive when it is used on the edge by a taller defensive player who possesses long limbs and exceptional upper-body strength. Note that the swim move described in the previous paragraphs is an outside swim move. If the blocker over-commits to the outside, the inside swim move is also an effective move. To execute the inside swim move, the pass rusher follows the same coaching points described in the previous paragraphs—the only difference is the obvious switch of right and left, as the inside swim move is a mirror image of the outside swim move.

The depth at which the quarterback sets up is the third consideration of the pass rusher. The pass rusher should keep the quarterback in sight as he engages the blocker. If the quarterback sets up at a shallow depth, he is going to release the ball quickly. The well-coached defensive lineman should learn to recognize the shallow drop and take the appropriate action. A shallow drop requires the pass rusher to limit his pass rushing technique to a power move or a quick rip to one side of the blocker. Also, by keeping the quarterback in his sight the pass rusher can adjust his pass rush angle, should the quarterback bring the ball down and begin to scramble.

A deep drop by the quarterback allows the pass rusher to use moves which involve more finesse. When the quarterback sets up on a 5-step or 7-step drop, the pass rusher should recognize that he has a chance to record a sack or a hurry. Defenders rushing from the defensive end positions should always maintain a tight outside-in leverage on the quarterback. The general rule to pass rushing while maintaining an awareness of the quarterback's location is this: *Focus on the blocker, but make sure you can see the quarterback.*

The disparity between the physical size of the pass rusher and pass protector is another important consideration when executing a pass rush technique. Generally, a defender should not attempt a swim move unless he is taller than the pass protector. A taller pass protector has the leverage to defeat the swim move. Shorter, bulkier, defenders should hone their bull rush, club and under move, and push-pull move. These three moves are tailored for athletes who possess power and bulk. Good speed rushers come in all sizes, as the technique is such that it diminishes the effect of the size. Normally, the taller the athlete the better his speed rush will be. This is because of his increased leverage ability. The usually tall offensive tackle cannot afford to lean on a taller speed rusher; however, his height advantage over a shorter defender can allow him the luxury of hitting downward.

Pre-snap keys may be the most critical consideration of the pass rushing defender. Our defensive linemen are trained to observe the stance mechanics and split distances on every scrimmage down. Many offensive linemen are coached to sit back in their stance on a passing play. We take full advantage of this type of offensive line coaching. Buddy Ryan once said that the secret to having a great defense is to play the run when they are going to run, and the pass when they are going to pass. We adhere fully to this philosophy. If an offensive lineman tips off to us that he is going to drop into a pass set, we throw our short power step technique out the window. You can believe that the 46 pressure defensive scheme has a provision for the "big first step" of the defensive lineman whenever a pre-snap key determines that the opponent is going to pass. Keep in mind that we are an attack defense—and an attack defense doesn't sit in the foxhole when the opponent shows his intention. Other pre-snap keys include formation tendencies, motion tendencies and situational tendencies. It is our job as coaches to examine our opponent's tendencies and extract any valuable piece of information that will allow us to *play the run when they are going to run and the pass when they are going to pass.*

CHAPTER 7

LINEBACKER AND STRONG SAFETY PLAY

VERSUS THE RUN

The 46 pressure package requires the services of a strong safety who can play linebacker technique. It is no coincidence that our strong safety is one of the fiercest hitters on the team. While his alignment varies according to the front and secondary coverage calls, his primary alignment in the traditional 46 look is directly over the weakside offensive tackle, four yards from the line of scrimmage. In this alignment, his primary key is the fullback. Our revised 46 alignment puts him on the line of scrimmage just outside the tight end.

As discussed in a previous chapter, the 46 package, and our entire defensive concept as a whole, is built on the premise of getting the linebackers a free run at the ball carrier. The defensive lineman's primary objective is to occupy the offensive linemen and prevent them from obtaining leverage and pathways to the second level. The free-flowing linebacker concept is driven by the read philosophy of our defensive line techniques. For our linebackers to be able to fill windows and run to the ball, our defensive line attack philosophy must be a power-step, read technique and not the increasingly popular "big first step" attack technique.

Alignment:

The normal depth of our linebackers when playing off the line of scrimmage is 4.5 yards. You may find that the 4-yard depth is more appropriate for your players, as the acceptable range is from 4 to 4.5 yards from the line of scrimmage. Because we are a multiple defensive front, our linebackers align in multiple positions. However, regardless of the different positions at which the linebacker may be required to align (e.g., over the guard, over the tackle, etc.), the one constant is the headup alignment. We never want our linebacker to shade his alignment to one side or another. Our pointer system of play recognition helps our linebackers to get a jump into the flow of the play. If a linebacker is shaded to one side, he will be extremely susceptible to the jump-through block from the opposite side. For example, if he shades outside the primary blocker, the linebacker will be exposed to the jump-through from the inside. If he shades inside a primary blocker, he will be defenseless against a zone-reach block from the primary blocker. While our defensive linemen are allowed to shade and adjust according to a formation tendency or other dead key, our linebackers play from the headup position at all times.

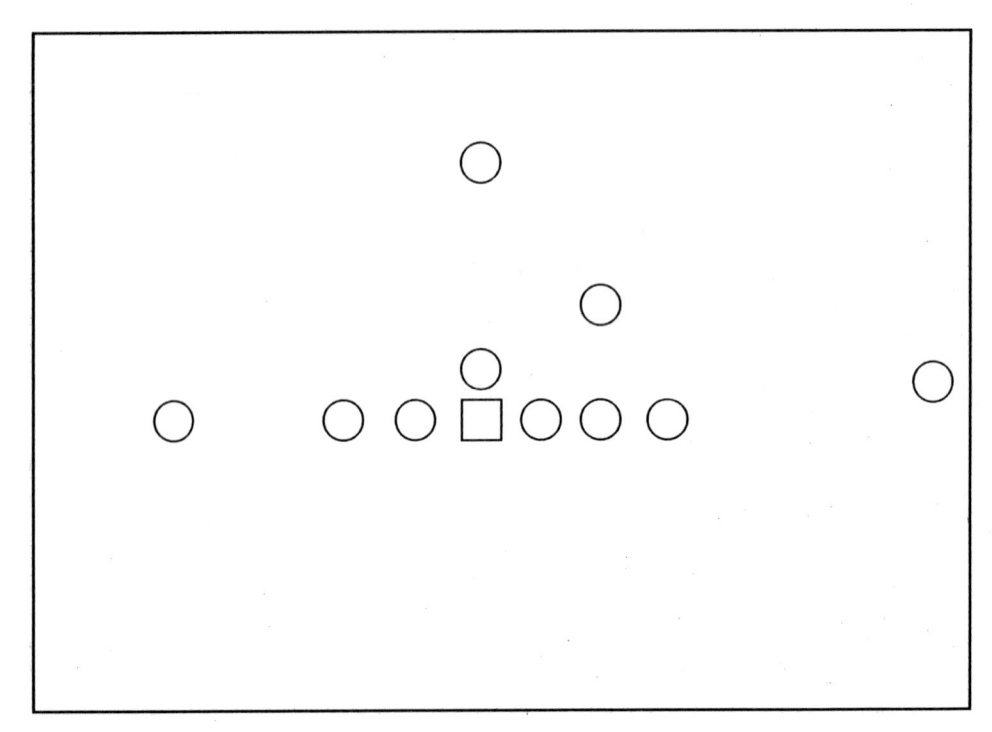

Diagram 7-1: The strong set I formation.

Initial movement:

Our linebackers take a pointer step (i.e., jab step) in the direction of the fullback's flow. This step puts him in a good leverage position against a jump-through blocker or a reach blocker. Just as importantly, the pointer step allows the linebacker to keep his shoulders square during the initial read. And by keeping his shoulders square during the initial read, he is able to redirect upon his recognition of an alarm such as a pull-away or pull-to.

Two-gap to one-gap:

Our linebackers play two-gap control. However, in the second it takes to seek and fill an open window, our linebacker usually becomes a one-gap player. He becomes a one-gap player when he correctly reacts to the 3 technique's action on flow toward him. In fact, many offensive formations and defensive front alignments tend to allow the linebacker to play a one-gap technique. Formations such as a strong set I cue the linebackers to favor the strongside gap, while the typical 46 alignment on the tight end allows the linebacker aligned over the strongside tackle (Mike) to be more conscious of beating the jump-through to the weak side.

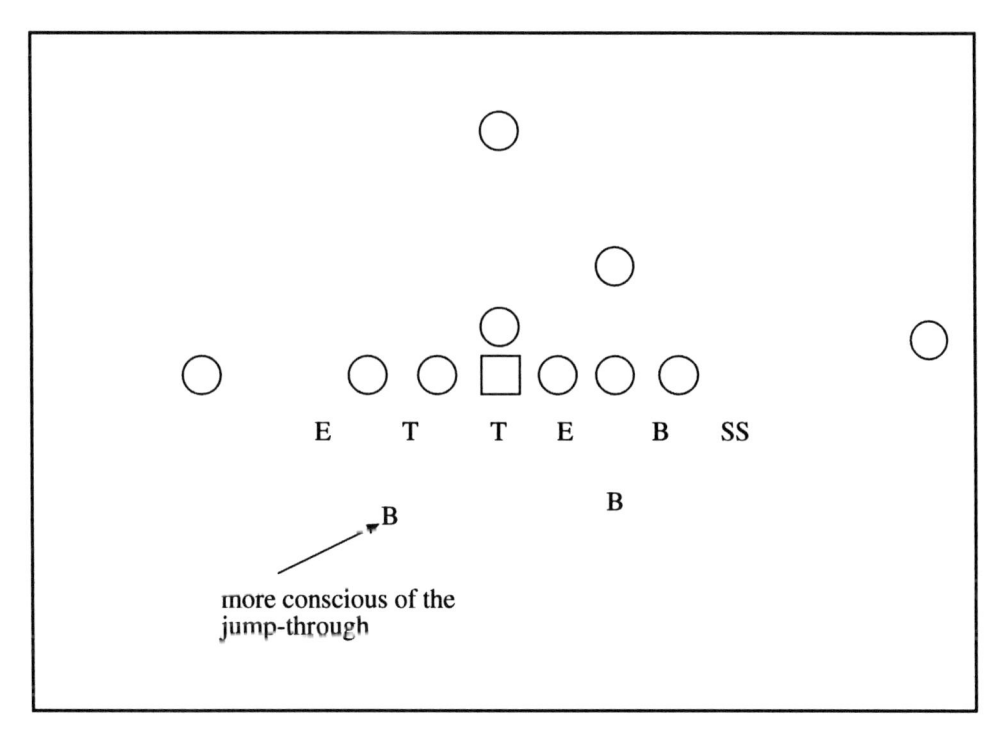

Diagram 7-2: The 46 alignment versus the strong set I formation.

The most common conversion of the two-gap linebacker into the one-gap linebacker occurs when the linebacker reads the action of the defensive tackle. For example, if the defensive tackle successfully defeats a reach block, the linebacker is "A" gap conscious. He makes sure the "A" gap is no longer a threat before he overruns the 3 technique. Remember, the 3 technique is responsible for a three-yard area to the outside; therefore the linebacker should be in no hurry to overrun a 3 technique. However, if the 3 technique fails in his assignment versus the reach block and is hooked, the linebacker must quickly get over the top as he overruns the 3 technique. He must replace the 3 technique in the "B" gap and continue to flow to the ball on an inside-out angle. In other words, our backside linebacker should overplay the reached 3 technique, but underplay the leveraged 3 technique.

In most situations, the action of the 3 technique determines the action of the linebacker. The one blocking scheme which doesn't require the linebacker to read the action of the 3 technique is the double team. Whenever the offensive tackle and guard double-team our 3 technique, we ask only that our linebacker scrape to a stack position behind the 3 technique. We feel that in most double-team scenarios, the tailback is coached to read the action of the playside linebacker. Our shaded 3

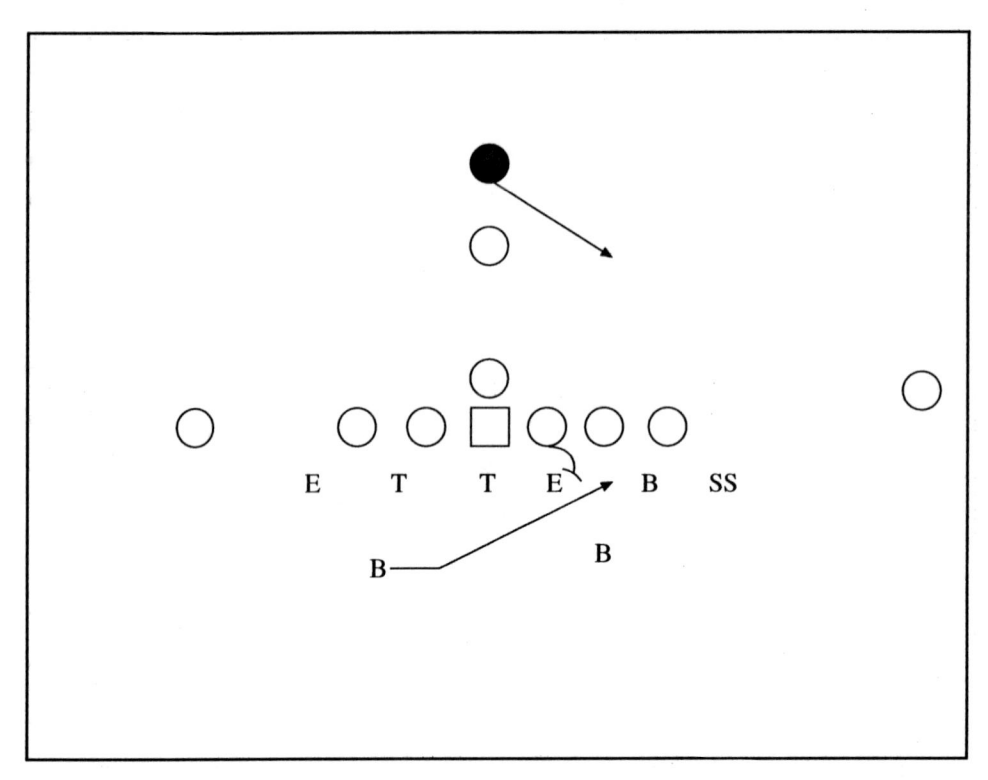

Diagram 7-3: The backside linebacker should overplay the reached 3 technique.

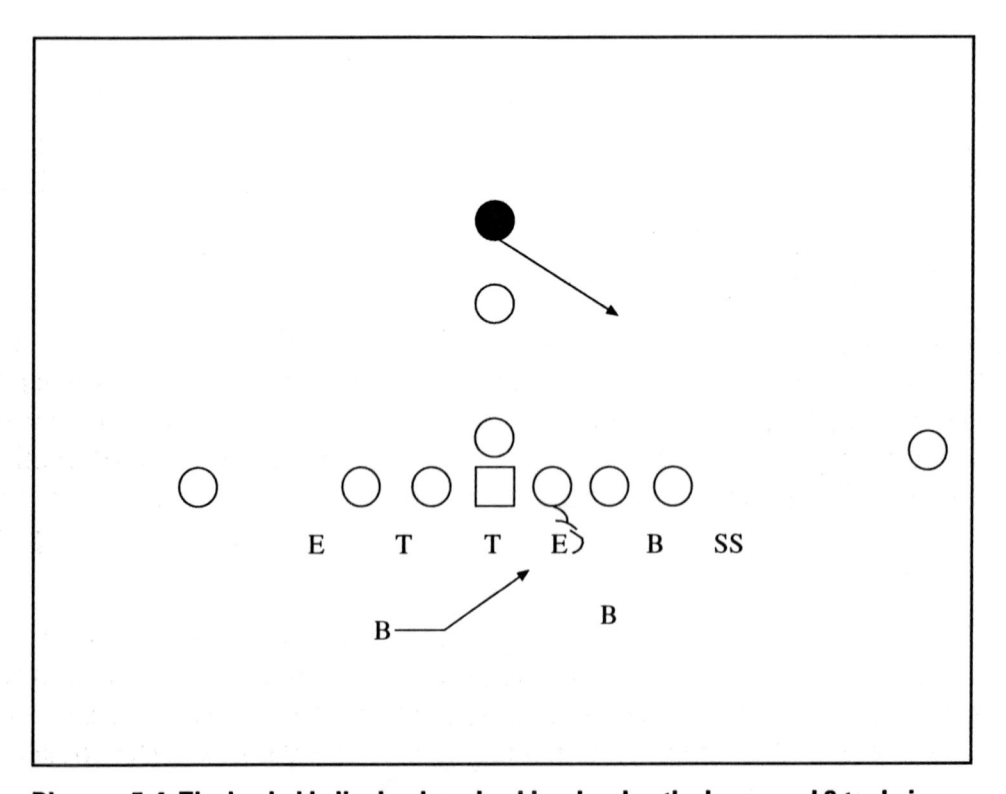

Diagram 7-4: The backside linebacker should underplay the leveraged 3 technique.

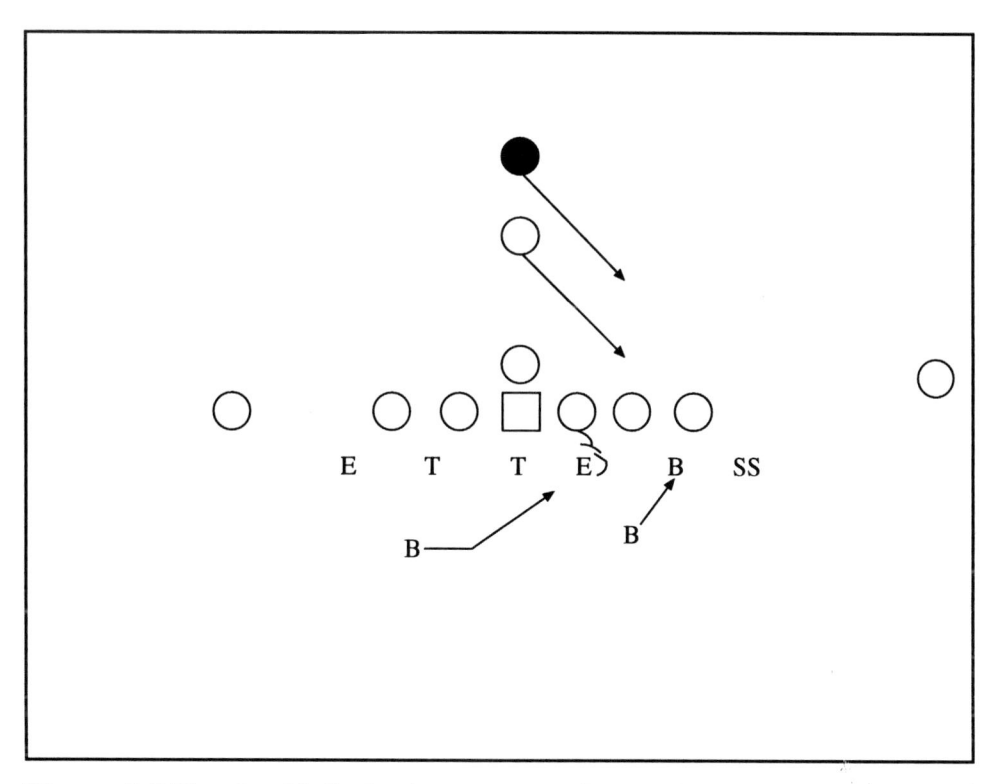

Diagram 7-5: The playside linebacker scapes to the outside linebacker's inside heel.

technique will get his hips in the "B" gap and stalemate the double team. Consequently, the I-formation tailback should look to cut it back to the inside. If our linebacker stacks behind the doubled 3 technique, he can fall back in on the cutback, yet be in a good inside-out position to continue in his pursuit should the tailback attempt to bounce outside.

The pointer system:

Our linebackers play what we call the pointer system. In this system, whenever a linebacker or strong safety aligns at the traditional linebacker depth and alignment, he will key the fullback. If the fullback flows outside of the 3 technique and toward the linebacker, the linebacker will look to the nearside tackle box to pick up the action of the tackle. The specific point to which the linebacker looks on flow away is the heel of the inside leg of the nearest outside linebacker or defensive end. See Diagram 7-5.

If the linebacker reads flow away, the linebacker looks for a high-hat of the backside guard or a pull back toward him. Should the guard be pulling back toward him (a pull to read), the linebacker will stop, rock, and roll to pursue the ball carrier on an inside-out angle. If the read is a high-hat, the linebacker will look across to sight a dragging receiver and pivot to his drop zone.

This brings us to the two alarms of the linebacker—a high-hat or a pull. An alarm is a recognition of an opponent moving counter to the initial flow of the primary key or ball carrier. For example, if both backs dive to the opposite side of the ball, but a guard shows in a pull-back toward the offside linebacker, the guard is an alarm. The action of the guard sounds an alarm to the linebacker that something strange is happening: A bootleg, a counter trey, or a reverse, is likely. Responding to the alarm allows the linebacker to stop, rock, and roll back into position to successfully meet the new threat and make the play. Likewise, if the guard shows pass, the linebacker will get a high-hat read. Reading a high-hat with flow away cues the linebacker to look to junction a crossing receiver or sink to his drop zone and wall out a receiver. The high-hat read tells him that the play is a pass when his primary keys say it is a run. Basically, the function of the alarms is to alert the linebacker to the true nature of the play. By being alert to alarms, the linebacker will not allow himself to be fooled by deceptive play passes and counters.

Stopping the counter:

Few two-back plays (or one-back plays) cause more problems for the defensive coordinator than the counter trey—also known as the counter OG-T. Because of our sound rules for playing the counter trey, our linebackers are not vulnerable to the OG-T. In the 46 package, the strong safety is responsible for forcing the counter trey to the weakside. The Mike linebacker (i.e., middle linebacker) is responsible for closing the window between the pulling guard and tackle. If the counter trey is run to the strongside, the strong safety sounds the alarm by yelling "pull-pull." He then becomes the hitter as he shuffles into the window inside of the second puller. The Mike linebacker will close his normal window between the first and second puller, while the Sam (i.e., strongside linebacker) will force outside of the first puller (i.e., guard). The 46 scheme always provides a defender outside the first puller, between the first and second puller, and inside the second puller. As always, the rules remain likeable and learnable.

CHAPTER 8

DEFENDING THE OPTION

Many people mistakenly point to the 46 scheme's vulnerability to the option as a glaring weakness of the defensive package. We aren't sure where this rumor of a supposed weakness to the option originated, but you can probably guess that it was started by an option coach who didn't want to deal with the 46 on a weekly basis. The truth is: If properly coached, the 46 defense cannot only cope with the option attack, it will break it down and destroy any hope for success. In fact, stopping the option from the 46 pressure package requires only two defensive considerations:

- *Your defensive plan must be fundamentally sound.*

    Obviously, the 46 pressure package is a fundamentally sound plan of attack against the option. As a defensive coordinator, you should avoid rigging a "special" defensive plan versus the option. Every defensive scheme can be manipulated to meet the demands of stopping an explosive option attack. Generally, it is a bad idea and an unsound premise to structure a special defense for the option. With the 46 pressure defense, you don't need a special plan or a gimmick, you only need practice at the sound strategies available inside the package.

- *You must vary your plan of attack when facing the option.*

    To effectively counter an option scheme, you should present numerous "looks" to the basic attack. The 46 allows you to plan various strategies to attack the option. These looks are accomplished through varying the individual responsibilities of your perimeter and second-level players. For example, if the option team runs a load scheme at your weakside, your defensive end can attack a point inside the load blocker, he can attack a point outside the load blocker, or he can be responsible for the pitch. Just as the defensive end can be assigned different responsibilities, so can the free safety and linebacker. This mix of attack strategies can give a quarterback fits when he attempts to make his read and execute the option play.

As a 46 coach, you can be sure of one thing: Your opponent will try to attack you with the weakside option. Even teams who normally don't run option will install an option to run against the weakside of the 46 defense. Chuck-and-duckers will try it, wing-T teams will try it, I-based schemes will try it, and one-back teams will try it. We know the weakside option appears inviting to the opponent because of the strength of the 46's alignment on the formation's strong side. And because we are aware of our apparent weakness, we have a plan to bait our opponent into bad decisions at the option's point of attack. Decision-making, after all, is the essence of the option's success. If you force the quarterback to make bad decisions, you will destroy the option attack.

For our defense to force the perimeter with several looks, we need the free safety to be active versus the weakside run. This accomplished, we incorporate three rules for playing the weakside option. (These rules also apply to the strongside option.) The "three rule" system for playing the option states that in order to effectively defend against the option, we must have a player assigned to the following:

- *Inside the load blocker.*
- *Outside the load blocker.*
- *Pitch.*

A load blocker is a blocker who is responsible for blocking the defender assigned to the quarterback. Load options are characterized by a load blocker. If an option is a dive-option, the dive back is designated as the load; therefore, dive options fit within the classification of load option. Most coaches classify options into three categories; load, lead, and speed. Lead options are characterized by a blocker assigned to the defender who has pitch responsibility, while speed options are run from one-back sets and are characterized by the absence of either a lead or load blocker. If the offensive coordinator facing the 46 defense runs an option that is neither a load option, nor a dive-option, the quarterback should check his major-medical plan for disability coverage. Versus the 46, the weakside option without a load blocker (e.g., lead option, speed option) is not only ineffective, but hazardous to the quarterback's career. Attempting the strongside option against the 46 defense—be it load, lead, or speed—is an equally bad decision.

Not only are our option rules a problem for the offense, they are fun to execute because they are aggressively and simplistically performed. They fit perfectly in our overall concept of keeping things likeable and learnable. The following chart details the defensive rule responsibilities against the weakside option.

The blue call versus the weakside option:

As outlined in Chart 8-1, the blue call requires the defensive end to play outside the load blocker. An important coaching point to this requirement is the defensive end's responsibility to make a play, not just occupy a blocker. A priority of the 46 defensive scheme is to never trade one for one. By not trading one for one, we mean that the defender is to never settle for occupying a blocker and securing an area on the field. We don't want any defender, particularly a perimeter defender, to trade his body for a position on a

	Will	End	Free Safety
Blue	inside the load	slow-play the pitch	outside the load
Tango	slow-play the pitch	inside the load	outside the load
Sally Blue	inside the load	outside the load	play the pitch
Sally Tango	outside the load	inside the load	play the pitch

Chart 8-1: Rules for attacking the weakside option.

blocker. Option attacks are designed to provide one-for-one matchups on the perimeter. If our players fall into the trap of thinking their job is to simply occupy a blocker, the option attack will take advantage of their misconception.

The blue call is a field call made prior to the snap, but you may choose to use it as your base plan against the option and simply make alternate calls at the line of scrimmage. The primary objective of the blue call is to ensure that we get a 2-on-1 advantage against the quarterback keep. Our defensive end uses his alignment width (i.e., two yards from the tackle) to keep his outside leverage and control a two-yard window to the outside. Because he is the force player, he plays outside the load but doesn't trade one for one.

Meanwhile, the playside 3 technique and the Will linebacker will play inside the load blocker in an effort to tackle the quarterback. The 3 technique will likely get a reach block read from his guard. If the 3 technique reads a reach by the guard, he should work his hips into the "B" gap and maintain outside leverage. Getting his hips into the hole puts him into position to be able to shed the guard and tackle the quarterback. (Remember, don't trade one for one.) The Will linebacker is singled by the tackle as he reads the fullback flow toward him. His pointer takes him to the inside leg of his defensive end as he keeps his outside arm free. In attacking the tackle, the Will linebacker attempts to fit snug underneath the load blocker. As the following diagrams show, the option attack weakside is in a pickle when our 3 technique defeats the reach and our Will linebacker attacks his pointer and defeats the tackle. For the offense, a worst-case scenario is realized when the quarterback makes a mistake and pitches off the first defender that shows our 3 technique. Pitching off the 3 technique would allow the Will linebacker to continue on to the pitch while the defensive end immediately breaks to the tailback on the pitched ball. And, don't forget—the free safety is flying upfield outside the load. Basically, pitching off the 3 technique gives us three defenders for the pitch. Indeed, the best-case scenario against a 3 technique loose in the "B" gap is the quarterback eating the ball for a loss. It is clear that if our 3 technique executes his top priority of not getting reached, the base-blocked option is an offensive option only in the choice of how to take a loss.

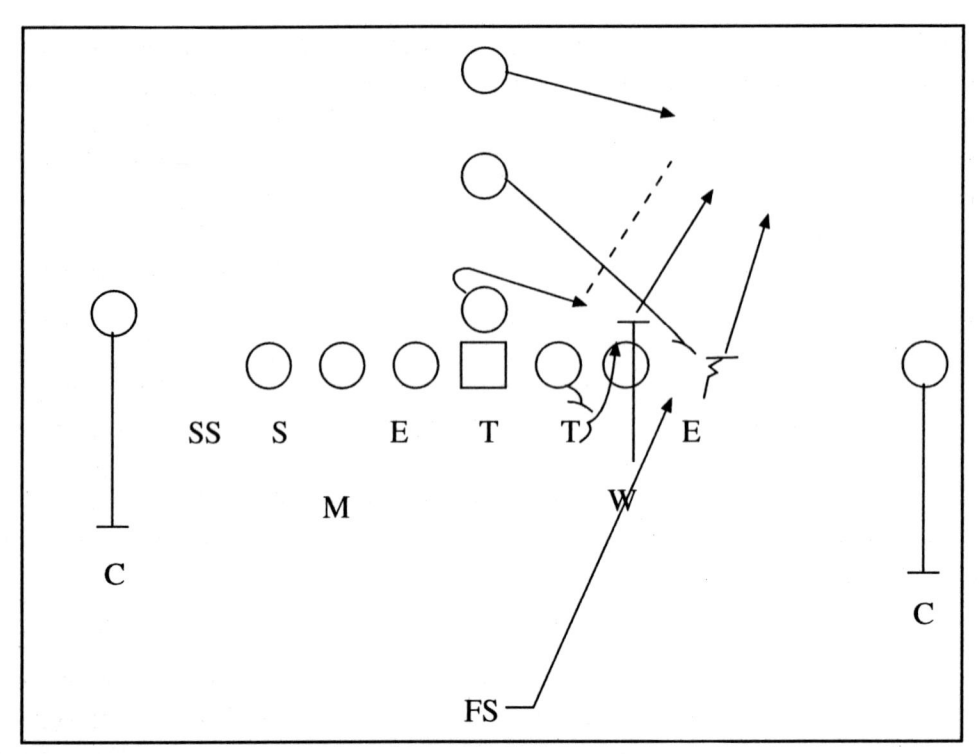

Diagram 8-1: The 3 technique's ability to play the reach block is critical to defensive success against the option.

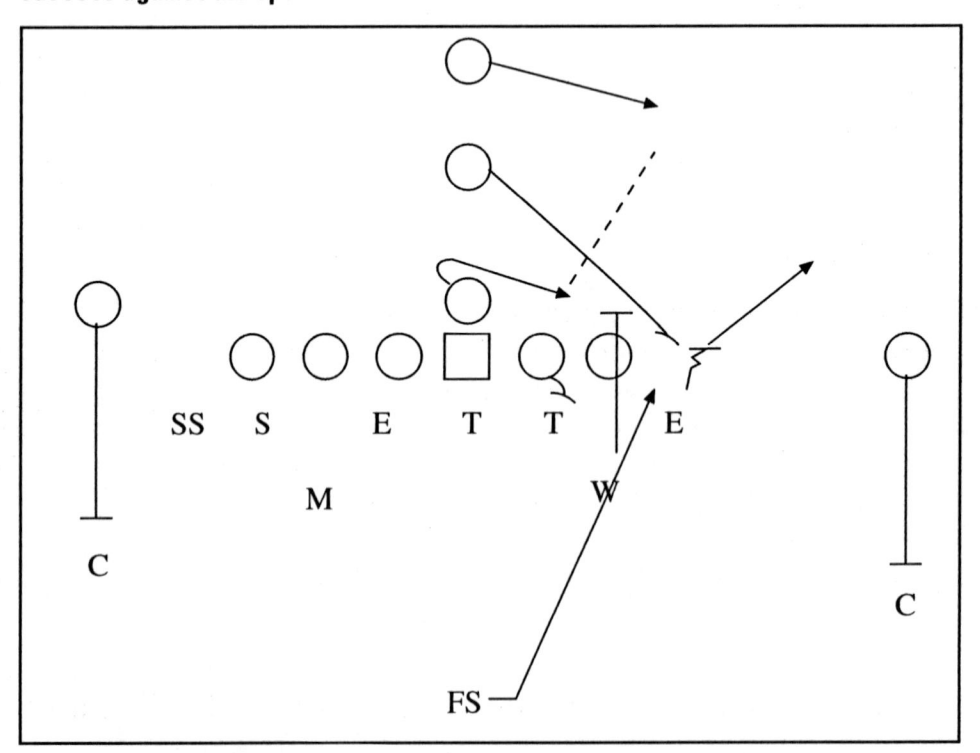

Diagram 8-2: The Will linebacker attacks the tackle and fits inside the load block.

Knowing that the premise of our defense is to not be reached at the 3 technique, some teams will veer block the load option. In this case, the Will linebacker will get a down block read from the tackle as he chips through the 3 technique to cut off the fast flowing Mike linebacker. Unfortunately for the offense, the combo scheme will likely free two defenders. First, the Will is free to fill inside the load blocker and take the quarterback. If the load blocker attempts to load the linebacker, the linebacker will cause a train wreck as he meets the fullback at the line of scrimmage. In any case, the 3 technique will disrupt the combo scheme as he reads the reach and throws his hips into the hole, establishing a "B" gap barrier to prevent the tackle from chipping to the next level. When the tackle gets his hips into the tackle and prevents the chip, the Mike is given a free lane to the football. Mike becomes a free-hitter as the backside tackle and nose prevent a jump-through from the guard and center. Therefore, if the front-line defenders all do their job well against a veer blocking scheme, both the Will and the Mike will be free to flow to the quarterback. The free safety will put the icing on the cake as he fits outside the load while the defensive end slow-plays, favoring the pitch.

An important coaching point for the slow-playing defensive end on the blue call: He cannot afford to overemphasize his slow-play technique. You don't want your defensive end to get into a position in which he is required to rely on his foot speed to run down a tailback. As the force player, he should never lose outside leverage on the tailback. Emphasize to all your players that the force player must never sacrifice leverage for technique. Naturally, he must stay on his feet and keep his butt back as he fends off the blocker. His back foot should be staggered back as he plays his technique. Keeping the outside foot back not only protects him from being cut, it keeps his hips open so that he can break at an angle down the line of scrimmage. Whenever a defensive end—or any front player—breaks to a cover a pitchman, he should open to the sideline so that he can intercept the pitchman anywhere from 3 yards behind the line of scrimmage to 5 yards in front of the line of scrimmage.

The tango versus the weakside option:

A second way to play the weakside option is the tango call. The tango call changes the responsibility of the Will linebacker and the end; the free safety's responsibility remains the same as the blue call. On the tango call, the defensive end will crash down through a point on the tackle's hip. Actually, his line of attack takes him through the front part of the tackle's hip. This angle keeps him down inside and facilitates his wrong-shoulder attack technique. If the dive block shows or if a guard attempts to pull toward the defensive end, the end will use the wrong-shoulder technique. By using the wrong-shoulder technique, the defensive end will spill any action to the outside. The Will linebacker will read the flow and read the closed window in front of him as the defensive end crashes down. Upon recognition of the flow toward him, the Will should fit off the defensive end's butt and get into position to slow-play the pitch. The Will should make sure that he positions himself in the proper posture for slow-playing; outside foot back, shoulders

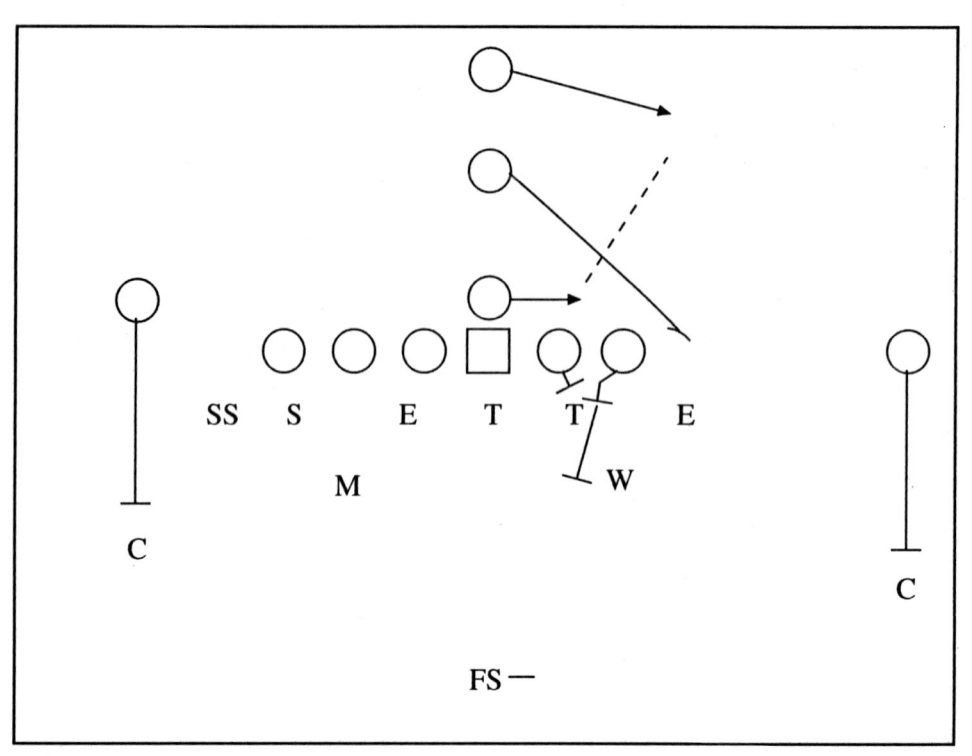

Diagram 8-3: Some teams will attempt the veer blocking scheme.

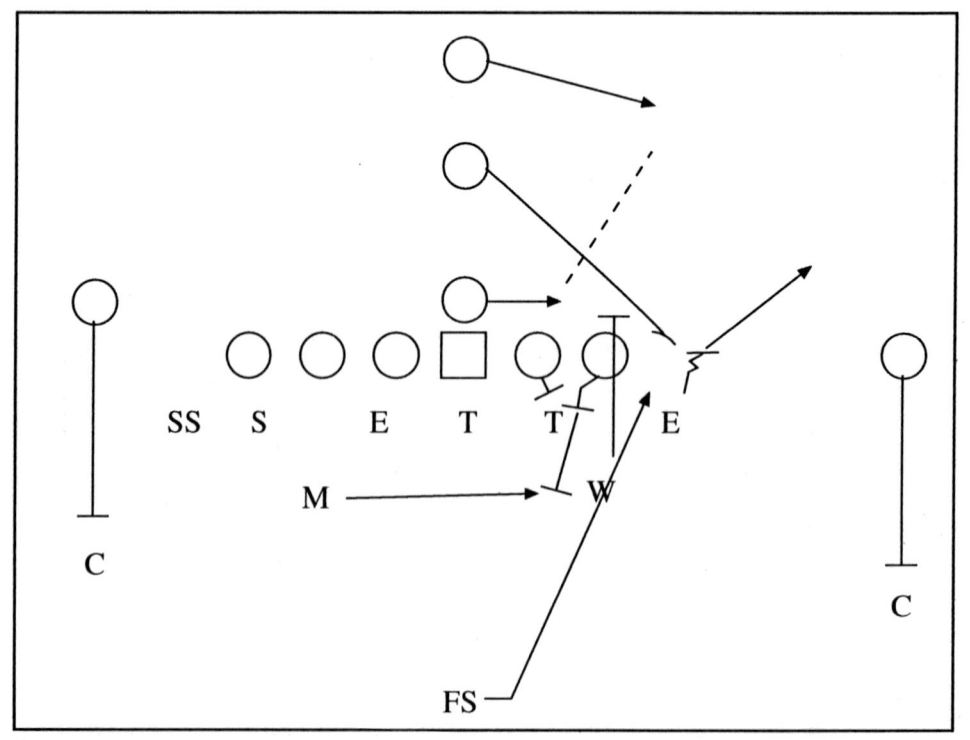

Diagram 8-4: One possible defensive reaction to the veer blocking scheme.

72

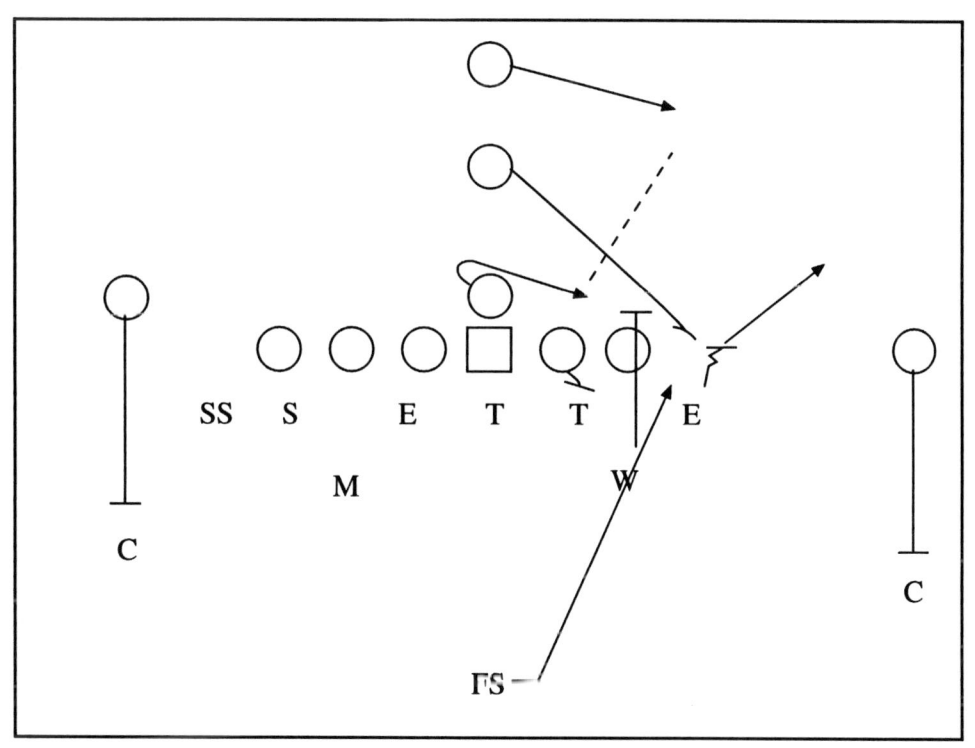

Diagram 8-5: The proper angle for a defensive end breaking to the pitch.

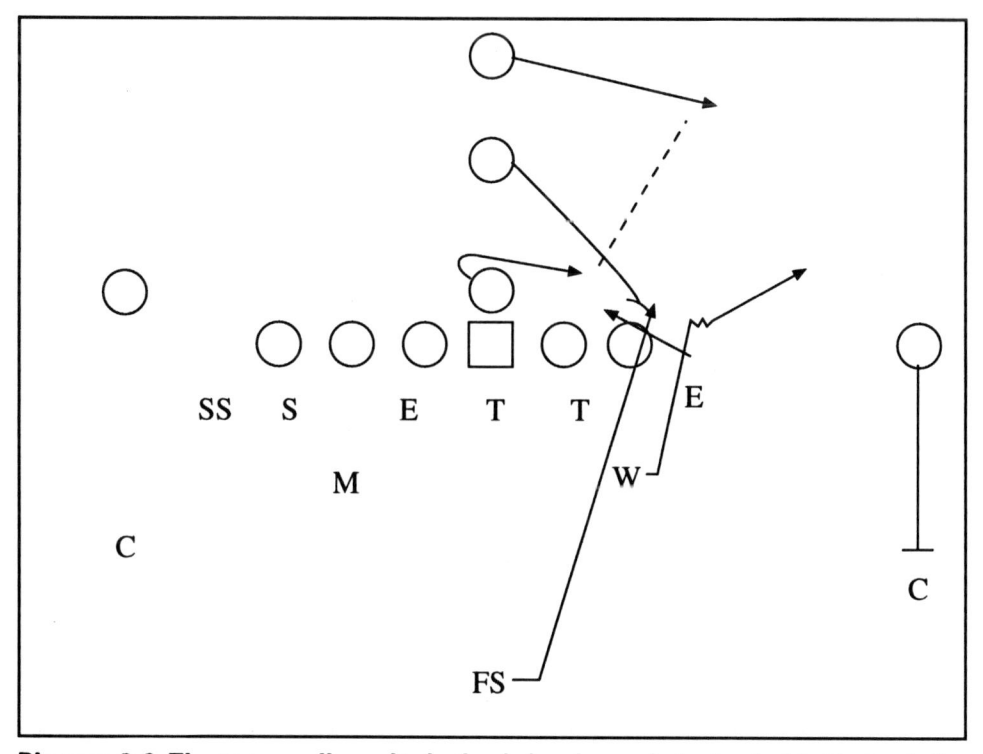

Diagram 8-6: The tango call results in the defensive end playing inside the load, the free safety playing outside the load, and the Will linebacker slow-playing the pitch.

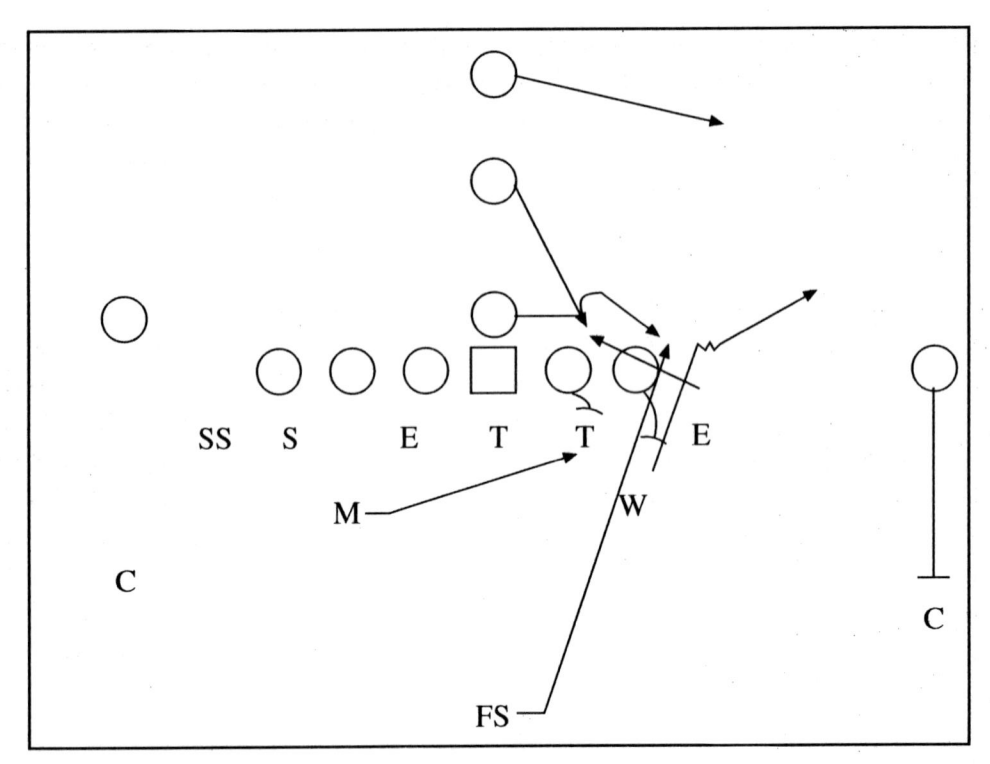

Diagram 8-7: The tango call versus a dive option.

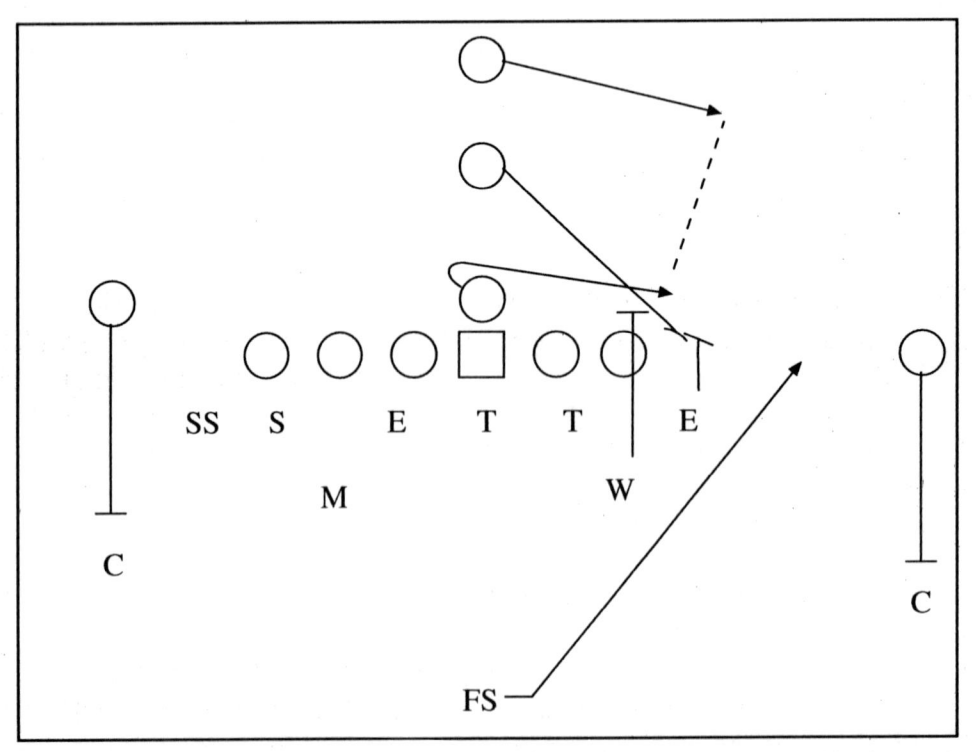

Diagram 8-8: The Sally blue call results in the Will linebacker playing inside the load, the weakside end playing outside the load, and the free safety taking the pitch.

slightly turned outside, on the line of scrimmage. Assuming the proper posture ensures that the linebacker can effectively break on the pitch at any time during the slow-play. Like the defensive end in the blue call, the Will linebacker cannot afford to stay in the slow-play mode too long. He must maintain leverage on the tailback, even if he has to prematurely break out of his slow-play. On the tango, the free safety will execute his same blue responsibility and play outside the load.

The tango call is an excellent change-up from the blue call. You should run the tango when you want to force the quarterback to pitch fast. Against a normal load option, a well-executed tango call should result in the free safety becoming a free hitter on the pitch. If the dive option shows, the free safety will fill the window on the quarterback as the defensive end attacks the dive. On the dive option, the quarterback will see the defensive end crashing down. He will react by pulling the ball and attacking the defensive end—who is slow-playing the pitch. The quarterback should respond to the defensive end's slow-play by turning up with the ball. At that point he will be met by the free safety filling outside the load. Should the remaining defensive linemen do their job and prevent the jump-through blocks, the free safety will have help from the Mike linebacker fast-flowing as a free hitter.

The Sally blue call versus the weakside option:

If the quarterback is a threat, another good change-up is the Sally blue call. The Sally blue puts the Will linebacker inside the load, the defensive end outside the load, and the free safety on the pitch. Coupled with effective 3 technique play, the Sally blue call provides solid pressure on the quarterback without the fast-play crashing technique from the defensive end. Both the Will linebacker and the 3 technique can secure the area inside the load blocker, while the defensive end plays a strong technique outside the load blocker. In essence, three defenders are available to take the quarterback while the free safety sprints to the pitch.

Because the Sally blue isn't a fast-play tactic and because of the availability of three defenders on the quarterback, the defensive end has the freedom to play games with the quarterback. A good strategy for the defensive end is to turn his head and dropstep outside as if he is bailing out of a slow-play to the pitch. This action baits the quarterback into turning up—straight into the 3 technique and Will linebacker. The defensive end can then run a bullet at the quarterback after faking the bailout. We tell the bulleting defensive end to hit the quarterback high for maximum impact.

You should realize that once the offensive coordinator picks up on the free safety's pitch responsibility, he will assign the wide receiver to crack the free safety. The cornerback should alert the free safety to any crack path by yelling "crack-crack-crack." After alerting the free safety, the cornerback should replace the free safety and take the pitch himself. The cornerback should alert the free safety to any pre-snap keys to an impending crackback. A tight receiver split or a short motion toward the formation indicates that a crackback block is likely to occur.

A crackback block can occur against a linebacker as well as a free safety. In the case of the Sally blue or blue call, the crackback on the linebacker is an unsound strategy. However, in the case of a tango or Sally tango, the crackback on the Will is an effective strategy. Similarly, the crack can be executed against the defensive end. And if the defensive end has the pitch on a blue call, the crack could be effective against the defensive end. A good rule for the cornerback recognizing the crack is to squeeze the crack blocker and yell the crack alert to the inside players. After squeezing the crack, the cornerback is in position to play whatever develops. Generally, the cornerback should take the pitch whenever a crackback is attempted —regardless of the crack blocker's target.

The Sally tango call versus the weakside option:

The fourth change-up versus the weakside option is the Sally tango call. On the Sally tango call, the end fast-plays inside the load, the Will plays outside the load, and the free safety plays the pitch. It is important for the Will linebacker to attack the line of scrimmage with his horse saddled. He doesn't have time to play any quarterback games; he must be able to break immediately on the pitch. Against any tango, the quarterback should pitch the ball quick. A quick pitch puts pressure on the Will linebacker to assist the free safety. Nevertheless, you should not overcoach the Will on this call. He has an outside the load responsibility; thus, he has quarterback as a primary responsibility. You should simply make the Will aware that a tango normally forces the quarterback to pitch it quick, and a quick pitch frees the Will to fly to the pitch along with the free safety.

The blue call versus the strongside option:

While it is an unlikely offensive strategy, the strongside option may indeed be part of an option attack game plan. As we stated in Chapter 1, the 46 scheme has a plan for every situation and style of offensive attack; therefore, we have a plan for the strongside option. The blue call on the strongside mirrors the weakside blue strategy—the obvious difference is the personnel who executes the call. Instead of the defensive end slow-playing the pitch, as with the weakside blue call, the strong safety slow-plays the pitch on the strongside blue call. And because of the presence of a tight end, we have some specific adjustments to the execution of the strongside blue call.

The major adjustment of the blue call when run on the strongside involves the teamwork of the Sam and Mike. The Sam linebacker and Mike linebacker work together to fit inside the load block. Neither Sam nor Mike can be assigned an exclusive option responsibility because of the tight end's capability to block—and thus eliminate one of the linebackers. Because of the tight end's obvious capability, we have integrated a trade-off procedure between the Sam and Mike. Basically, the plan calls for the Mike to "play off" the Sam. In other words, the Mike linebacker reads the action of the Sam, along with the action of the tight end. This is a simple task for the Mike, since one of his pointers is

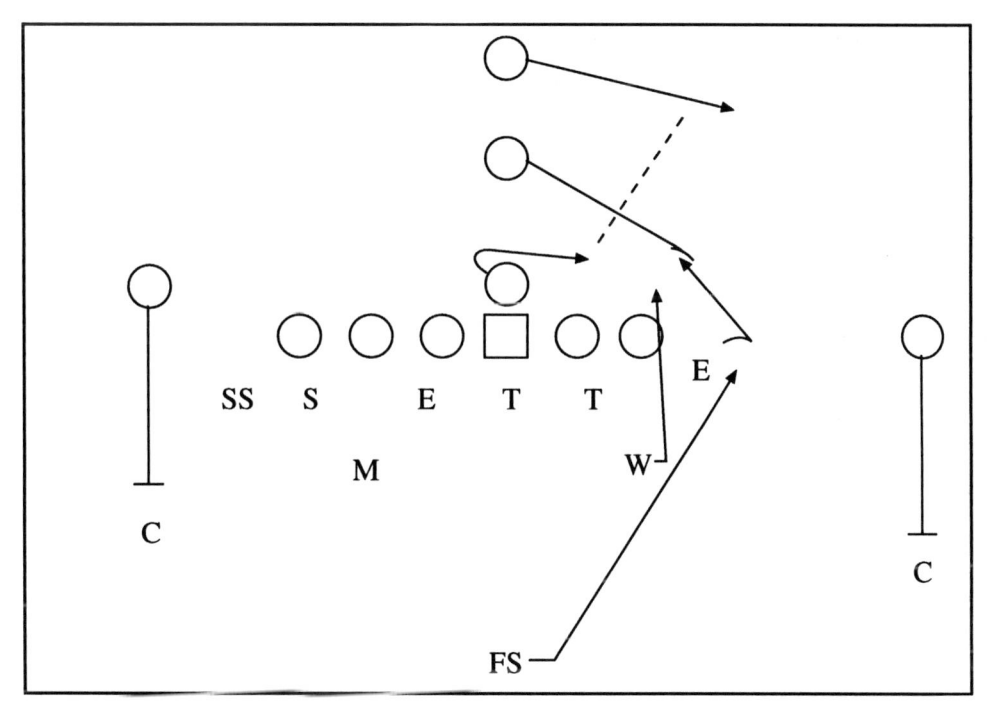

Diagram 8-9: On the Sally blue call, the defensive end has an opportunity to fake a slow-play favoring the pitch.

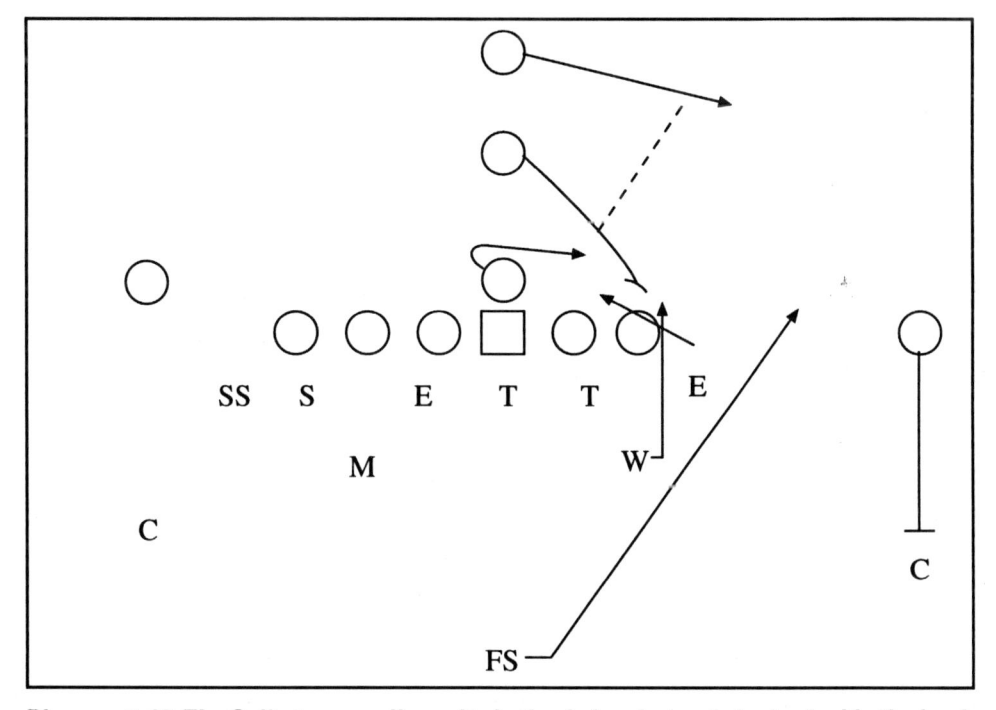

Diagram 8-10: The Sally tango call results in the defensive end playing inside the load, the Will linebacker playing outside the load, and the free safety playing the pitch.

the Sam linebacker's inside leg. (For more information on pointers, see Chapter 7.) As shown in Diagrams 8-11 and 8-12, the action of the tight end dictates the action of the two linebackers.

If the tight end blocks the Sam linebacker, the Mike fits outside the Sam. We use the word fit, to describe the hip-to-hip relationship of Mike's ideal position to Sam. The linebacker who operates from a position off the line of scrimmage tends to commit one error: He scrapes but doesn't fit tightly to the defensive lineman. Failing to fit properly leaves a gap between the two defenders. This gap is one defensive breakdown that an option quarterback is especially adept at exploiting.

In Diagram 8-11, the tight end blocks the Sam. The Sam becomes a 1-on-1 player against the tight end. Mike reads the Sam engaging the tight end and recognizes the closed window. (See open-closed windows in Chapter 7.) A closed window cues the Mike to fit outside the Sam linebacker.

In Diagram 8-12, the tight end releases outside of the Sam. In this diagram, the tight end is releasing outside to hook the Mike. Upon reading the flow, Mike throws his eyes to his flow—to pointer—Sam's inside leg—and reads the Sam widening with the tight end. Because the window is open, Mike attacks the line of scrimmage to fit inside the Sam linebacker.

As stated earlier, our base plan requires the strong safety to slow-play the load option—favoring the pitch. It is unlikely that the tight end will attempt to reach block the strong safety who is aligned in the 46 package. However, should the tight end attempt to reach him, the strong safety would simply maintain his outside leverage and skate outward for the pitch. In this scenario, the Sam would be free to play outside the load. Consequently, Mike would read the Sam outside and fit inside the open window. Diagram 8-13 illustrates the defensive reaction to the tight end attempting to reach block the strong safety.

Sam's widening with the release of the tight end as shown in Diagram 8-12 is only one possible technique Sam may employ. Another—probably more common—technique available to the Sam linebacker is to simply take the quarterback on any arc release option. (An arc release option is an option in which the tight end releases outside; an arc release is also known as an arch release.) Since this tactic is a standard eight-man front strategy against the lead option, it fits well within the dynamics of the 46 package. In this strategy, the Sam plays a solid "C" gap control technique and sits for the quarterback. The Mike then reads the closed door and fits outside the Sam linebacker. Against the inside veer scheme, the Sam's "C" gap control technique is the preferred strategy.

Diagram 8-14 shows the inside veer scheme versus the 46 alignment. While the inside veer dive option scheme has several blocking adjustments available, none of the adjustments provide any negligible advantage for the offensive attack. Shown in Diagram 8-14 is the pure veer scheme: the tight end arcing for the force; the tackle blocking inside;

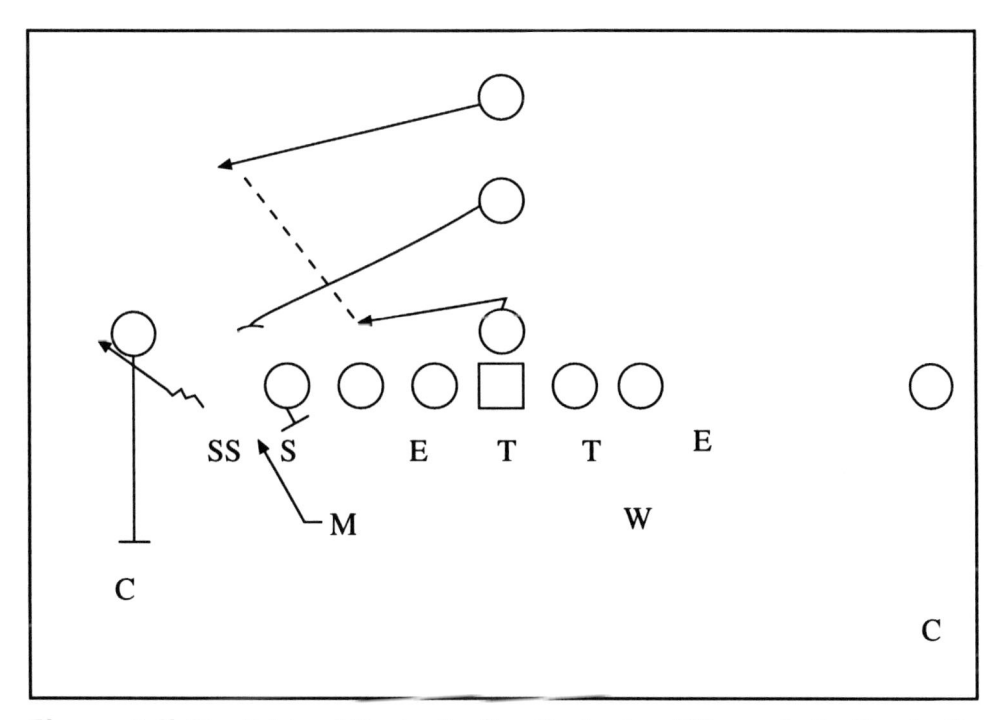

Diagram 8-11: The tight end blocks the Sam linebacker; Mike reads the Sam inside and fits tightly outside.

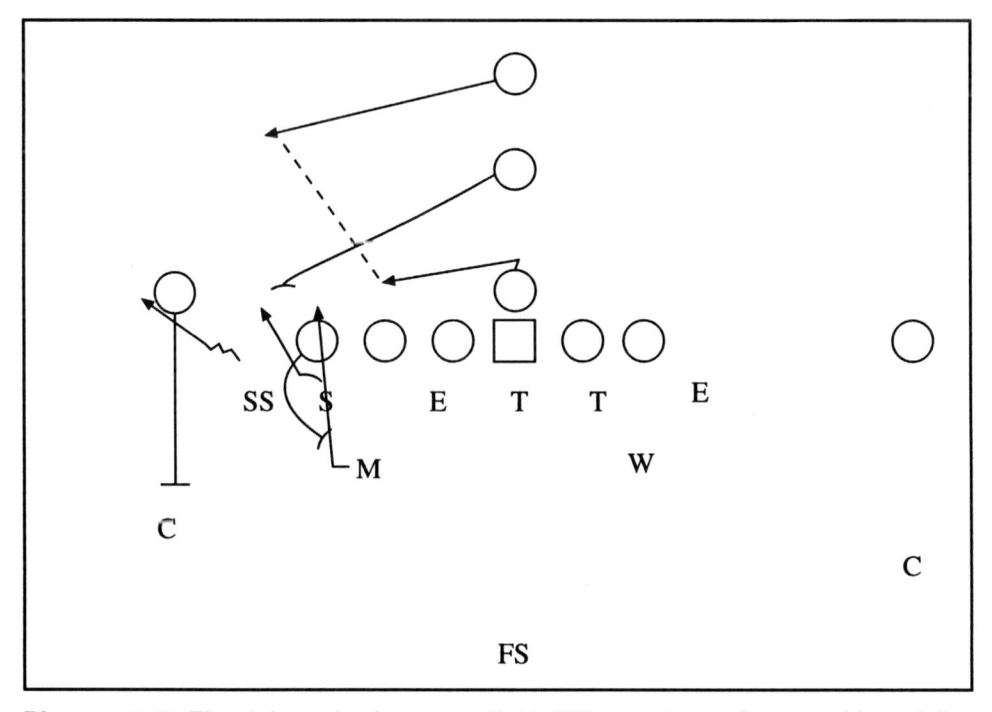

Diagram 8-12: The tight end releases upfield; Mike reads the Sam outside and fits tightly inside.

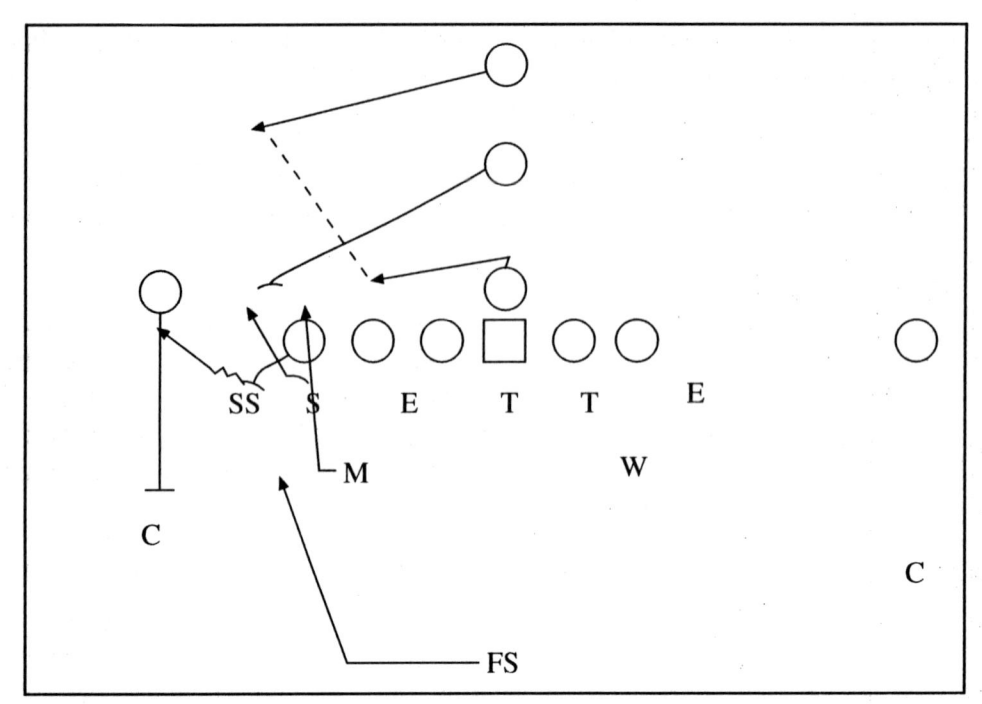

Diagram 8-13: The tight end attempts to reach the strong safety; the strong safety shucks the tight end and skates outward; Mike reads the Sam outside and fits tightly inside.

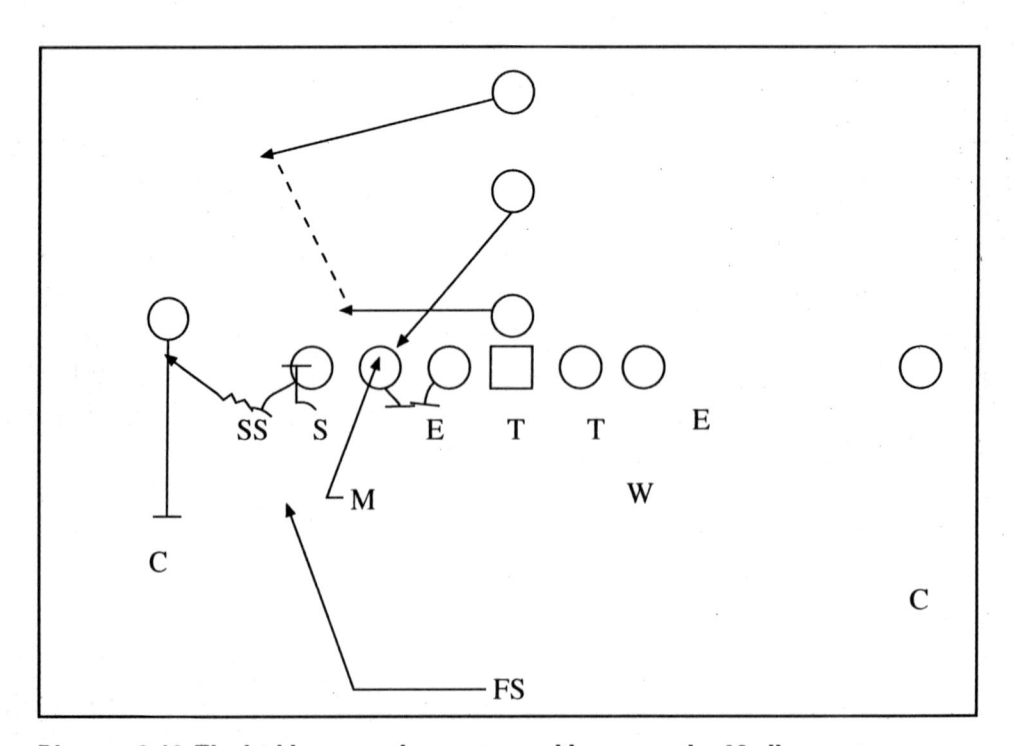

Diagram 8-14: The inside veer scheme strongside versus the 46 alignment.

80

and the guard blocking the man on him. As you see in Diagram 8-14, the pure veer scheme frees the Mike and Sam. Mike reads an open window and steps up to take the dive while Sam sits for the quarterback.

Naturally, the alternate defensive tactic against this scheme is to assign the Sam to close the "C" gap while Sam reads a closed window and scrapes. Diagram 8-15 illustrates this defensive tactic against the veer.

Both defensive tactics are simple to execute and highly effective. The two tactics give the veer quarterback two very different reads. When the Sam sits outside, the veer quarterback gets a "give" read—but the Mike is closing the window and attacking the diveback. When the Sam closes inside and takes the dive, the veer quarterback gets a pull read—but the Mike reacts to the closed window and scrapes to fit for the quarterback.

It is easy to see that no matter what the Sam does against the veer option, he isn't wrong. In this manner, the arc release by the tight end is a reactionary block. Like the 3 technique's reaction to the fold block, the Sam's reaction to the arc release is never wrong. The well-coached Mike linebacker simply responds to Sam's defensive reaction and fits accordingly.

The strong safety executes his pitch responsibility in deference to two coaching points: Versus load option and speed option, he should slow-play the pitch; versus lead option he should fast-play the pitch. The aforementioned designation of an option as a load option is characterized by the presence of a diveback or a running back assigned to block the defender assigned to the quarterback. Versus a load option, the strong safety wants to buy time for the pursuit to flow to the ball. Most load options are slower to attack the edge than either the lead or the speed option; therefore, the strong safety has the luxury of the time. Speed options are faster to attack the edge, but still not as much of a threat to the perimeter as lead options. More importantly, since a speed option is a one-back option, speed options are characterized by the lack of a blocker or diveback. Against a speed option, the strong safety's priority is to again buy time for the pursuit. Lead options are characterized by a blocker assigned to the force player. Basically, anytime a blocker attempts to block the strong safety, whether that blocker be a tight end, running back or wide receiver, the option is a lead option. Since the purpose of a lead option is to kick the ball out to the pitchman and get on the edge quickly with a lead blocker, the strong safety must fast-play the pitch. Against a lead option, the strong safety doesn't have time to shuffle outward in a slow-play technique; he must attack the lead blocker, defeat him, and make the hit on the pitchman.

One additional coaching point for the strong safety is the need for correctly diagnosing the lead blocker's angle of attack. It is this diagnosis that helps the strong safety distinguish the option as a lead or load scheme. If the blocker's angle is flat or arched outward, the blocker is attempting to get wide in order to execute a lead block on the force. If the blocker's angle is vertical (i.e., into the line of scrimmage), the blocker is not a threat to lead on the force. In the case of the latter, the option is properly diagnosed as a load option, and the strong safety slow-plays the pitch.

The technique of attacking the lead blocker of an option is called "dumping the pitch." To effectively dump the pitch, the strong safety must keep outside leverage on the blocker and stay on his feet. He must, above all else, stay on his feet and keep a tight leverage on the pitchman. He must refuse to take part in a 1-for-1 trade with the lead blocker. Excellent strong safety play against the lead option will destroy that component of the option attack.

The blue call for the strongside is an effective strategy against all types of option. It's a sound foundation for a solid defensive system against the strongside option—but it is only the first component of the 46's mechanism for defeating the strongside option.

The strongside tango call:

One alternative to the strongside blue call is the strongside tango call. The tango call to the strongside is very similar to the weakside tango call. Both tangos result in a fast-play on the quarterback from the edge. In the strongside tango out of the 46 front, the strong safety will knife inside through the tight end's hip. He should attempt to wrong-shoulder any pulling lineman or kick-out block and consequently spill the play to the outside. Since the strong safety is inside the load, the Mike slow-plays the pitch. As previously mentioned, the tango calls are mirrored, so the Mike's tango responsibility mirrors that of the Will's tango responsibility. Slow-playing the pitch is a tough responsibility from a linebacker position. Therefore, the linebacker should be heavy on his pointer to the outside. And knowing that the strong safety is spilling the off-tackle hole, the Mike should step to a wider pointer —more toward the inside foot of the strong safety. The wide pointer puts him on a better path to gain outside leverage and enables him to take the pitch more effectively. Meanwhile, Sam will play off the tight end's block and attempt to fit between the Mike and the strong safety—outside the load. Sam is helped by the free safety, who acts as a late alley filler, after checking the tight end dump route.

If the tight end releases, the Sam will widen with him and ride him outward. In this case, the Sam will slow-play the pitch. The tight end may be arc releasing to capture the Mike linebacker. If the tight end is releasing for the Mike, he will likely be successful; by alignment, he has the angle on the Mike linebacker. Therefore, whenever the tight end arc releases, Sam must ride the arc release outward and take on the assignment of the Mike— that is, slow-play the pitch. Mike will read Sam's response to the tight end's arc as he steps to his pointer. The window will consequently open up and Mike will fit inside of Sam. Sam and Mike will change assignments. Mike will assume the outside load responsibility, while Sam will slow-play the pitch.

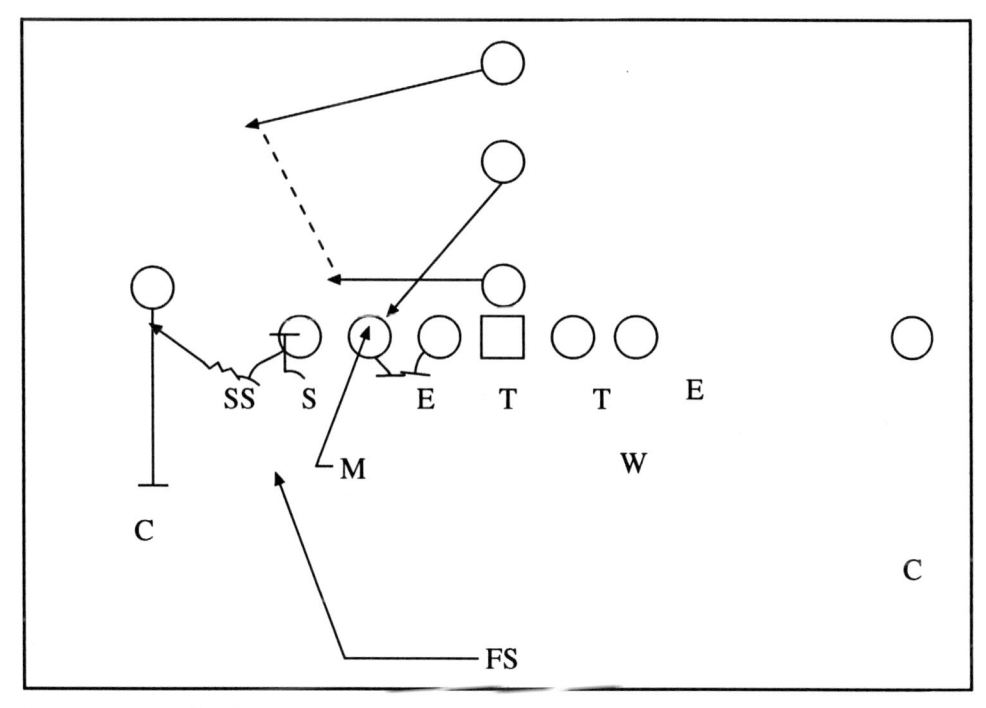

Diagram 8-15: Against the inside veer, the Mike attacks the open window as Sam sits for the quarterback. The strong safety is responsible for the pitch.

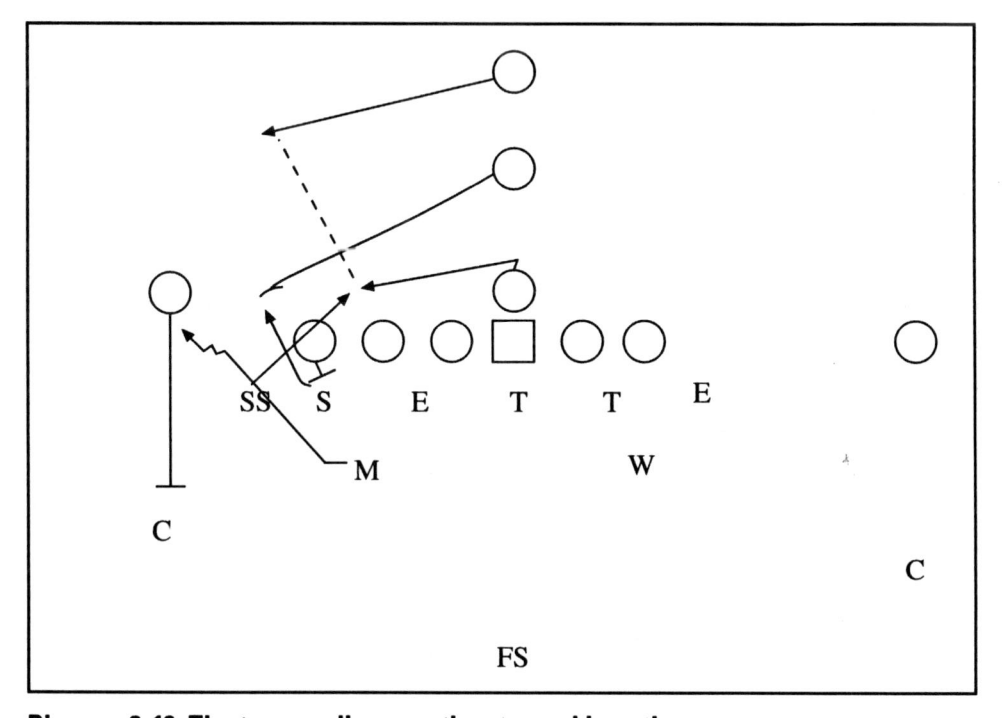

Diagram 8-16: The tango call versus the strongside option.

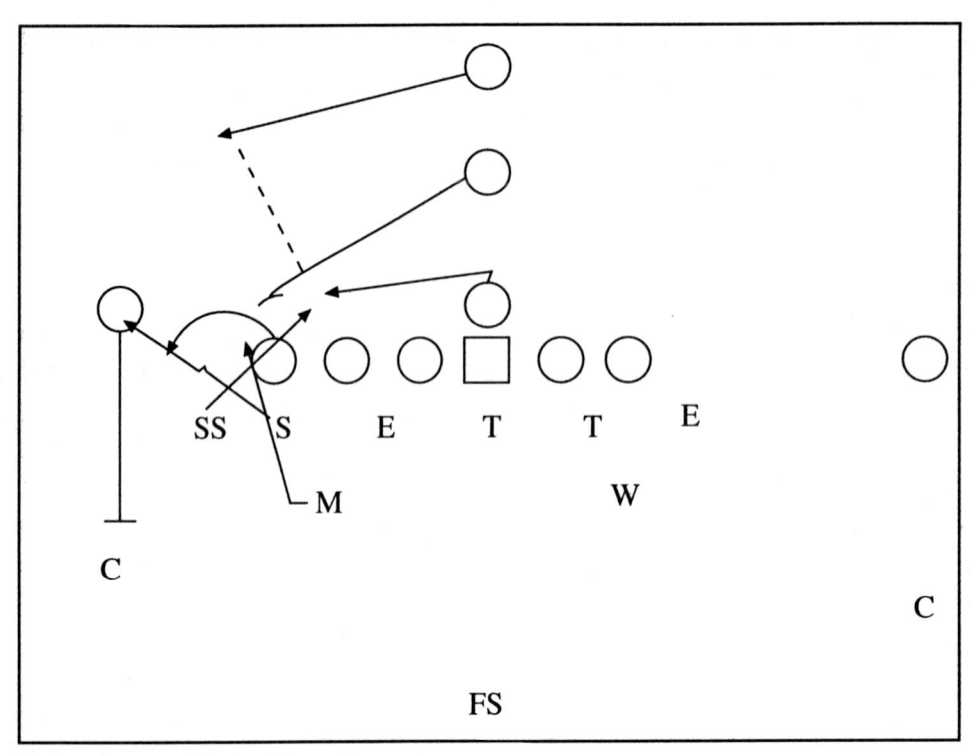

Diagram 8-17: Mike and Sam fit.

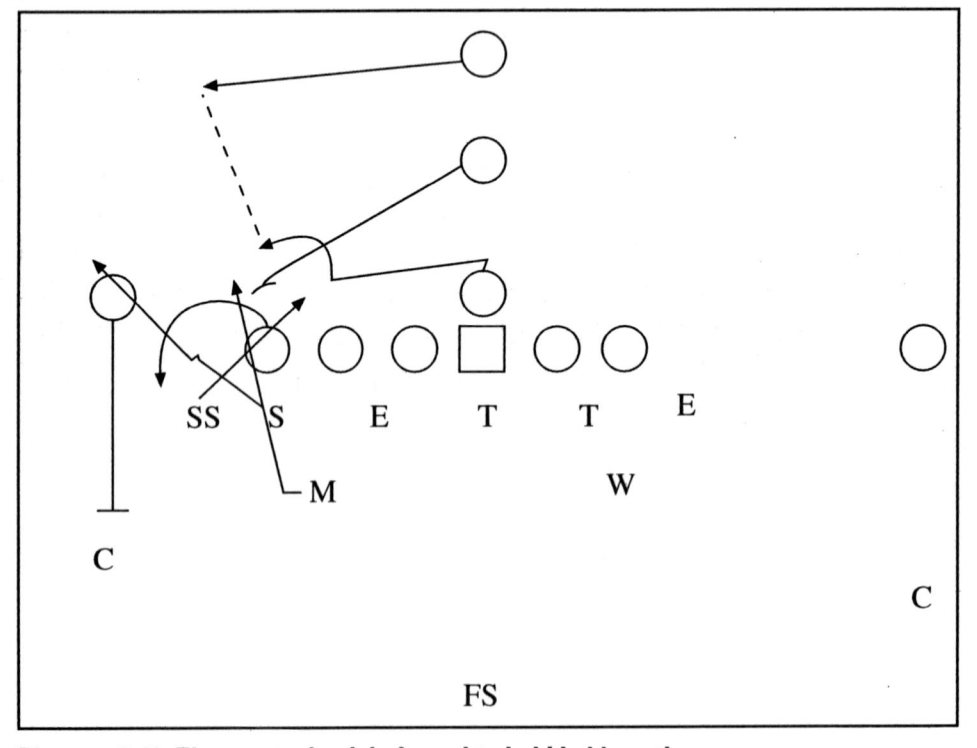

Diagram 8-18: The quarterback is forced to bubble his path.

Again, keep in mind an extremely important coaching point: *On a tango, the quarterback is being fast-played by the strong safety.* This indicates positively that the quarterback will pitch the ball quick on either a lead or speed option. And, even if the option is a load option—an option where a blocker is assigned to the defender who has quarterback responsibility—the quarterback will be forced to bubble (i.e., deepen his path) around the wreck caused by the strong safety.

What does all of this mean? It means that on a strongside tango, you should alert your Sam and Mike to be ready to break immediately to the pitch, should option show. A strongside tango will make the option resemble a quick pitch as the ball is kicked out quickly to the edge. Even a well-executed load block will result in the quarterback bubbling around the pile, allowing your 3 technique and free-hitting Will linebacker to get into the pursuit. A major cause of fumbles on the option is a hit from a member of the backside pursuit. You should emphasize to your people that the backside angle versus the option quarterback is an excellent opportunity for stripping the ball and delivering a devastating blow.

Other defensive choices versus the strongside option:

Other options versus the strongside option include stunting so that the tango call is turned inside-out. In other words, the strong safety can stunt underneath the Sam as the Sam steps outside to establish a sound slow-play position. Obviously, both the strong safety and Sam will have to adjust their alignment slightly in order to run this stunt effectively. You should coach your Mike that he will likely get an open window in the area of his outside pointer whenever the tango stunt adjustment is made. Naturally, an open window dictates the Mike filling the window in a good tackling demeanor.

Depending on the coverage, the Sam linebacker may cover the tight end man-to-man. This can free the free safety to get involved on the pitch, much in the same manner as the weakside option. This type of scheme can give you an extra man on the option, particularly if the tight end base blocks the Sam. Versus a load option with the tight end blocking Sam, the Sam linebacker can defeat the tight end and play off the block. You gain the free safety as an option player whenever you play a man-to-man technique with the Sam on the tight end.

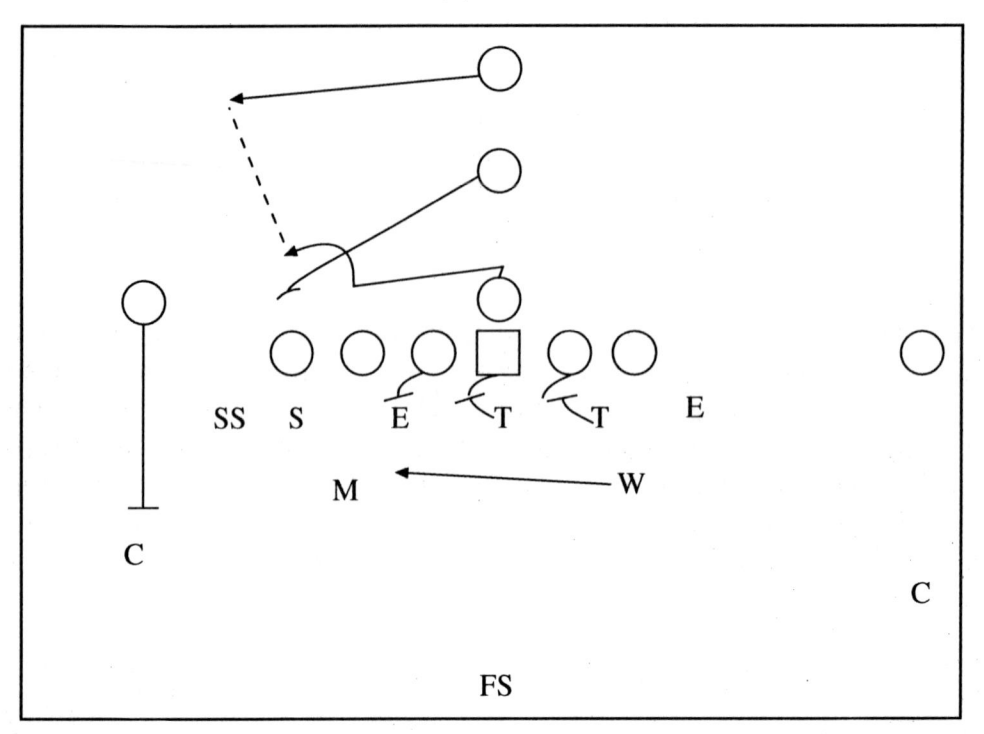

Diagram 8-19: The Will linebacker is a free hitter from the backside, if the defensive linemen do their job.

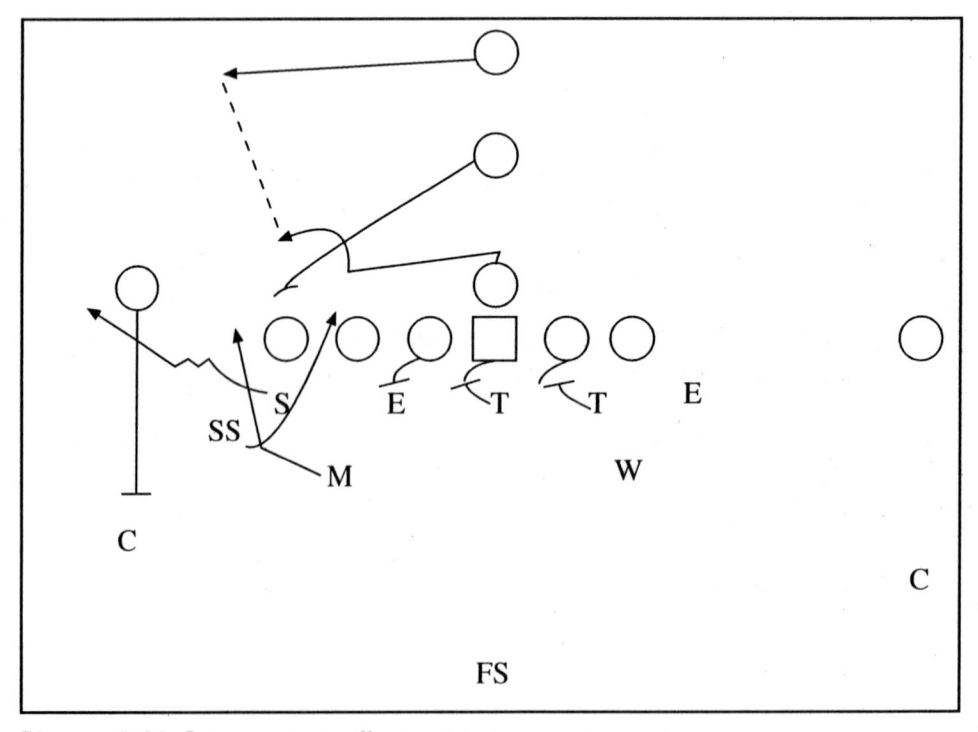

Diagram 8-20: A tango stunt adjustment.

CHAPTER 9

SECONDARY

The secondary package of the 46 defense is a multiple scheme which supports both zone and man-to-man (i.e., man) concepts. One hallmark of the 46 defense is the responsibility of the secondary to adjust to the formation changes. It is a characteristic of the 46 package to keep the front alignment static against various formations and adjust with the secondary personnel in order to avoid being flanked. With only slight variations of the linebacker alignments, the stability of the front alignment is consistent, regardless of whether the coverage call is a zone or man-to-man.

The primary coverage alignment and scheme of the 46 defense is what we call the chalkboard zone, or three-deep zone. The three-deep zone is called the chalkboard zone because it is the most common coverage scheme in football. Probably well over 95% of all high schools and colleges use some style of the three-deep zone.

The 46 zone coverage concept is built upon three foundations.

- *Landmark drops underneath.*

    As described in later paragraphs, the underneath droppers cover the four landmark zones. However, they don't simply drop to the landmarks without incorporating a read concept.

- *Read concepts over the top.*

    The three deep defenders, the cornerbacks, and free safety utilize read concepts over the top as they drop to cover the deep 1/3 zones.

- *The outside dropper carries the second receiver through the zone.*

    A critical coaching point to the effective Cover 3 scheme in the 46 package is the understanding and mastery of the "second receiver through the zone" principle.

Cover 3 deep zone techniques:

Position alignments normally range from 5- to 7 yards off the wide receiver for the cornerbacks. Exactly where in this two-yard range the cornerback aligns is dependent upon several factors, not the slightest of which is the defensive philosophy of the coordinator. Down-and-distance, the strength of the opposition's passing game, and the relative talent differential between the receiver and the defender are also factors which influence the alignment depth of the cornerback. Against a nub end (i.e., a single receiver side of the formation with the tight end being the single receiver) the cornerback should normally align at five yards deep and three yards outside the tight end (nub). In cover 3, the free safety aligns in a range from 10- to 12-yards deep.

While he normally aligns on the midline of the offensive formation, in certain situations the free safety adjusts his alignment laterally to a position over either guard. The depth of the free safety's alignment varies considerably according to the style of the offensive attack, the type of offensive formation, and the down-and-distance. For example, a wing-T attack demands an active participation by the free safety in stopping the running game. Against a wing-T, the free safety should align no deeper than ten yards from the line of scrimmage and focus intently on a predetermined lineman read. The lineman read is usually best determined by intense film study and may be either a covered or uncovered lineman. When facing a wing-T attack in a running situation, particularly aggressive coaches have been known to align the free safety as close as eight yards. An unbalanced formation may require the free safety to cheat to the unbalanced side. An unusually long down-and-distance or time-sensitive situation might require the free safety to deepen his alignment to as far as 20 yards off the line of scrimmage.

Two basic philosophies exist in the coaching community with regard to the three-deep zone concept. The first philosophy—and the simplest—is the philosophy of landmark drops. The second philosophy is pattern reading.

Shown in Diagram 9-1, landmark drops result in the coverage personnel dropping to a field landmark. In the landmark drop philosophy, the cornerbacks, free safety and underneath coverage personnel focus entirely on the ball movement. Dropping to landmarks has extremely limited value. While the concept is easily the simplest to coach and master, the principle of dropping to cover the field instead of the receiver patterns is extremely vulnerable against a well-coached and talented quarterback and receiver corps. Landmark drops surrender substantial passing yardage against even the simplest of passing attacks. In fact, the only thing landmark drops are good for is not getting beat deep. Even though the single advantage of landmark drops is constricted to covering the long ball, this advantage alone is substantial enough for many head coaches to demand the instruction of the three-deep concept in accordance with the landmark drop philosophy. And, as most coaches are aware, the level of play strongly dictates your level of coaching. As stated in chapter three, the principle reason for developing our comprehensive style of defensive line coaching and limiting the reads to two categories, rule reads and reactionary reads, was the limitations on coaching time at the college and high school level. In line with this sensitivity to coaching time and practice time, we firmly support the youth football coach's stance that he should teach the Cover 3 landmark drop philosophy. However,

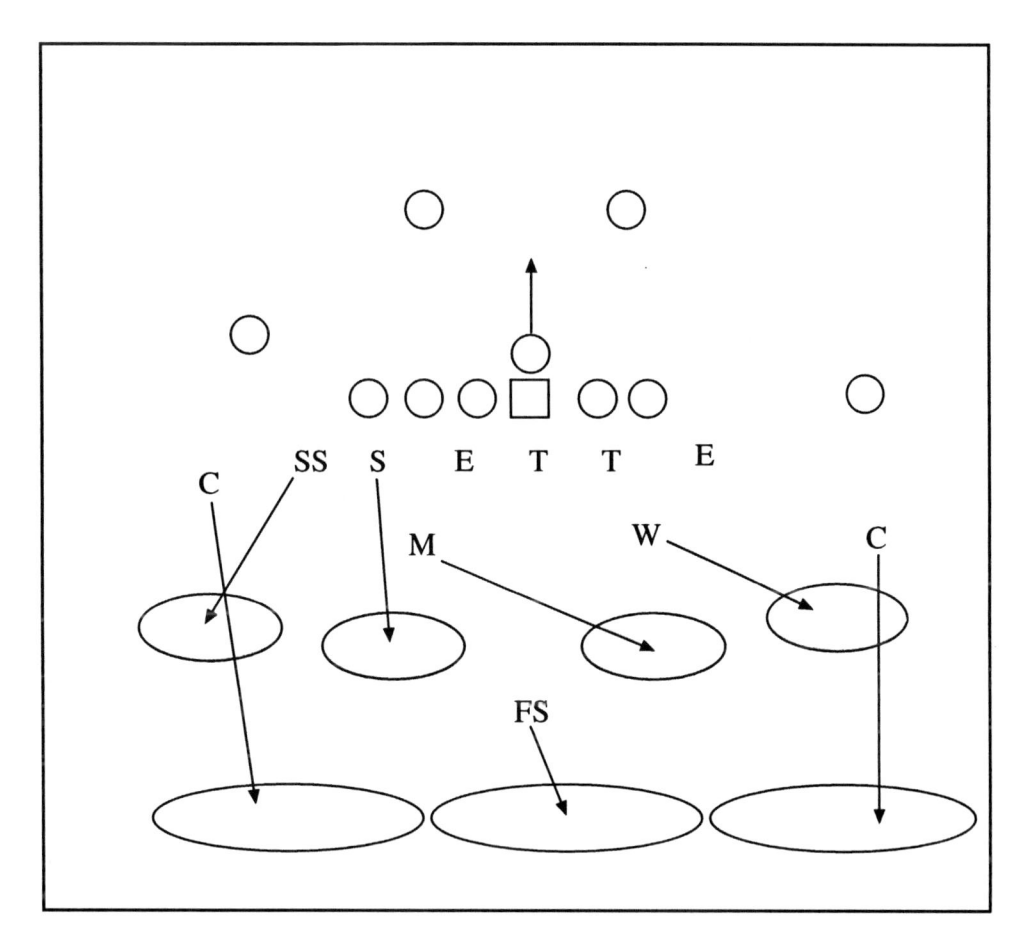

Diagram 9-1: The cover 3 landmark drops versus a dropback pass from the pro formation.

if the level of play is representative of solid passing attacks with moderate levels of execution, we have no doubt that you should incorporate the Cover 3 pattern reading philosophy into your teaching.

Pattern reading is actually a combination of landmark dropping and reading the receiver's routes. In fact, in order to effectively teach pattern reading, you must first teach your athletes to master landmark dropping. It is in their progression to the landmark—particularly for the underneath defenders—that the coverage personnel read the patterns of the key receiver. The defender's ability to landmark drop is the backbone of the pattern read concept.

A popular misconception about pattern reading is that the concept is complex and therefore difficult to learn. This belief is completely erroneous. In its simplest and most common form, pattern reading normally involves reading the route of a second receiver aligned to the side of the reading defender. For example, the cornerback aligned to the tight end/flanker side of the pro set would read the tight

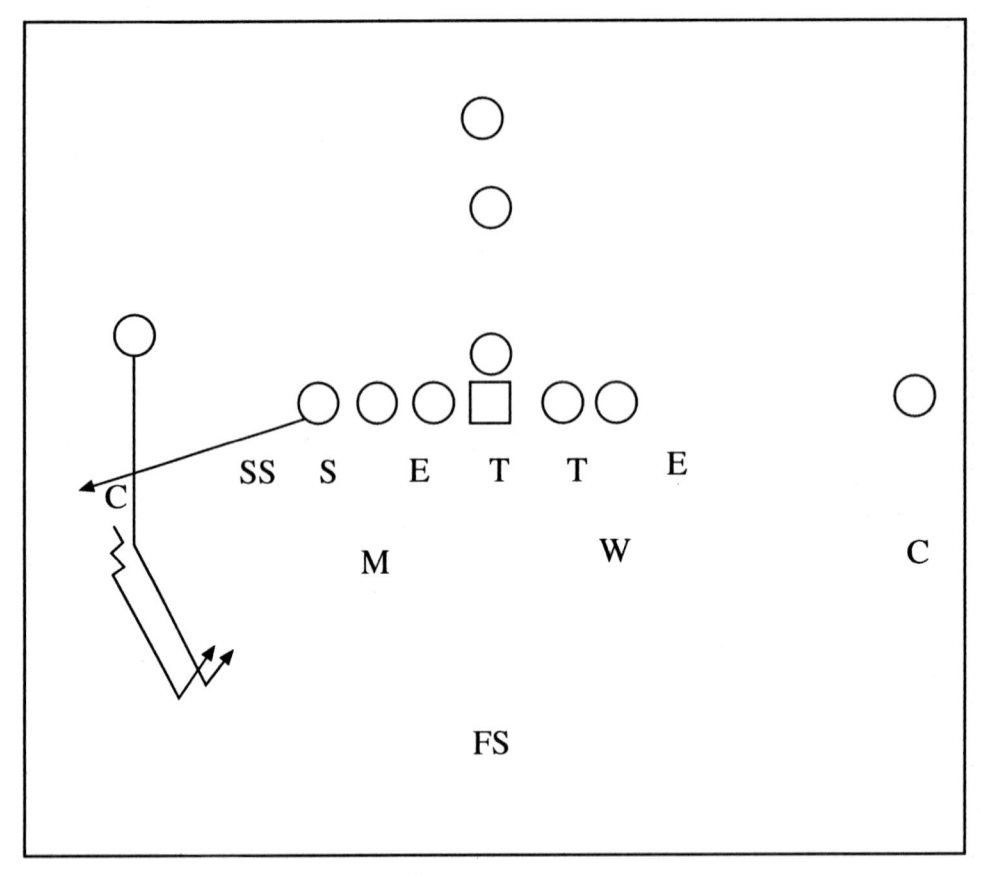

Diagram 9-2: The number two receiver runs an out route.

end's route. In our system of numbering the receivers, the second receiver from the sideline inward is designated as the number two read.

Because the pattern reading zone drop concept is much more precise, each position is instructed on the universal patterns and what they mean to the individual defender. Versus a dropback pass, the cornerback aligned on the strongside of the pro formation responds to the following universal pattern reads by the number two receiver:

- *Number two (the tight end) runs an out directly to the flat.*

    If the tight end runs a flat route, the expected combination is the curl route from the number one receiver (the flanker). This combination accounts for over 90% of the cumulative patterns in which the tight end runs a flat route. To stop the curl route of the flanker, the cornerback should drive to the flanker's upfield shoulder. A key coaching point: Whenever the number two receiver breaks out, the cornerback should immediately focus his attention on the number one receiver.

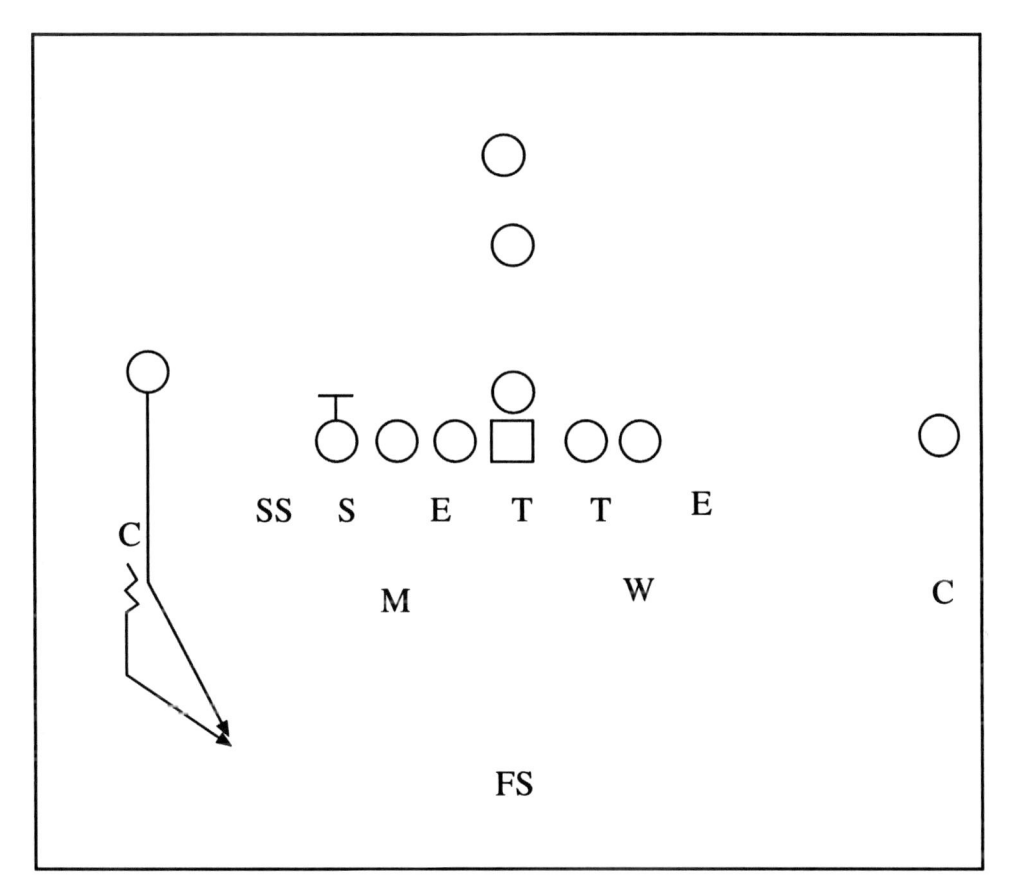

Diagram 9-3: The number two receiver blocks.

- *Number two (the tight end) blocks.*

    If the tight end blocks, several combinations are normally seen from the flanker. The three universal patterns from the flanker run in combination with the tight end blocking are the out, the stop-and-go, and the comeback. Whenever the number two receiver blocks, the cornerback should stay on top of the number one receiver. If the number two receiver breaks on an out route, the cornerback should drive on his upfield shoulder to challenge the receiver. If the number two receiver breaks upfield on a deep route, the cornerback should again drive on the receiver's upfield shoulder.

- *Number two runs a vertical route.*

    If the tight end runs a vertical route (i.e., a route straight upfield), the cornerback glances at the flanker to determine his intentions. If the flanker stutter-steps, his intentions are to break inside. The opponent

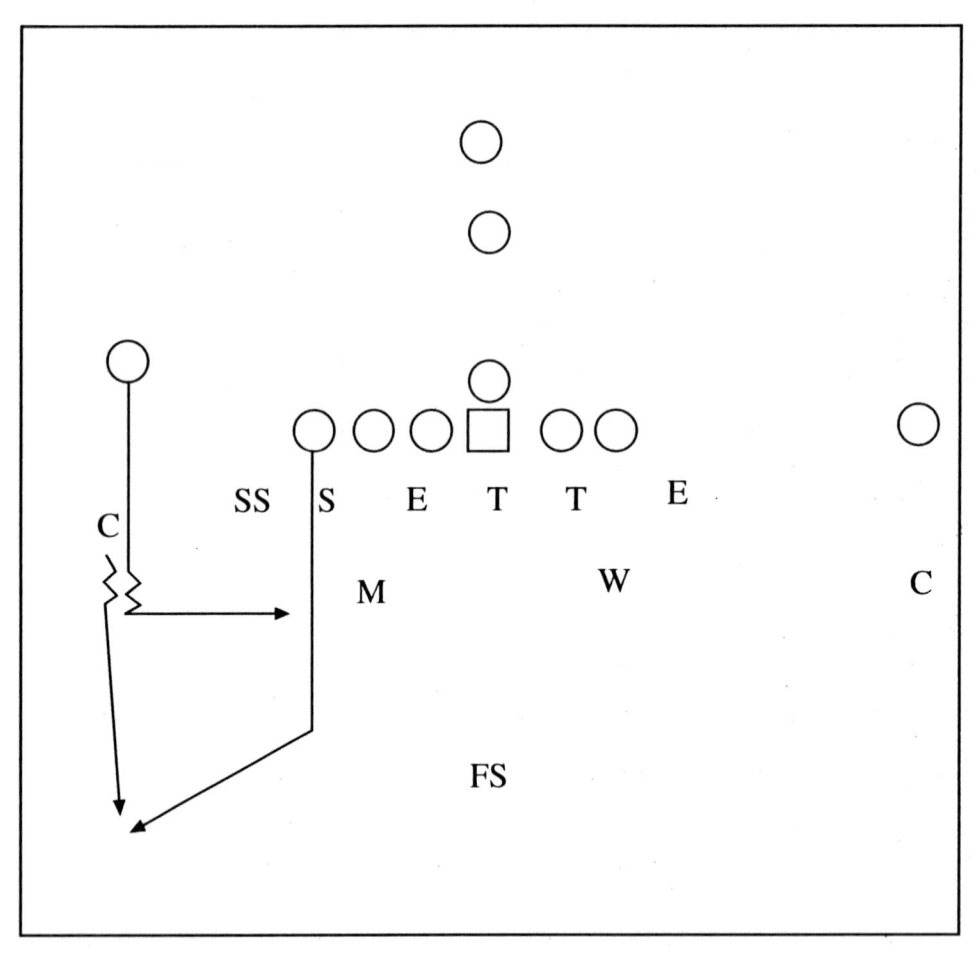

Diagram 9-4: The number two receiver runs a vertical route and the flanker stutters.

hopes that the flanker's inside break will bait the cornerback into settling to jump the flanker's route. By settling and dropping his hips, the cornerback would be vulnerable to being beaten deep by a corner route of the tight end. A stutter-step by the number one receiver is indicative of an impending corner route by the number two receiver. Another common combination is the double vertical pattern. If the cornerback glances and notices that the flanker is full-stride on a vertical path, the cornerback must stay in the middle of his 1/3 zone and maintain the proper cushion. He should attempt to stay in a position that will allow him to break on the deep ball thrown to either receiver. In the case of a double vertical combination, the cornerback's technique reverts to a pure landmark drop technique as he covers 1/3 of the field.

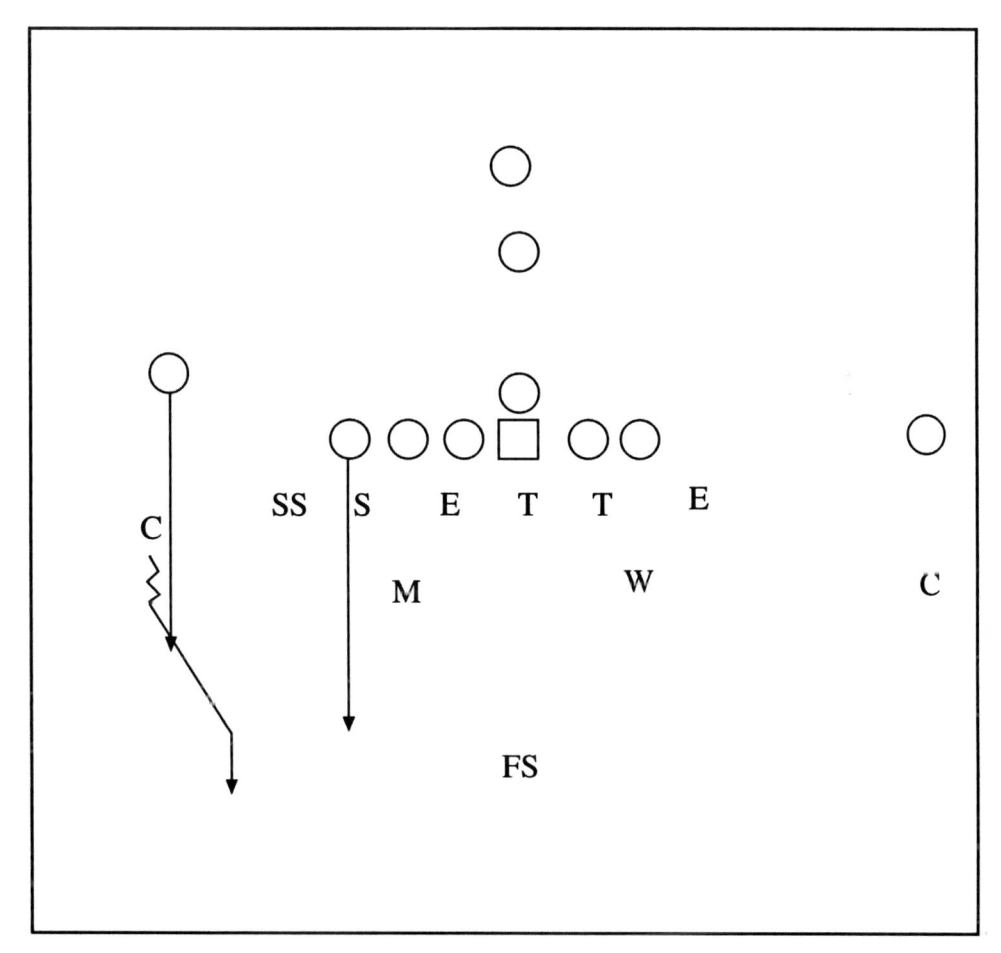

Diagram 9-5: The number two receiver runs a vertical route and the flanker runs a vertical route.

Against the flop formation (i.e., twins), a formation in which two wide receivers align on the same side, the read rules remain consistent (Diagram 9-6). The only difference is in who is identified as the number two receiver. In the flop formation, the inside receiver is number two.

Shown in Diagram 9-7, the cover 3 base adjustment to the flop formation calls for the cornerback to flip-flop to the two-receiver side. While better coverage adjustments are available in the 46 coverage package, a "play it" call which dictates that the coverage be played without a check-off would result in both cornerbacks aligned over the two wide receivers.

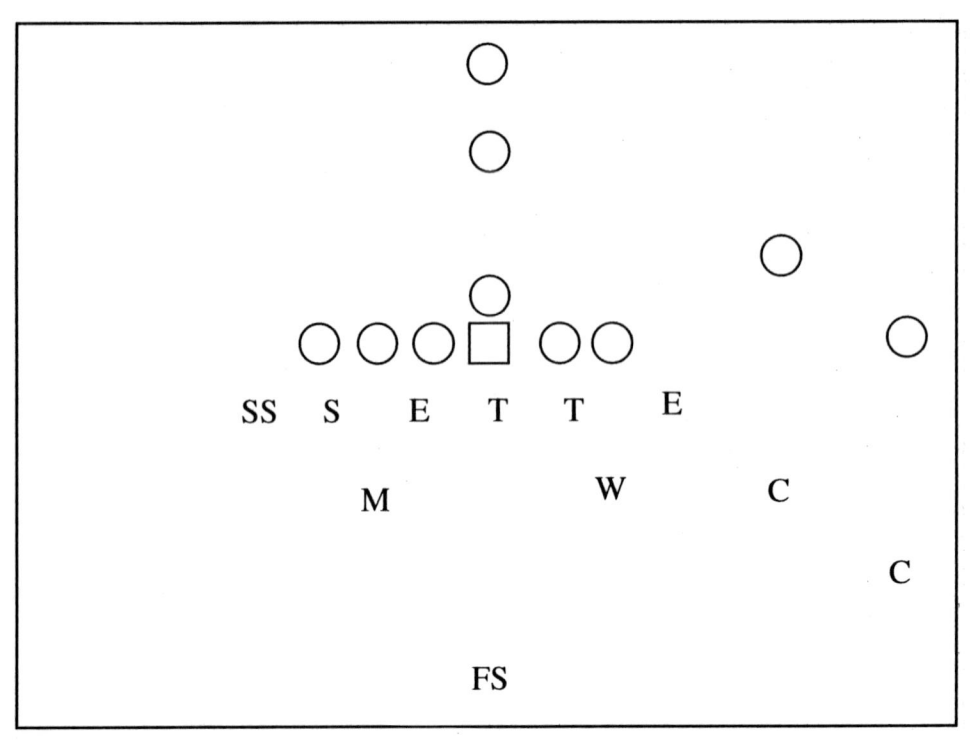

Diagram 9-6: The cover 3 adjustment to the twins formation.

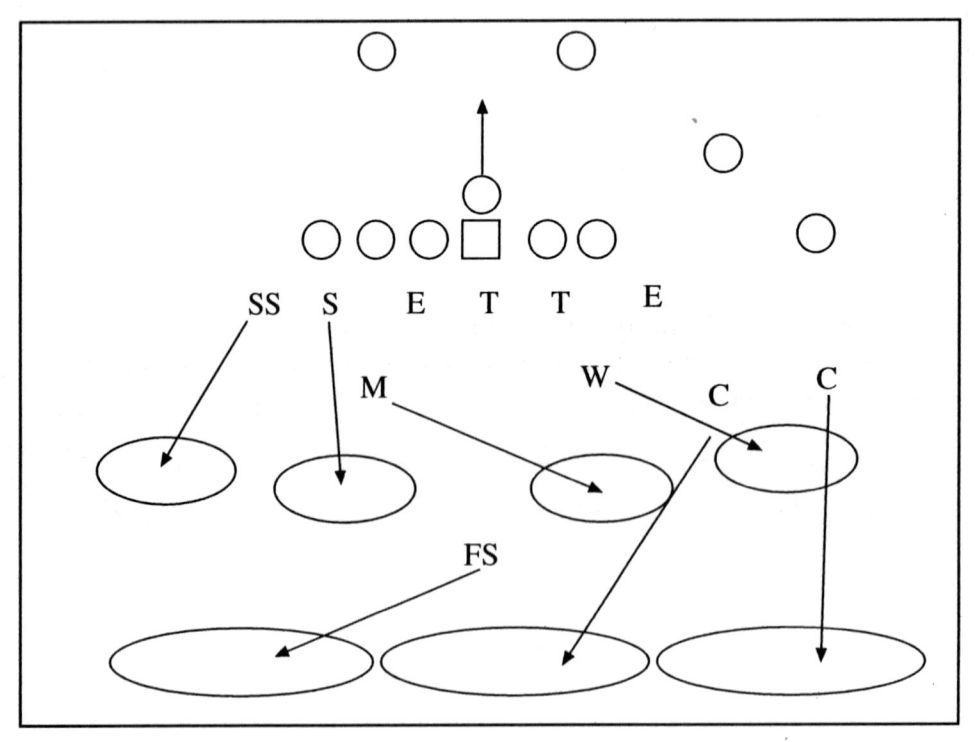

Diagram 9-7: The cover 3 landmark drops versus a dropback pass from the twins formation.

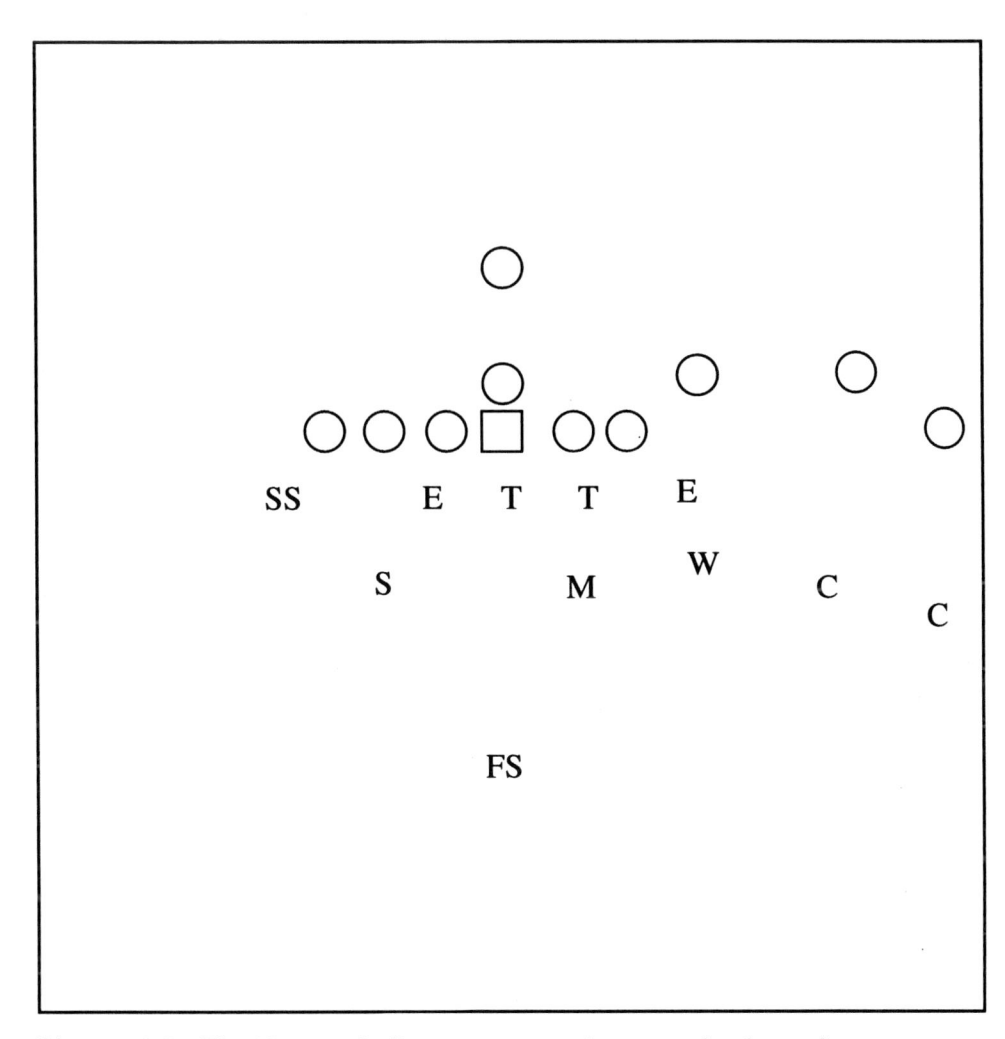

Diagram 9-7a: The 46 cover 3 alignment versus the open trips formation.

Obviously, the pro formation and the twins formation are only two of the fundamental offensive sets. While other formations present different problems for the cover 3 scheme, the underneath coverage defenders do not vary their drops according to the formation. In fact, the underneath zone drops are consistent for every underneath defender, regardless of the offensive formation. The cover 3 alignment against other common formations is shown in Diagrams 9-7b through 9-7e.

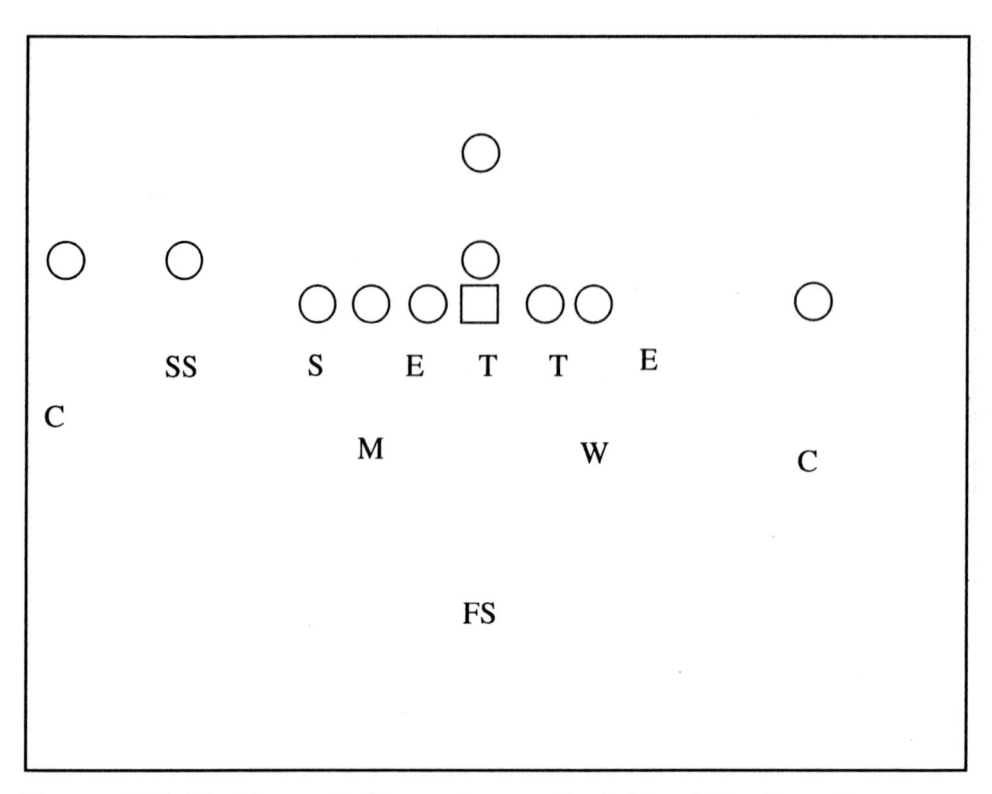

Diagram 9-7b: The 46 cover 3 alignment versus the tight end trips formation.

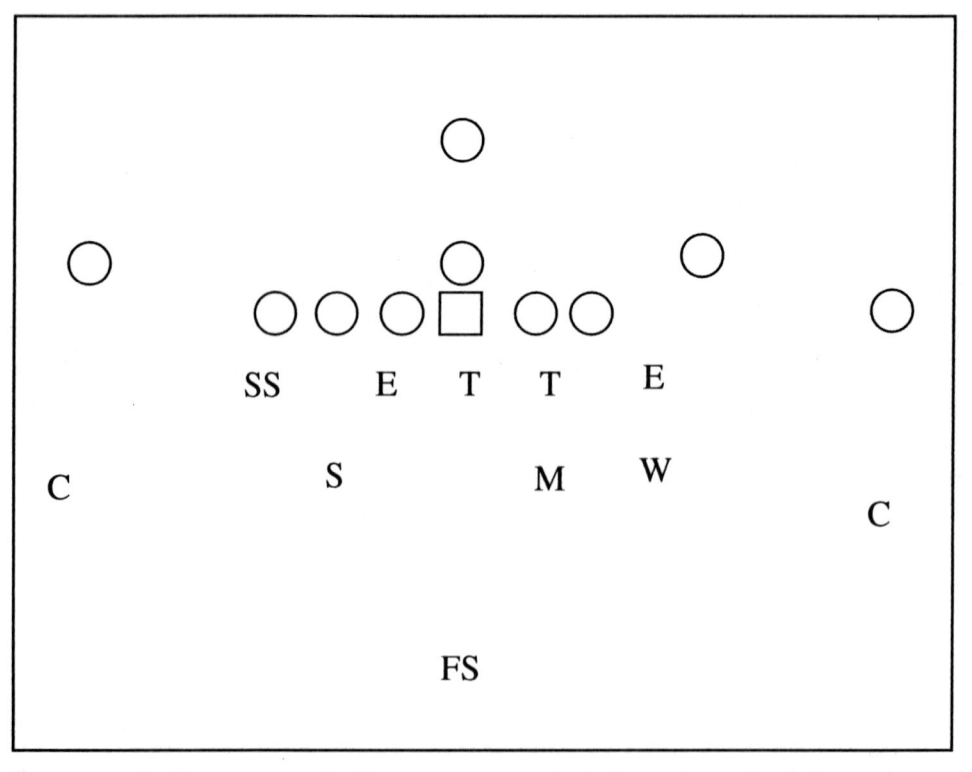

Diagram 9-7c: The 46 cover 3 alignment versus the balanced one-back formation.

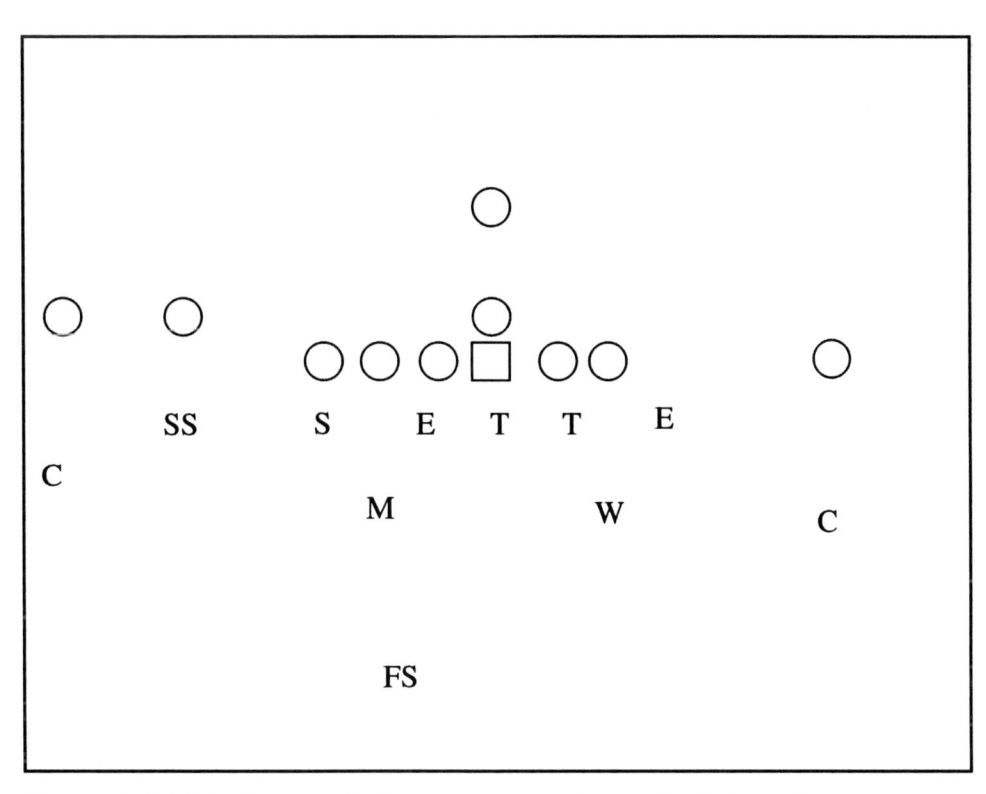

Diagram 9-7d: The 46 cover 3 alignment versus the one-back formation.

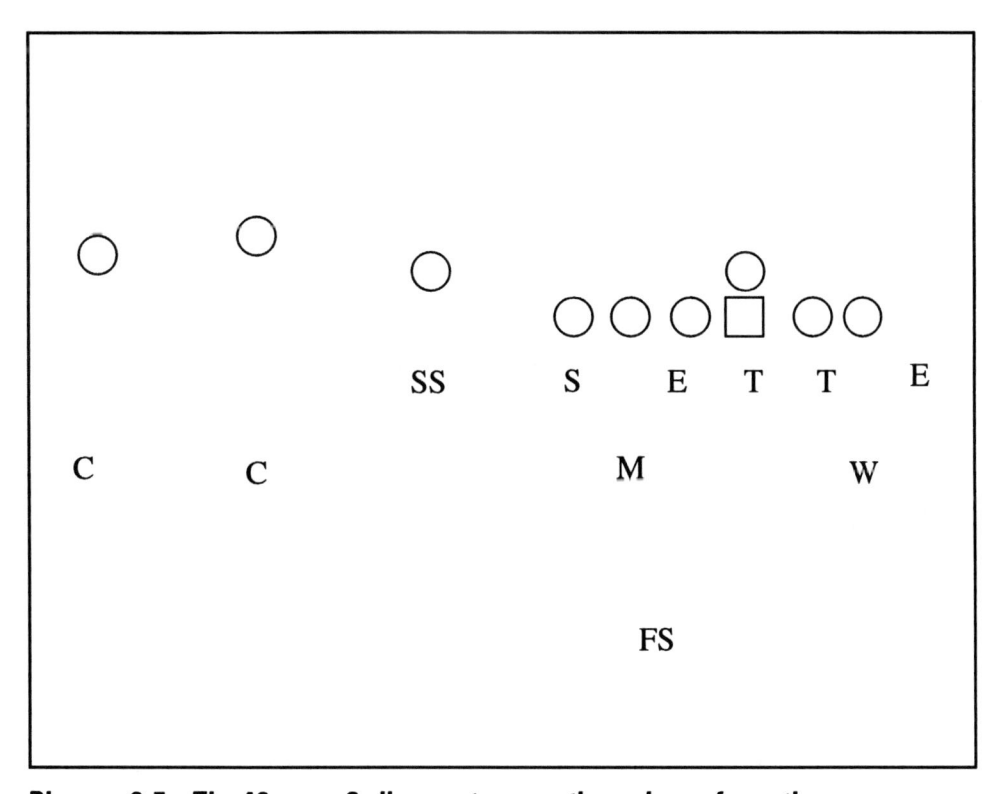

Diagram 9-7e: The 46 cover 3 alignment versus the end over formation.

Cover 3 underneath zone techniques:

As previously shown in Diagram 9-1, the four underneath coverage defenders are the three linebackers and strong safety. Four zones are covered by these four underneath defenders. Versus the dropback pass, the underneath defenders are characterized primarily as landmark droppers who incorporate pattern read concepts. Their landmarks are the four common zones: the strong curl, the strong hook, the weak hook, and the weak curl. The curl zone corresponds to the numbers painted on the field while the hook zone corresponds to the area just inside the hash marks. From his base alignment on the tight end, the Sam linebacker drops to the strong curl zone. The Mike linebacker drops to the strong hook zone.

The four underneath defenders should adhere to the following rules of underneath pass coverage:

- *Drop to a depth ranging from 12- to 15-yards.*

- *Never break on a shallow route until the ball is thrown to the shallow receiver.*

- *Carry the second receiver through the zone.*

When dropping to his zone, the underneath dropper should use the same key as the deep coverage personnel—the number two receiver. For example, when the Will linebacker drops to the weak curl, he reads the action of the number two receiver and peeks at the number one receiver. His primary key is the number two receiver, but he should be able to diagnose the action of the number one receiver—should the number two receiver provide no threat.

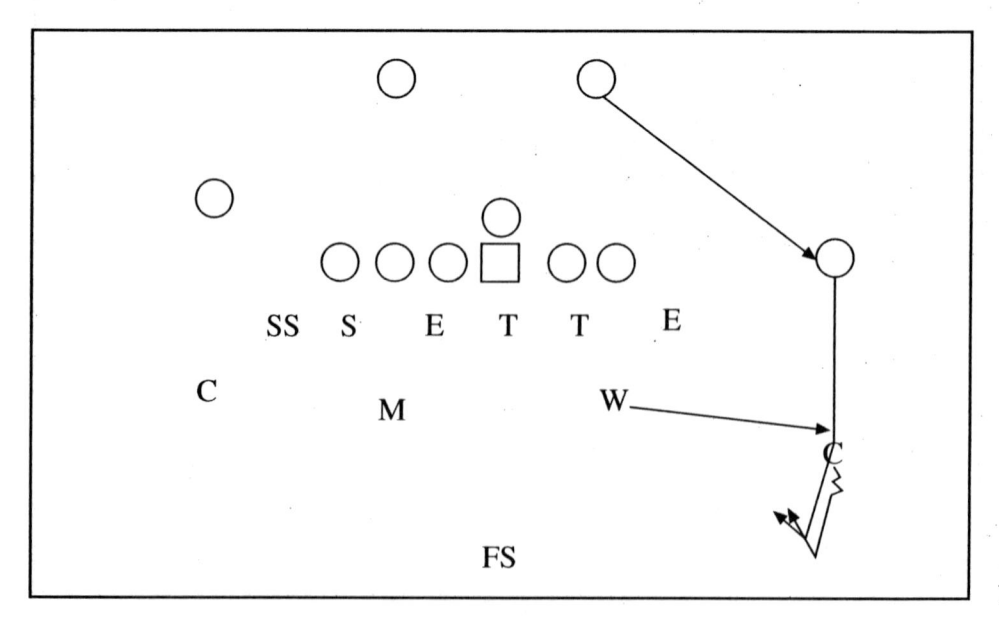

Diagram 9-8: The number two receiver runs an out route.

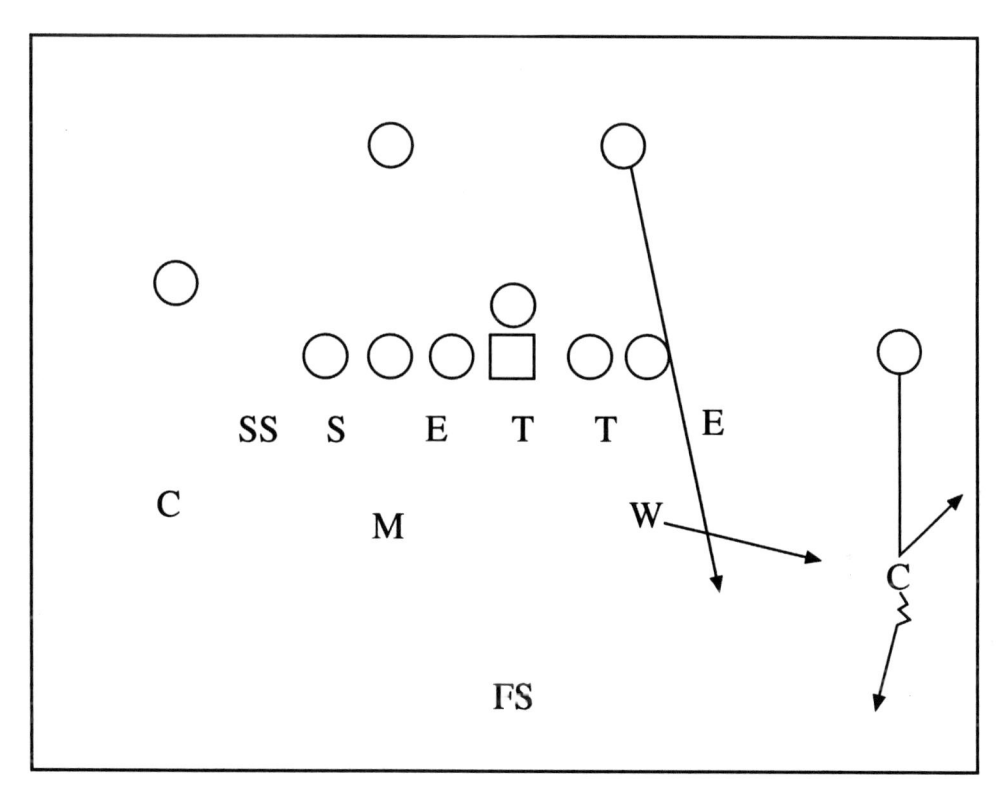

Diagram 9-9: The number two receiver runs a vertical route.

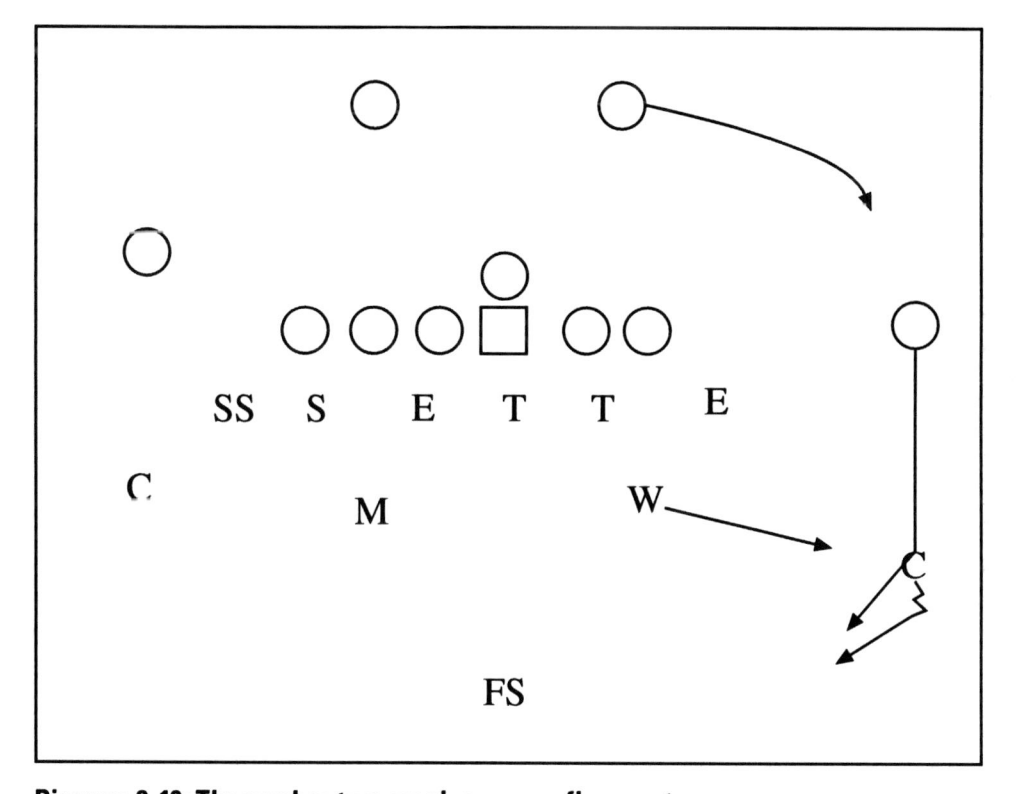

Diagram 9-10: The number two receiver runs a flare route.

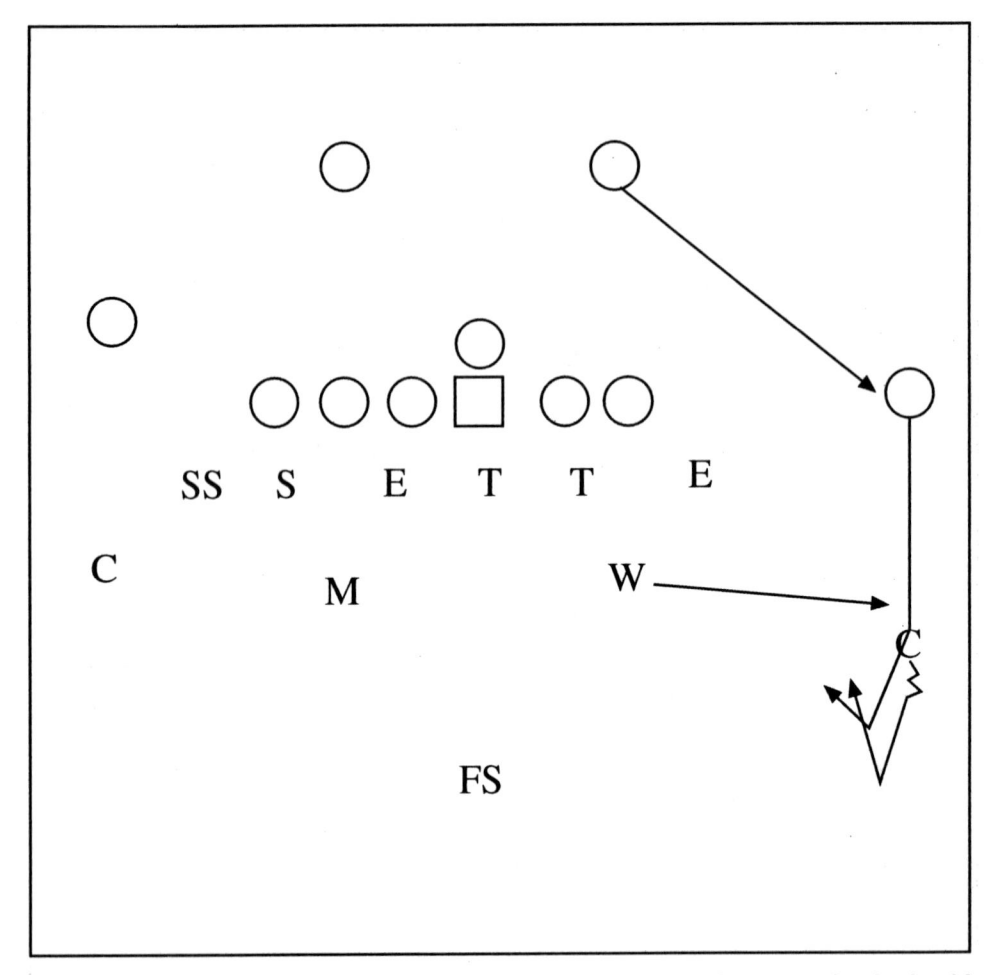

Diagram 9-11: The number two receiver runs an out route; the cornerback should expect a curl route by the number one receiver.

If the number two receiver continues through the flat zone and turns up on a vertical route, the number two receiver is a serious threat to the pattern-reading coverage concept. Consequently, the underneath dropper's adherence to the "carry the second receiver" rule is critical in order to maintain the integrity of the deep coverage.

As stated in a previous paragraph, the cornerback reacts according to one of three universal pattern reads, and each pattern read is cued by the action of the number two receiver. If the number two receiver runs a flat route, the cornerback is prompted to squeeze the route of the number one receiver and indeed challenge the expected curl route by the number one receiver. Considering the aggressive play of the cornerback in relation to the flat route by the number one receiver, the deep outside 1/3 is vulnerable to a conversion of the flat to a wheel route.

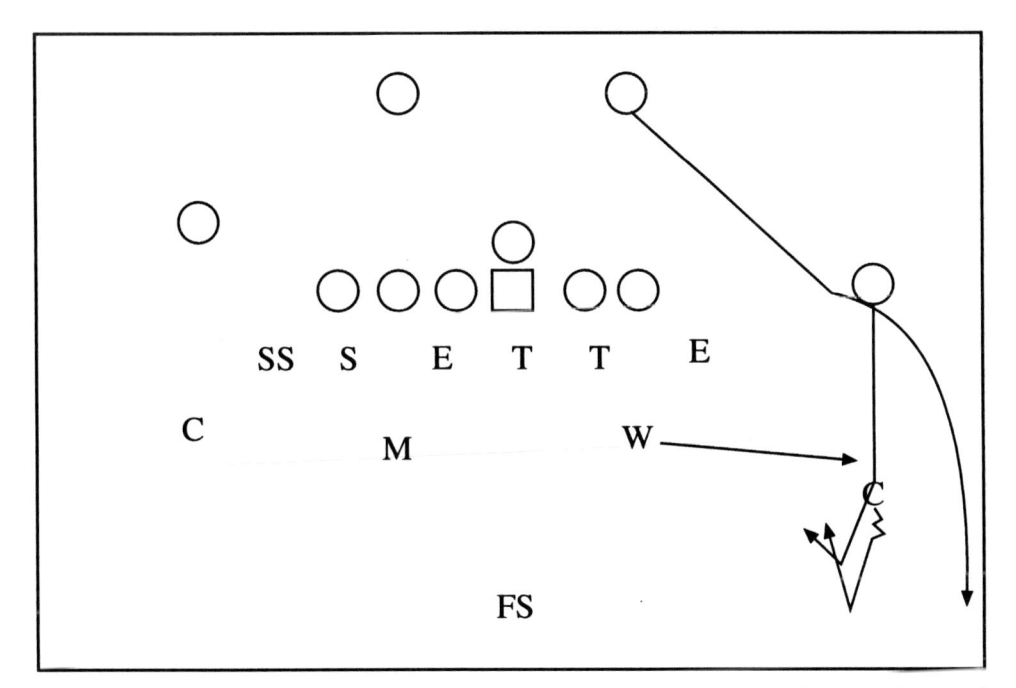

Diagram 9-12: The number two receiver converts the flat route to the wheel route.

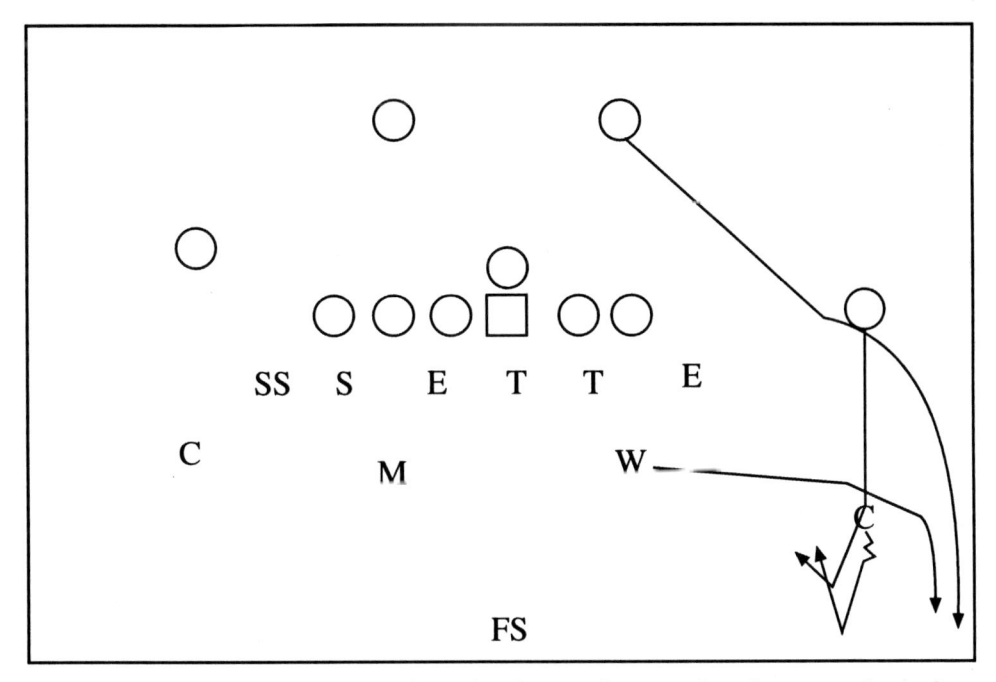

Diagram 9-13: Will responds to the wheel route by carrying the second receiver through the flat zone.

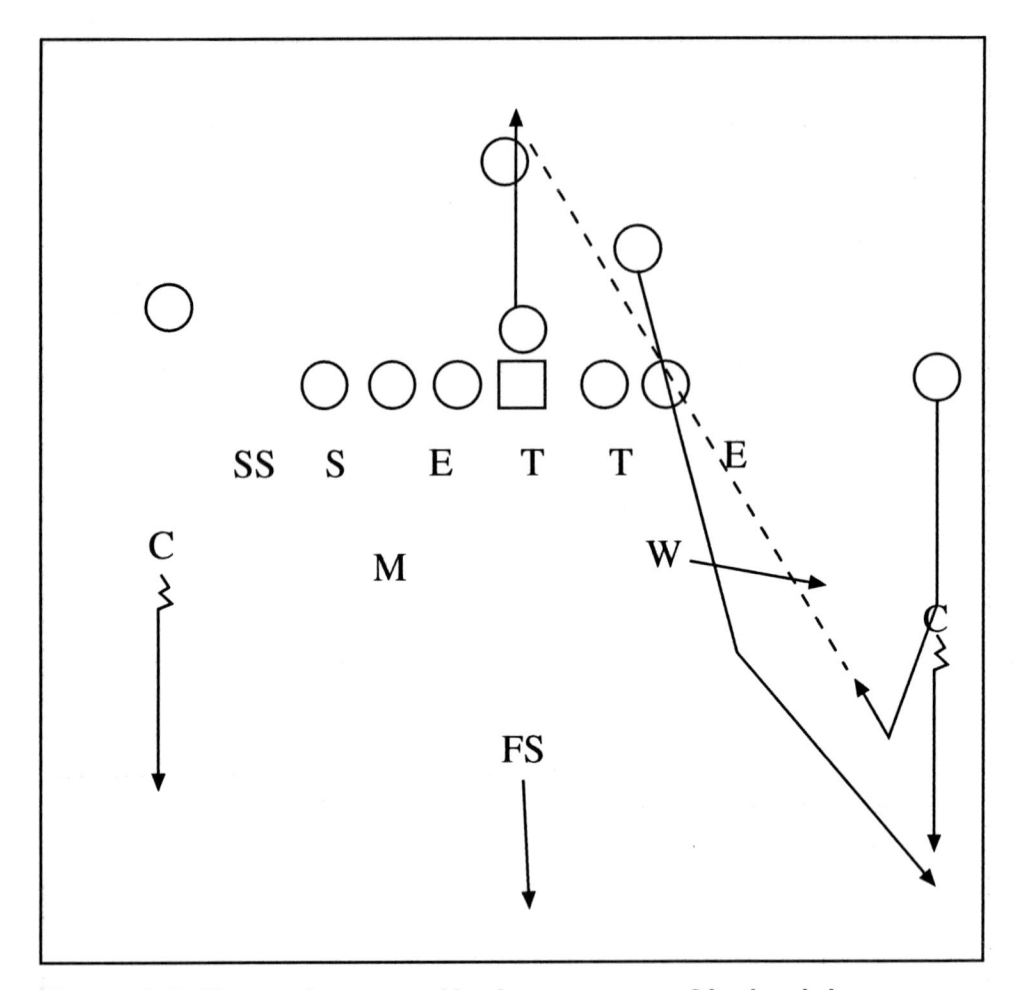

Diagram 9-14: The smash route combination versus cover 3 landmark drops.

The vulnerability of the deep outside 1/3 is eliminated by the underneath defender executing his technique of carrying the second receiver through the zone. By carrying the number two receiver through the zone, the underneath defender provides eye-to-eye coverage on the wheeling number two receiver.

On the surface, the strategy of assigning an underneath defender to cover a receiver on a deep route seems risky. However, with competent coaching and the proper personnel placement at the linebacker positions, this particular system of aggressive pattern reading in the cover 3 scheme gives you the best three-deep coverage available. The alternative to pattern reading is blanket landmark dropping and a soft, ineffective three-deep scheme which covers deep, but covers nothing else. If your objective in cover 3 is to simply cover the three deep zones every down, your secondary will be ruthlessly sliced apart by intermediate 15-17–yard underneath patterns (e.g., smash combinations, dig routes, and deep curl routes).

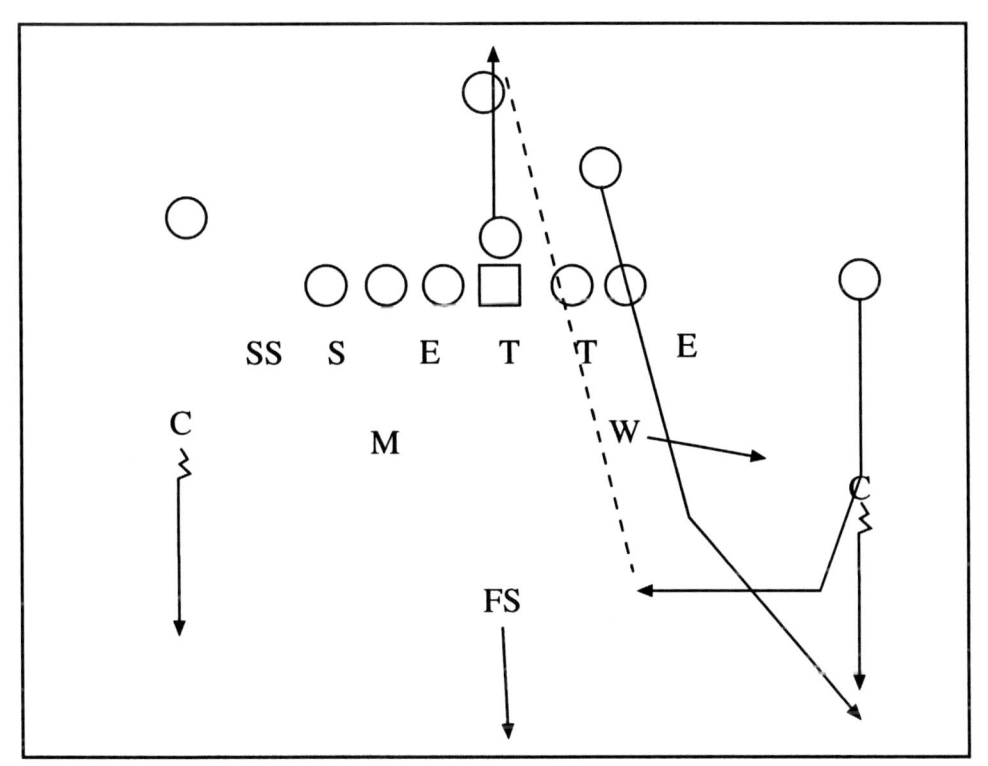

Diagram 9-15: The dig route versus cover 3 landmark drops.

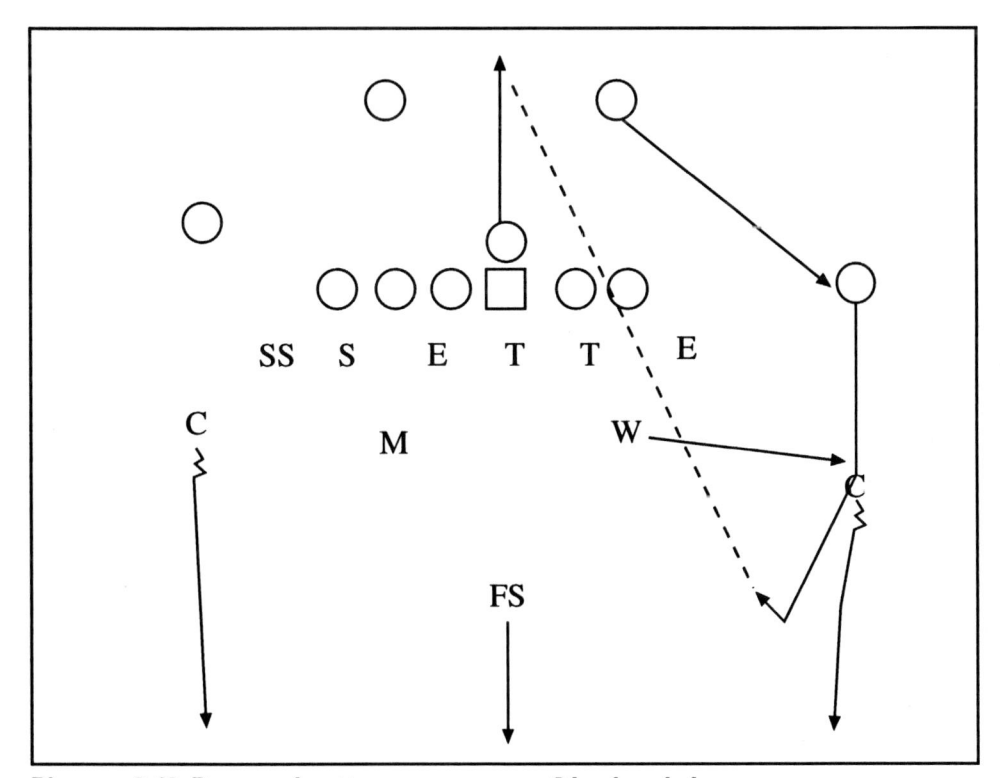

Diagram 9-16: Deep curl pattern versus cover 3 landmark drops.

103

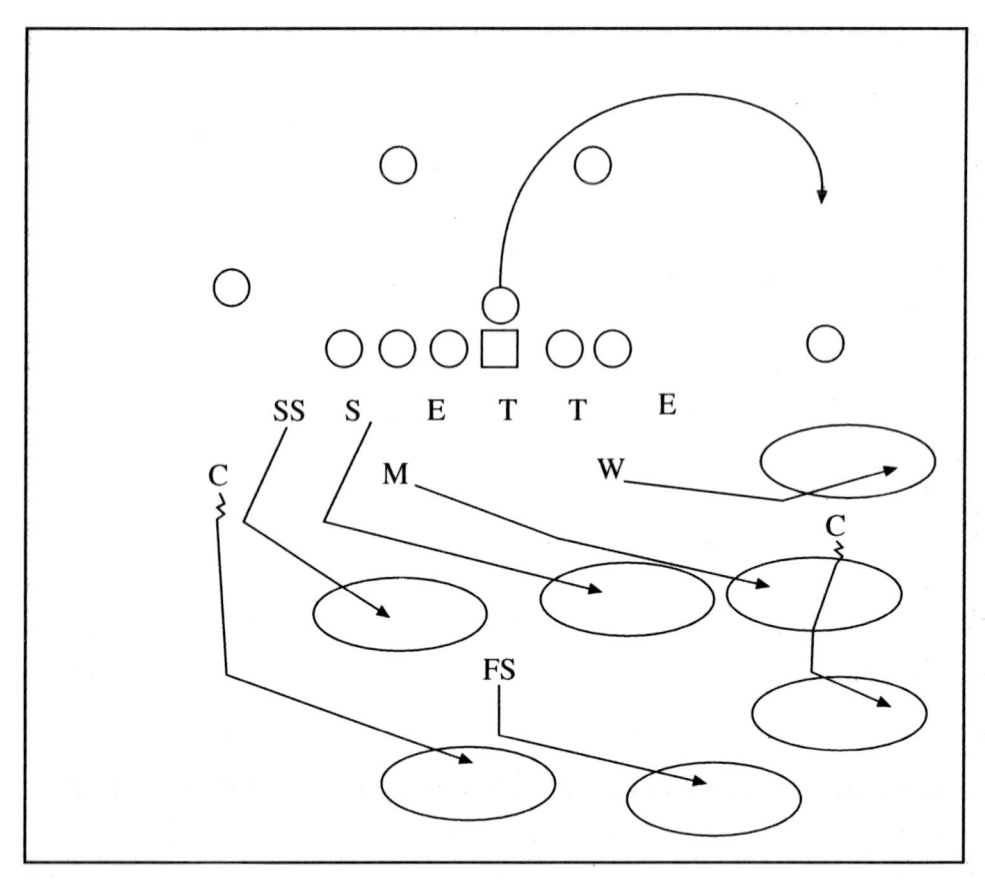

Diagram 9-17: The zone coverage defenders slide with the ball movement outside the tackle box.

Sliding the underneath coverage:

If the quarterback rolls to one side of the field or is flushed out of the pocket, the underneath coverage defenders will slide their zones in the direction of the quarterback's movement. Against a quarterback who is rolling out on the snap, the underneath defenders will initially open to sprint to their regular landmarks. Once the quarterback reaches the tackle box or demonstrates a clear intention to move outside the tackle box, the defenders begin to move in the direction of the quarterback's movement. Diagram 9-17 illustrates this concept as the quarterback is shown breaking outside the tackle box on the right defensive perimeter. In this particular case, both the underneath and deep zone defenders would slide their zones with the quarterback's movement. The deep zone defender's movement is less pronounced than the underneath defender's movement. The deep zone defender slides to a lesser degree with the quarterback because of the fact that the longer the quarterback holds the ball, the greater the chance he will throw back across the grain. Deep defenders should slide slightly over in the direction of the quarterback's flow, but they must continue to be aware of receivers who are moving downfield into the deep zones.

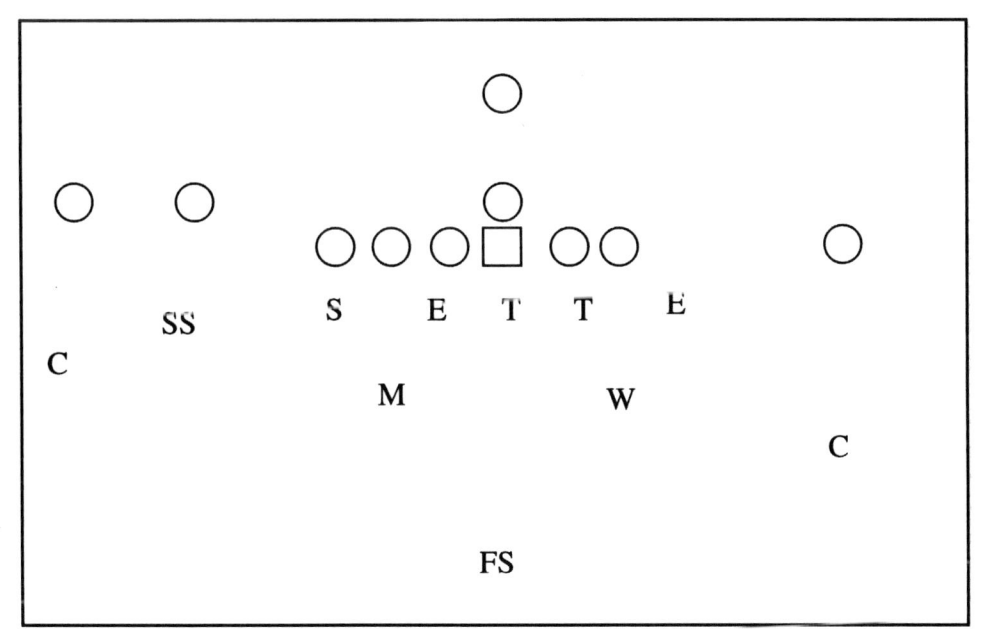

Diagram 9-18: The 46 loaded zone alignment versus the tight end trips formation.

Laying off the crossers:

One important coaching point to the underneath coverage is the fact that the underneath droppers must not chase crossing routes. The three-deep zone coverage is structured around the landmark drops of the linebackers and strong safety. If an underneath defender were to chase a crossing route, he would open up a seam in his designated zone.

If an underneath dropper recognizes a crossing route, he should yell out a warning to his teammates and, if possible, collision the receiver as he moves to his primary zone. He should not go out of his way to collision a receiver or allow his junction of the receiver to delay his progress to his primary zone. Crossing receivers, particularly shallow crossing routes, usually indicate the accompaniment of another companion crossing route which is more threatening. The underneath linebacker should learn to look through the crossing route, as well as opposite the crossing route, to search out any receiver looking for a hole in the defender's primary zone.

The loaded zone:

While cover 3 is referred to as the generic chalkboard zone, cover 3Z is called the loaded zone. In theory, the loaded zone is a combination zone and man philosophy. Against the strong side of the formation, the loaded zone is a pure zone concept. Against the weak side of the formation, the loaded zone is a man-to-man concept. Cover 3Z is structured from a three-deep alignment. It is a coverage that may be run as an automatic against three wide receivers aligned to one side of the ball (i.e., trips). Cover 3Z gives you the advantage of outnumbering the strength of the formation with a 5-on-3 advantage. On the

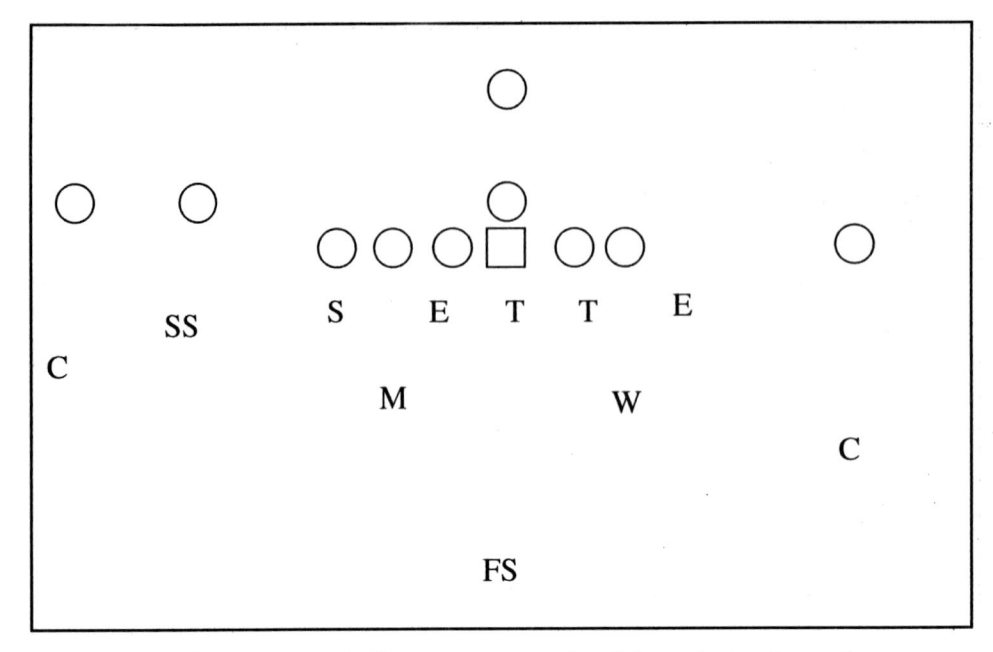

Diagram 9-19: The 46 cover 3 alignment versus the tight end trips formation.

backside, the man-to-man principles give you a 3-on-2 advantage.

As Diagrams 9-18 and 9-19 show, the initial alignment of the three-deep zone and the loaded zone defenders is the same. However, the alignment is where the commonality between the two schemes begins to fade. The loaded zone concept is initiated by the free safety. Just prior to the snap, the free safety opens his hips to the weakside of the formation and feints a pre-snap roll to the deep 1/2 zone. In moving to the weak side, the free safety invites the quarterback to look to the strong side and throw a post route behind the free safety. This tactic of bailing the free safety out alone has enabled us to get a high number of interceptions in the 3Z coverage. In faking a weakside roll, the free safety must not drift past the hash marks. He must be able to pivot back to the inside and square up to cover his middle 1/3 zone.

The principal difference between the three-deep zone and the loaded zone is in the landmarks of the underneath droppers. As stated in a previous paragraph, the landmark drops of the chalkboard three-deep are as follows:

- *Strong safety* —drops to the strong curl (the numbers).
- *Sam linebacker*—drops to the strong hook (inside the hash marks).
- *Mike linebacker*—drops to the weak hook (inside the hash marks).
- *Will linebacker*—drops to the weak curl (the numbers).

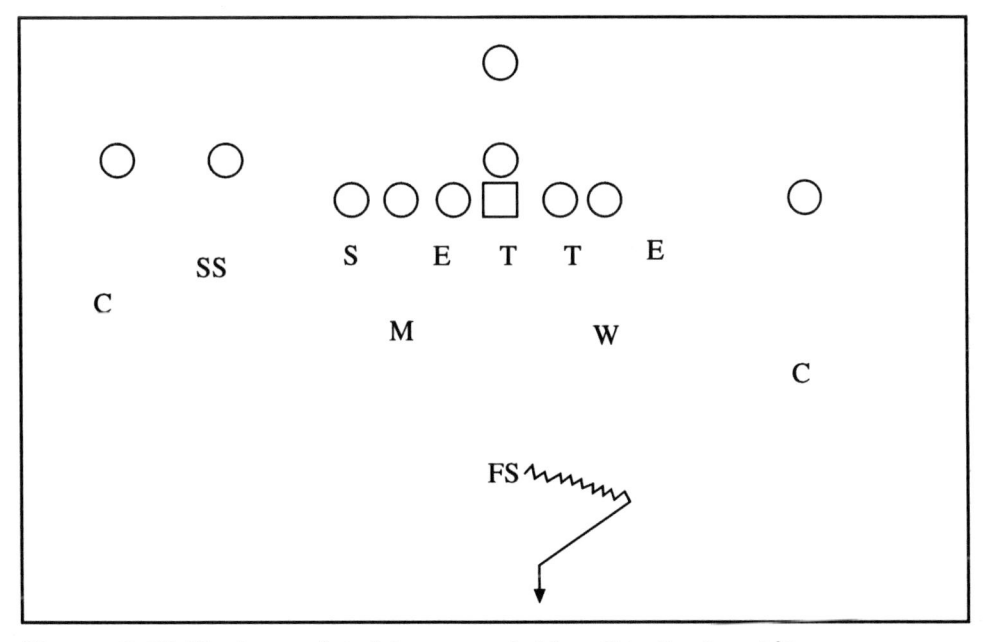

Diagram 9-20: The free safety fakes a weakside roll to the deep 1/2 zone.

Versus a three-receiver set to the tight end side, the landmark drops or techniques of the loaded zone are as follows:

- *Strong safety*—drops to the strong divider (underneath the numbers and seven yards from the sideline).
- *Sam linebacker*—drops to strong curl, but is responsible for man coverage on the second crossing receiver.
- *Mike linebacker*—drops to the strong hook, but is responsible for man coverage on the first crossing receiver.
- *Will linebacker*—makes a "zip" or "zip go" call, depending on the type of backfield set.

An obvious difference between the three-deep zone and the loaded zone is the sensitivity of the loaded zone to the side of the formation strength. Against a three-receiver set to the tight end side (e.g., tight end trips, etc.), the strong safety and Sam linebacker are pure zone droppers. Against the same three-receiver set from the loaded zone, the strong safety and Sam linebacker are pure man-to-man defenders in a banjo type of coverage on the tight end and nearback. Also in cover 3, the cornerbacks play on either side of the ball as they normally would align against a pro formation; whereas in cover 3Z, the cornerbacks align to the same side of the ball as they normally would align against a twins formation. Probably the most glaring difference between the cover 3 scheme and the cover 3Z scheme is the inside cornerback's underneath coverage responsibility against the three-receiver set to the open side (i.e., the side opposite the tight end).

As the information with regard to the comparative underneath responsibilities suggests, the loaded zone responsibilities are much more flexible than the rigid landmark drops of the chalkboard three-deep zone. With that flexibility comes a greater responsibility of reading the routes of the receivers. Each of the three linebackers must read the patterns as they open to drop to their landmarks and respond accordingly to the receiver routes.

The coverage can best be broken into two dimensions, a strong side and a weak side. The strong side of the coverage is the side aligned to the three receivers, while the weak side is the single or two-receiver side. It is important to note that it is the number of the receivers—not the location of the tight end—which dictates the strength of the formation. On the strong side of a tight end trips formation—any type of pro formation with three receivers aligned on the strong half of the formation—the Sam and Mike work together to guarantee close coverage on both the first and second crossing routes through the underneath zones. The strong safety will fly out on a flat path to the divider, which is seven yards from the sideline and underneath the numbers.

In reading the crossing routes to determine the identity of the second crosser, the Sam linebacker must first recognize the first crosser. Once Sam recognizes the first crosser, he should look outside for a second crosser. Since the most dangerous threat is the multiple-receiver side, Sam should look first outside to the strong side of the formation. If no second crosser is seen breaking from the three-receiver side, Sam can then swivel his head and look across the formation through the first crossing route. If a second crosser is breaking across the formation from the weak side to the strong side, Sam would then pick up the second crosser. Versus a three-receiver threat from the tight end side, it is important to note that generally, the second crosser will originate from the strong side—the side closest to the Sam linebacker.

Mike will open to the three-receiver side and move to his strong hook landmark. Mike will quickly pick up the action of the first crosser and cover him man-to-man. The first crosser will almost certainly originate from the three-receiver side—in this case, the tight end side. Note that Mike should generally drop to a shallow strong hook landmark and settle early, since the first crosser is usually a shallow crossing route.

As described in a previous paragraph, the dynamics of the coverage vary significantly according to whether the formation is a pro type of set or a twins type of set. Against a pro type of set, the weak side of the 3Z coverage is manned by the Will linebacker and the deep cornerback aligned on the open side (i.e., away from the tight end) of the formation. The weak side of the 3Z coverage against a twins type of set is manned by the Sam and the strong safety aligned on the tight end side of the set.

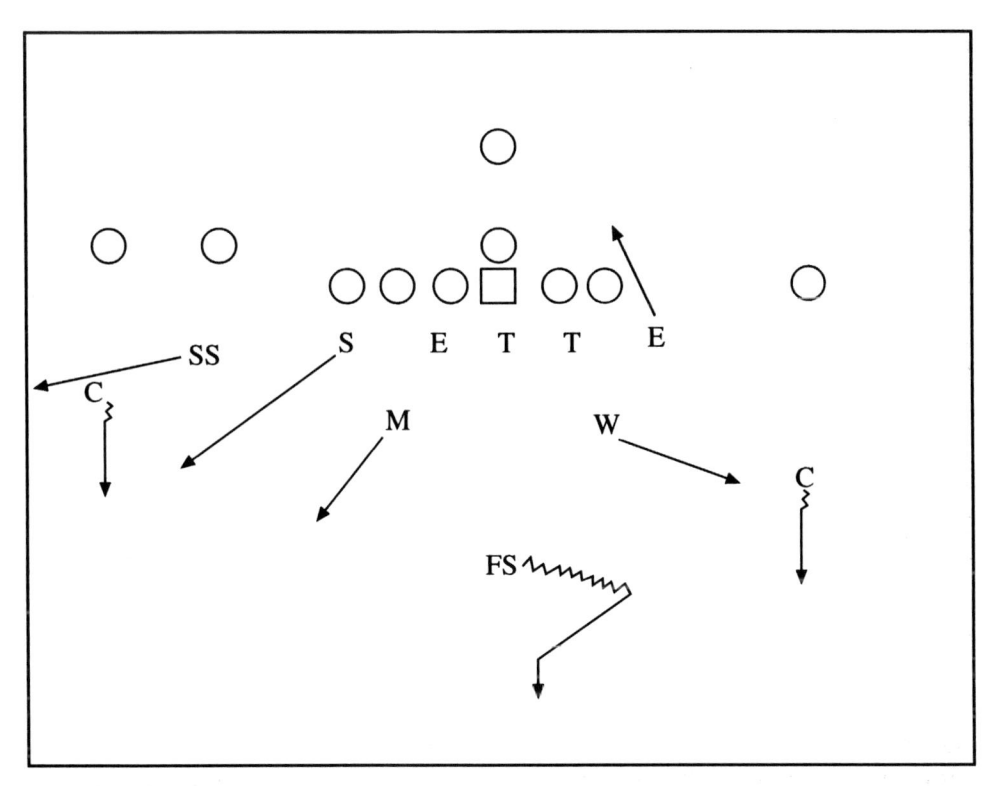

Diagram 9-21: Cover 3Z landmark drops versus a tight end trips.

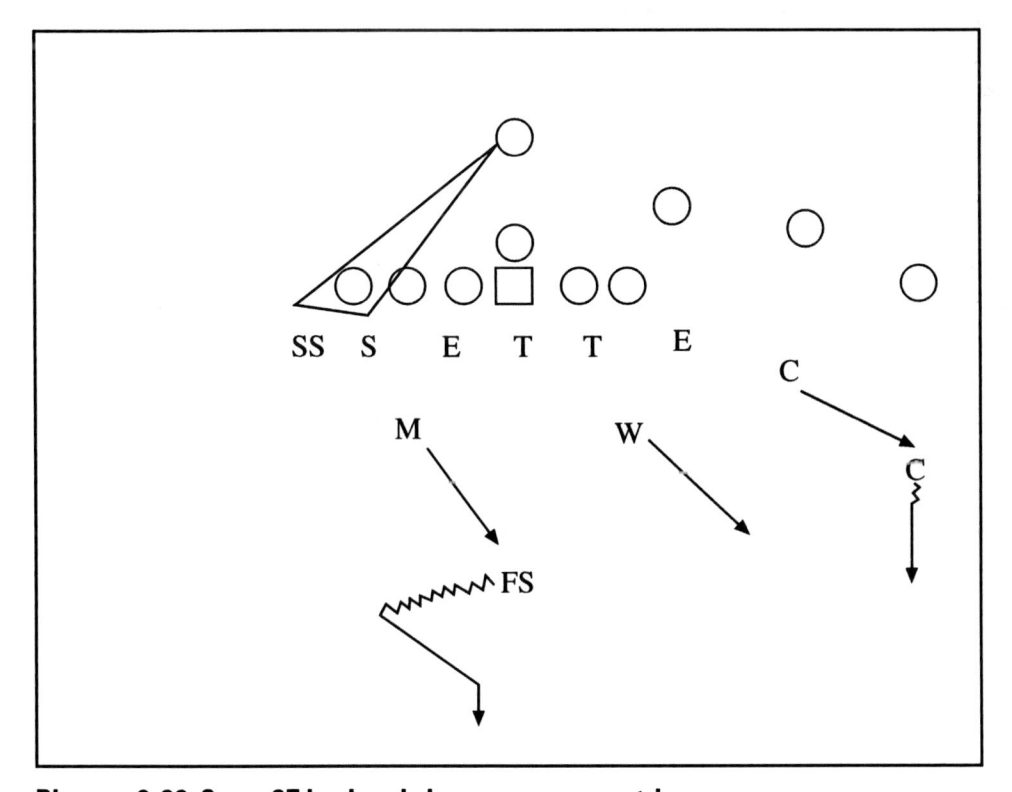

Diagram 9-22: Cover 3Z landmark drops versus open trips.

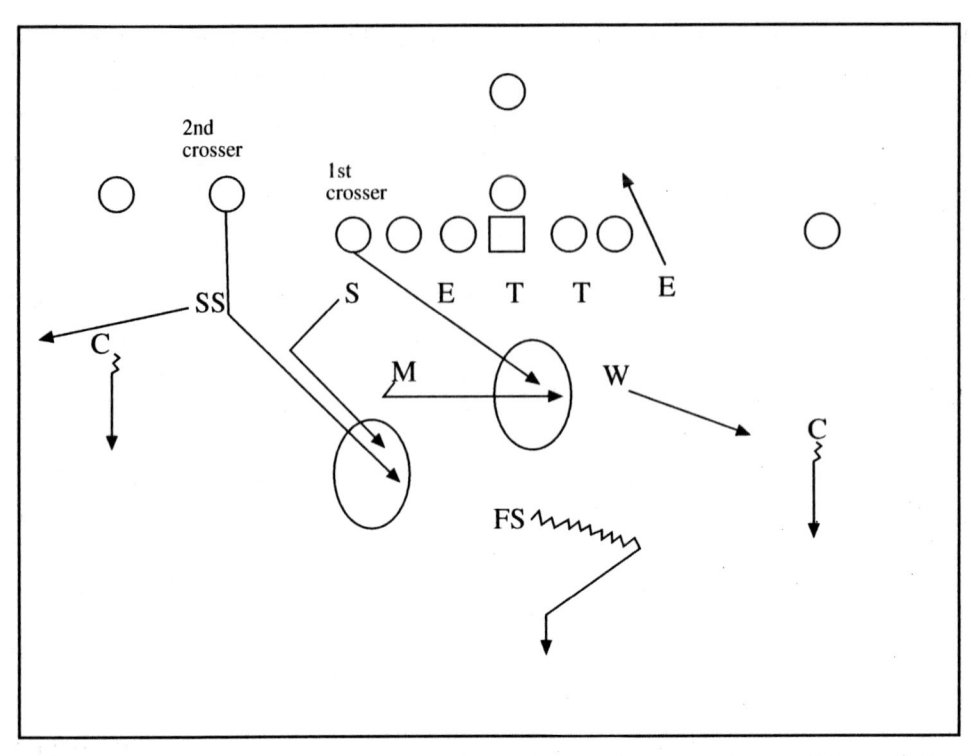

Diagram 9-23: Sam and Mike cover the first and second crosser from a tight end trips formation.

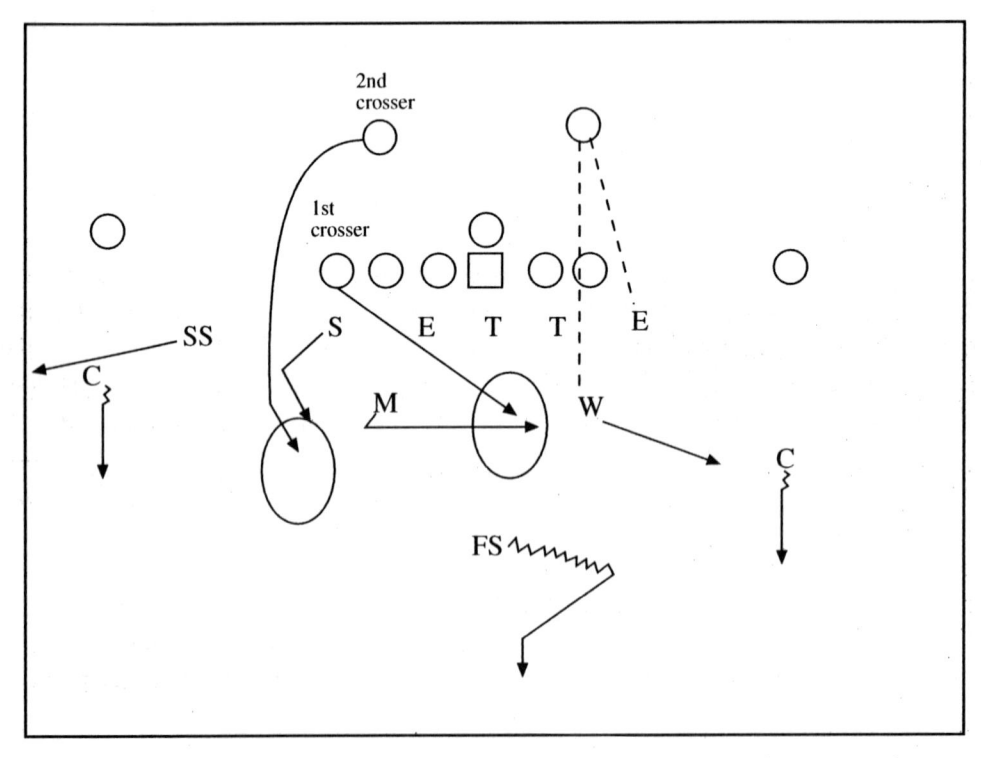

Diagram 9-24: Sam and Mike cover the first and second crosser from a pro formation.

When the three receivers are set to the open side, the dynamics of the loaded zone are very different from the standpoint of personnel assignments. Against a twins type of formation where the three receivers are aligned on the open side, both cornerbacks align on the open side. The inside cornerback becomes an underneath dropper while the outside cornerback covers the deep 1/3. Against the twins or open trips formation, the drop assignments are as follows:

- *Strong safety* — jams the tight end with both hands, forcing an inside release. If the tight end releases outside, the strong safety covers him man-to-man. If the tight end blocks or releases inside, the strong safety covers the second receiver out from the backfield.

- *Sam linebacker* — jams the tight end and covers him on a vertical release from an inside-out position. Unless the tight end releases across the face of the strong safety, the Sam linebacker covers the tight end man-to-man. If the tight end sets for a pass block, the Sam linebacker will rush.

- *Mike linebacker* — drops to the strong hook, but is responsible for man coverage on the first crossing receiver.

- *Will linebacker* — drops to strong curl, but is responsible for man coverage on the second crossing receiver.

- *Inside cornerback* — drops to the strong divider (underneath the numbers and seven yards from the sideline).

The techniques of the inside cornerback and the Will linebacker versus the twin set are identical to the strong safety and Sam linebacker versus the pro set. In reading the crossing routes to determine the identity of the second crosser, the Will linebacker must first recognize the first crosser. Once Will recognizes the first crosser, he should look outside for a second crosser. Since the most dangerous threat is the multiple-receiver side, Will should look first outside to the strong side of the formation. If no second crosser is seen breaking from the three-receiver side, Will can then swivel his head and look across the formation through the second crossing route. If a second crosser is breaking across the formation from the weak side to the strong side, Will would then pick up the first crosser. Versus a three-receiver threat from the open end side, it is important to note that, generally, the second crosser will originate from the strong side—the side closest to the Will linebacker.

Mike will open to the three-receiver side and move to his strong hook landmark. Mike will quickly pick up the action of the first crosser and cover him man-to-man. The first crosser will almost certainly originate from the three-receiver side—in this case, the open side.

To better communicate the principles of the weakside scheme of the 3Z coverage, we will examine first the 3Z coverage against the pro type of formation. On the weakside of the pro type of formation such as open trips, the Will linebacker and defensive end work together to cover the nearback. The weakside cornerback understands that he is likely to be left on an island, alone in his man-to-man coverage of the split end. In order to get the greatest benefit out of the scheme, the Will linebacker makes one of two calls to the defensive end. He can make either a "zip" call or a "zip-go" call.

If the nearback is aligned in a position which would allow him to release freely into a pattern, the Will linebacker makes a zip call. The zip call results in a banjo type of defensive coverage scheme between the Will and the defensive end. The parameters of the defensive end's responsibility on the zip call are as follows:

- *If the nearback releases outside, the defensive end covers the nearback.*
- *If the nearback blocks, the defensive end rushes directly at the nearback.*
- *If the nearback releases inside the defensive end on a vertical path, the defensive end rushes the quarterback.*

The parameters of the Will linebacker's responsibility on the zip call are as follows:

- *If the nearback releases outside, the Will works to an inside-out trail position on the split end.*
- *If the nearback blocks, the Will works to an inside-out trail position on the split end.*
- *If the nearback releases inside the defensive end on a vertical path, the Will covers the nearback from an inside-out position.*

A zip-go call is made when the nearback is not in a threatening position to release into a pass pattern. Diagram 9-28 shows a backfield set against which the Will linebacker would make the zip-go call. Whenever the backfield is set toward the tight end side, the call should be a zip-go call. A zip-go call assigns the nearback to the defensive end prior to the snap of the ball. No read of the nearback's action is needed to determine who will cover the nearback. Since the nearback is not in a threatening alignment, the defensive end can handle covering him without a problem.

The weakside scheme of the 3Z coverage versus the twins type formation is the same in application as the loaded theory, but it involves different coaching points for several defenders. For example, instead of the Will and defensive end working together to cover the nearback from the open side, the strong safety and the Sam will work together to cover the tight end and nearback from the nub-end side of the formation.

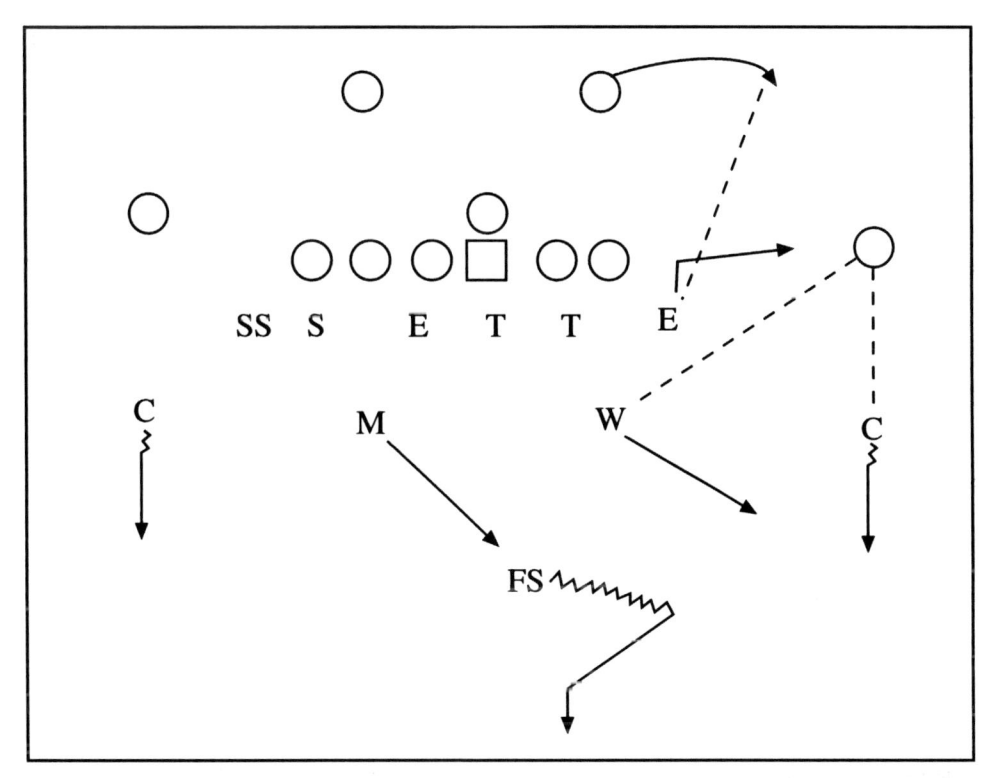

Diagram 9-25: The nearback releases outside.

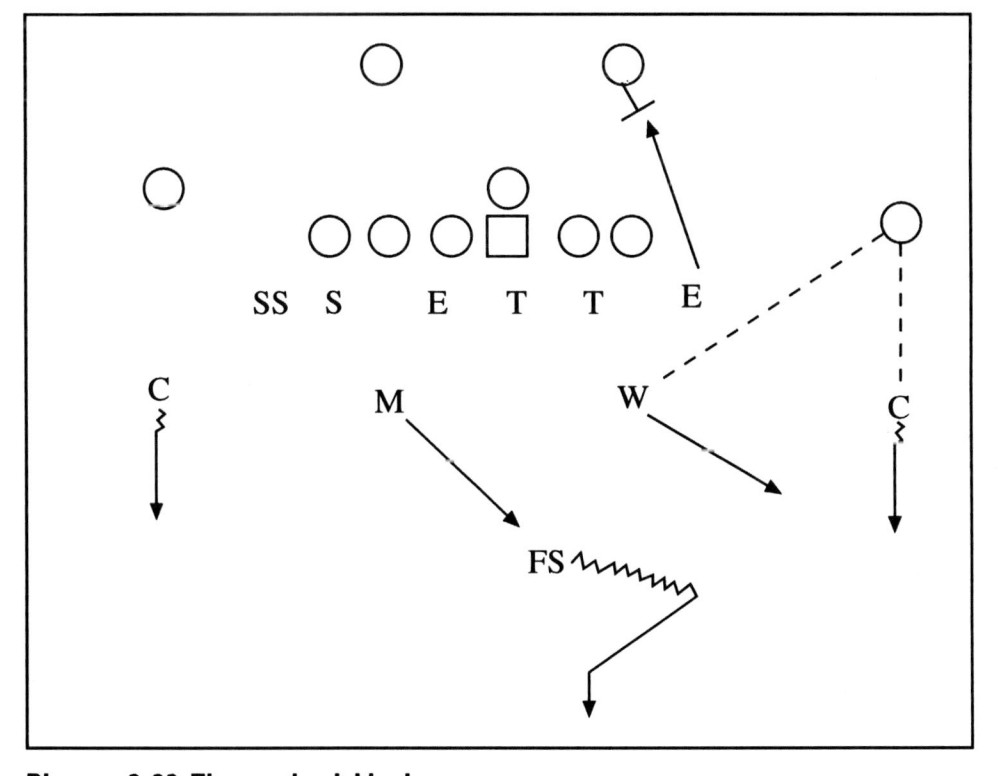

Diagram 9-26: The nearback blocks.

113

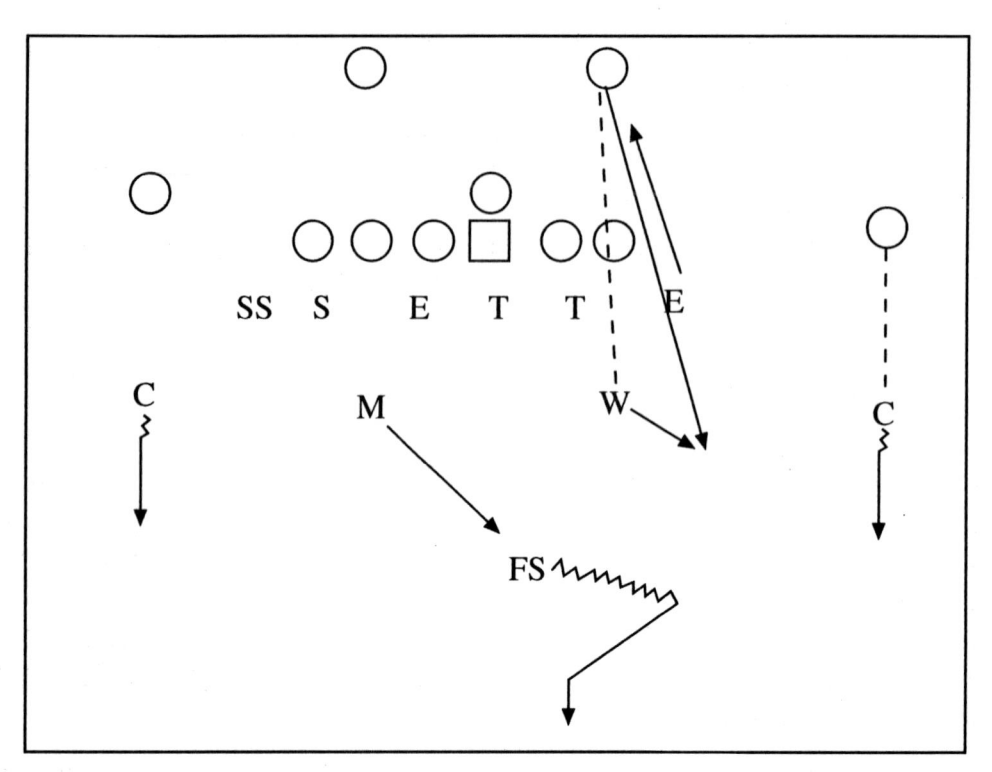

Diagram 9-27: The nearback releases on a vertical route.

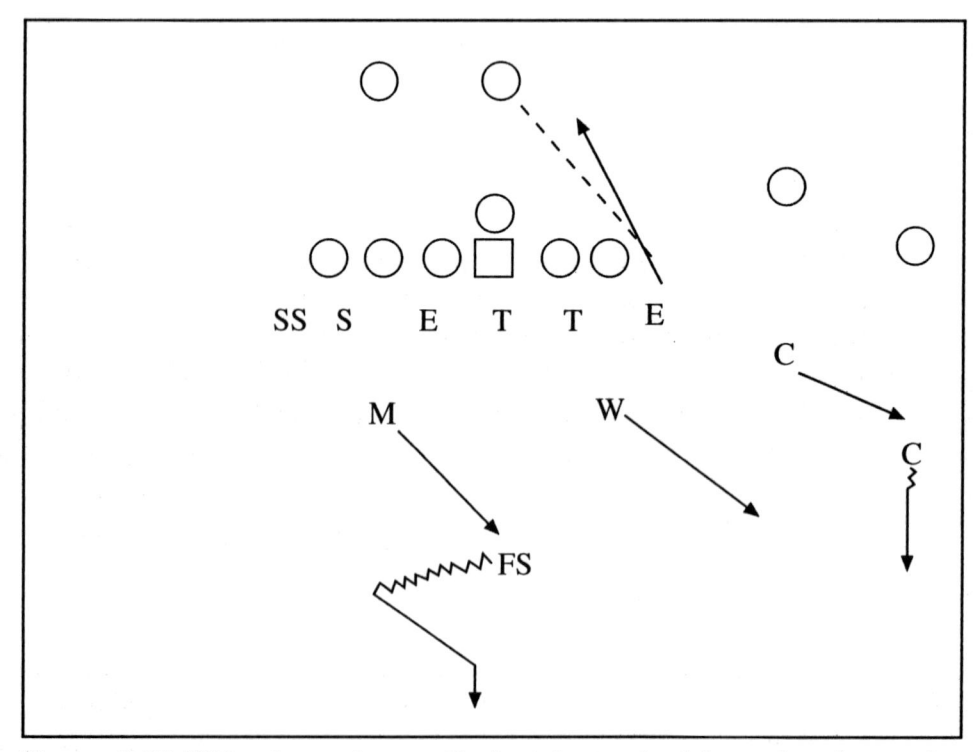

Diagram 9-28: Will makes a zip-go call when the nearback is not in a threatening alignment.

The strong safety's two-fold objective is to jam the tight end and cover him man-to-man if he attempts to cross the strong safety's face. Meanwhile, the Sam linebacker jams the tight end from an inside-out angle and has the responsibility of covering the tight end on any vertical release upfield or crossing route. The strong safety and Sam work a banjo technique on the tight end and the nearback. If the tight end releases outside and the nearback runs a vertical, the strong safety will match up on the tight end while the Sam linebacker covers the nearback. If the tight end releases inside the strong safety and the nearback runs a flat pattern, the Sam linebacker covers the tight end while the strong safety covers the nearback.

Man-free coverage:

The most effective pressure coverage scheme in the 46 package is the man-free coverage, or what we call "single." In theory, the man-free coverage scheme supports a 5-man rush. However, practically speaking, the man-free scheme allows for either a 5-man, 6-man, or 7-man rush without the need for a specific supplemental blitz call. In fact, versus a full maximum protection scheme with the tight end and both backs staying in to block, the single scheme gives you an 8-man rush. Diagrams 9-32 through 9-38 show the man-free alignment versus the various sets.

Generally speaking, our base coverage philosophy includes the "corner-over" alignment rule. The corner-over rule states that whenever a twins formation is presented, the two cornerbacks will align on the same side. For example, against a twins formation the cornerbacks will cover the split end and the flanker in the slot. The man-free coverage doesn't make exceptions to the corner-over rule.

However, if the formation is a tight end trips formation with a backside split end, the weakside cornerback obviously cannot abandon the split end to move over to the trips side. Therefore, in the case of the tight end trips formation shown in diagram 9-35, the Will linebacker acts as the adjuster and aligns on the number two wide receiver. To this end, Will is coached to move to the tight end side whenever three or four receivers align on that side. Having Will move to the tight end side is actually a simple adjustment. Mike simply alerts the Will linebacker (Will, himself, is also trained to be alert to the formation) to the presence of the tight end trips or tight end quad set and Will adjusts accordingly. Will should understand that he is always involved in coverage against any trips formation, be it a tight end trips or open-end trips. Versus the tight end trips, Will moves over to the strong side and covers the number two receiver; versus the open-end trips, Will covers the number three receiver. Diagrams 9-35 and 9-38 illustrate this coaching point.

While most 46 defensive coaches favor the single-coverage scheme because of its simplicity of adjustments and the free nature of the middle safety, the greatest rewards of single coverage are found in the pressure aspect of the coverage. As

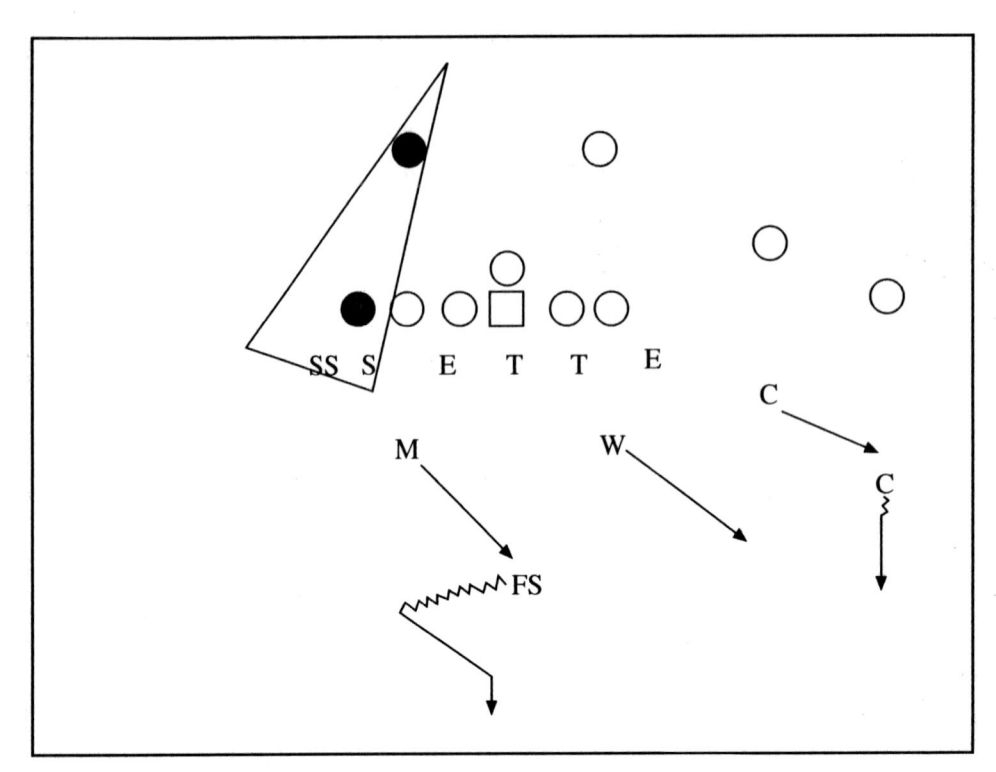

Diagram 9-29: The strong safety and Sam are responsible for covering the tight end and the nearback.

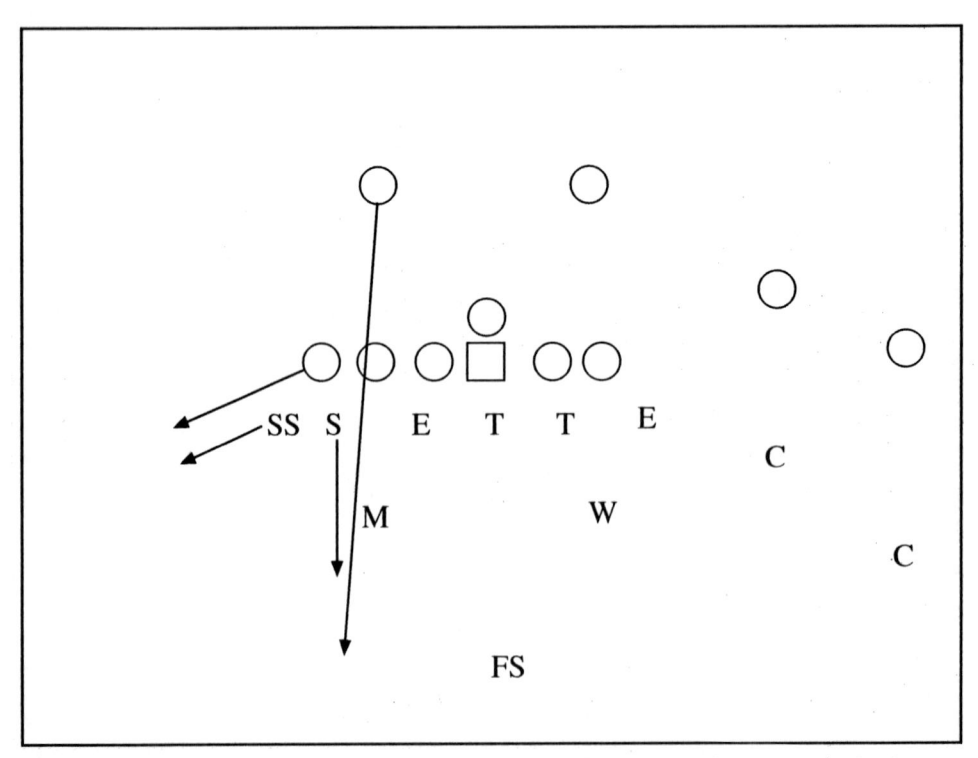

Diagram 9-30: The tight end releases outside and the nearback runs a vertical.

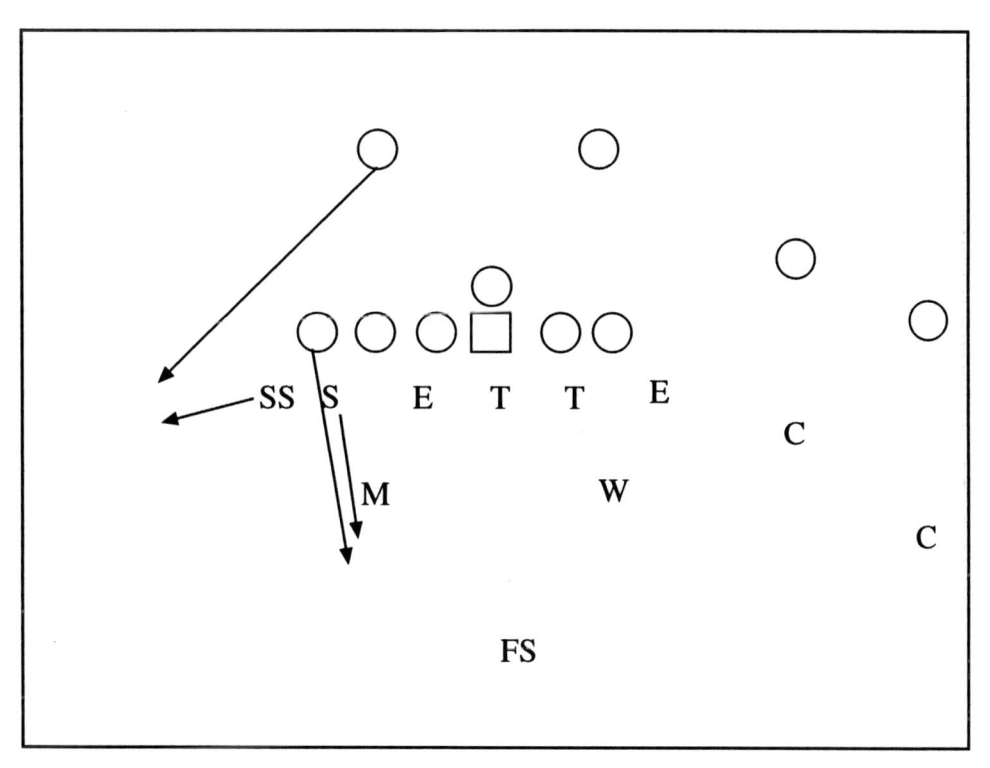

Diagram 9-31: The tight end releases inside the strong safety and the nearback runs a flat pattern.

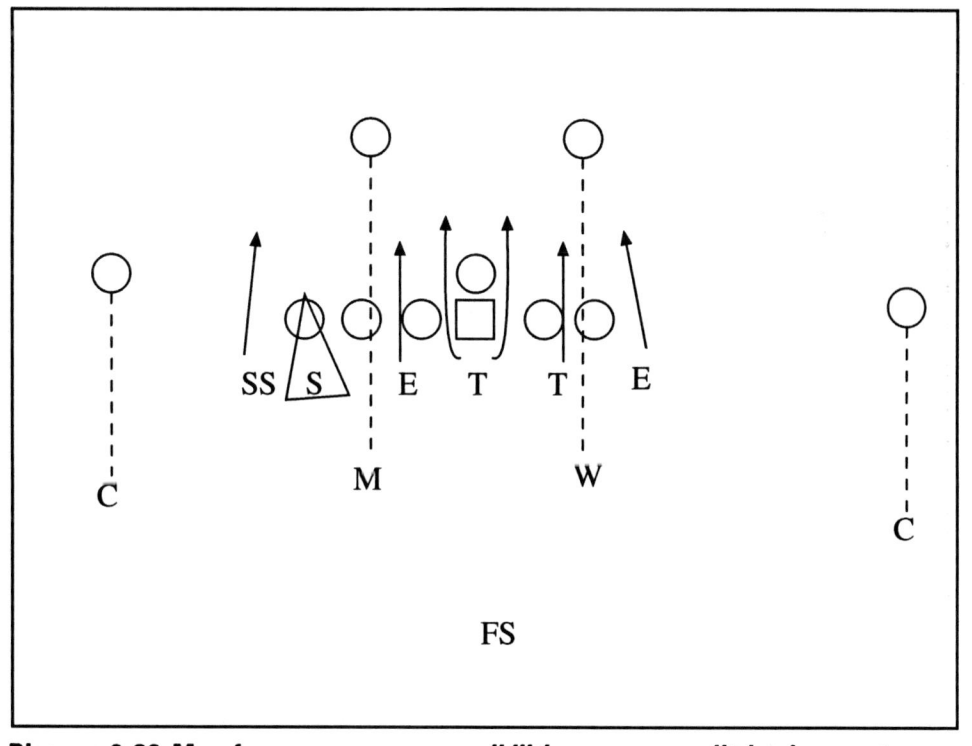

Diagram 9-32: Man-free coverage responsibilities versus a split-back pro set.

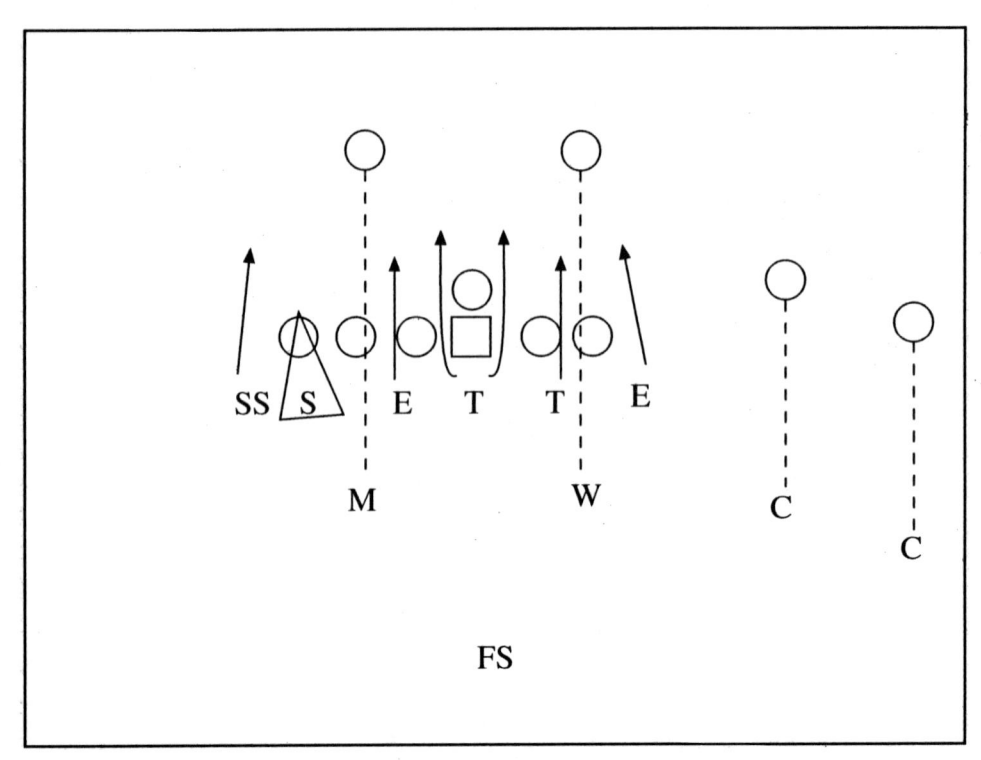

Diagram 9-33: Man-free coverage responsibilities versus a split-back twins set.

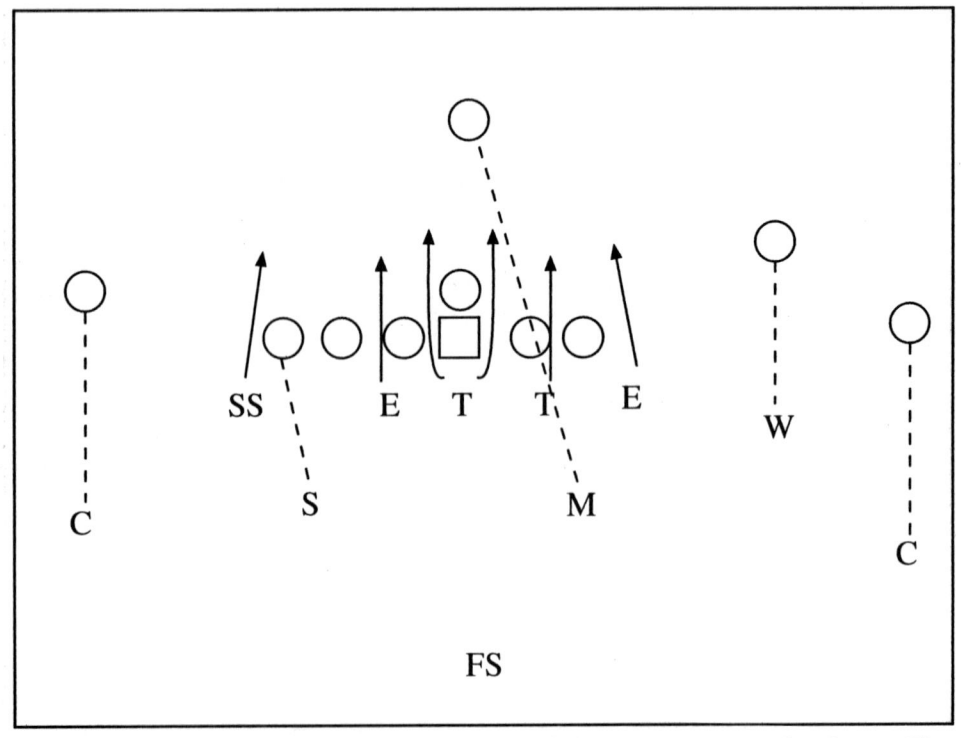

Diagram 9-34: Man-free coverage responsibilities versus a one-back set. The Jayhawk adjustment is shown.

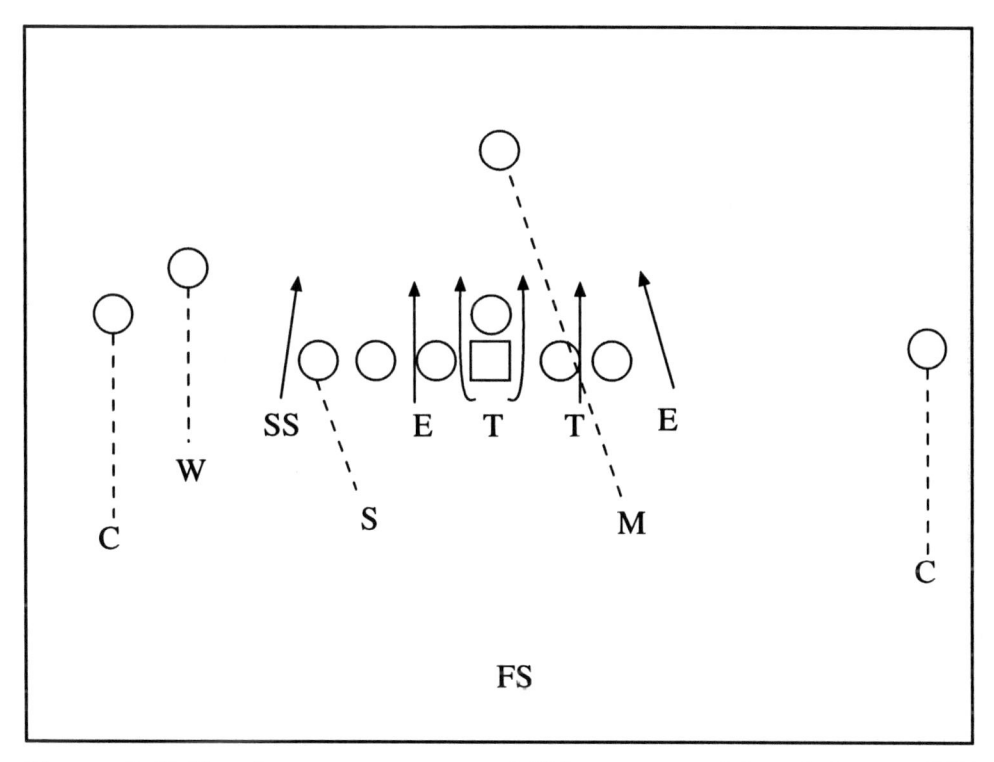

Diagram 9-35: Man-free coverage responsibilities versus a tight end trips set. Will acts as the adjuster. The Jayhawk adjustment is also shown.

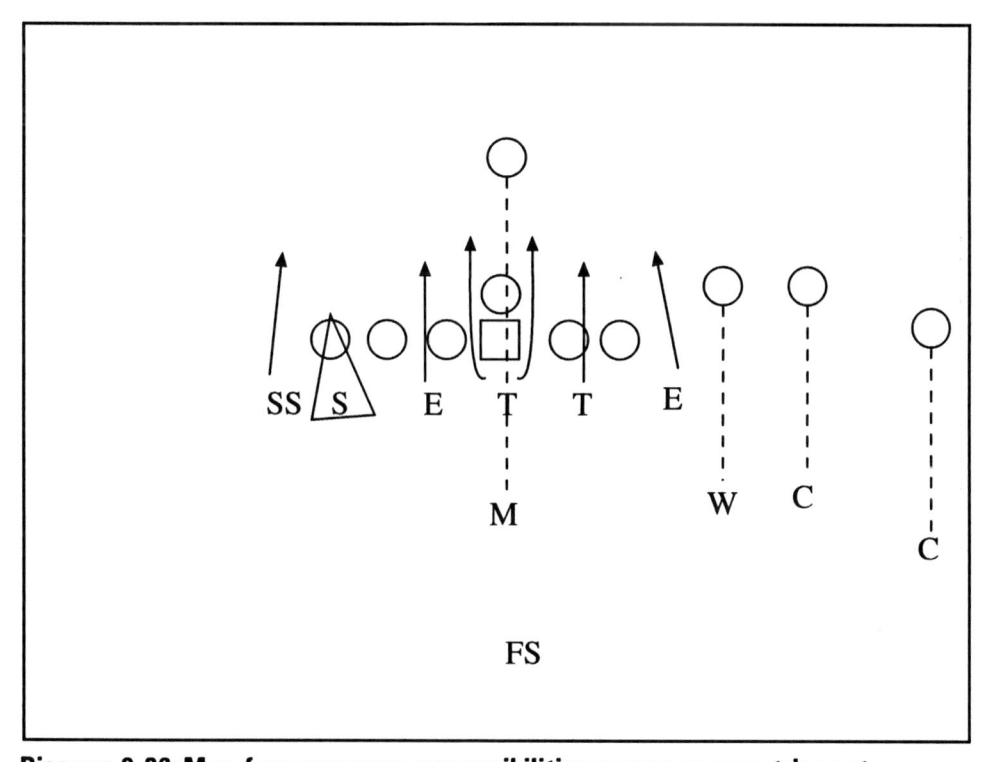

Diagram 9-36: Man-free coverage responsibilities versus an open trips set.

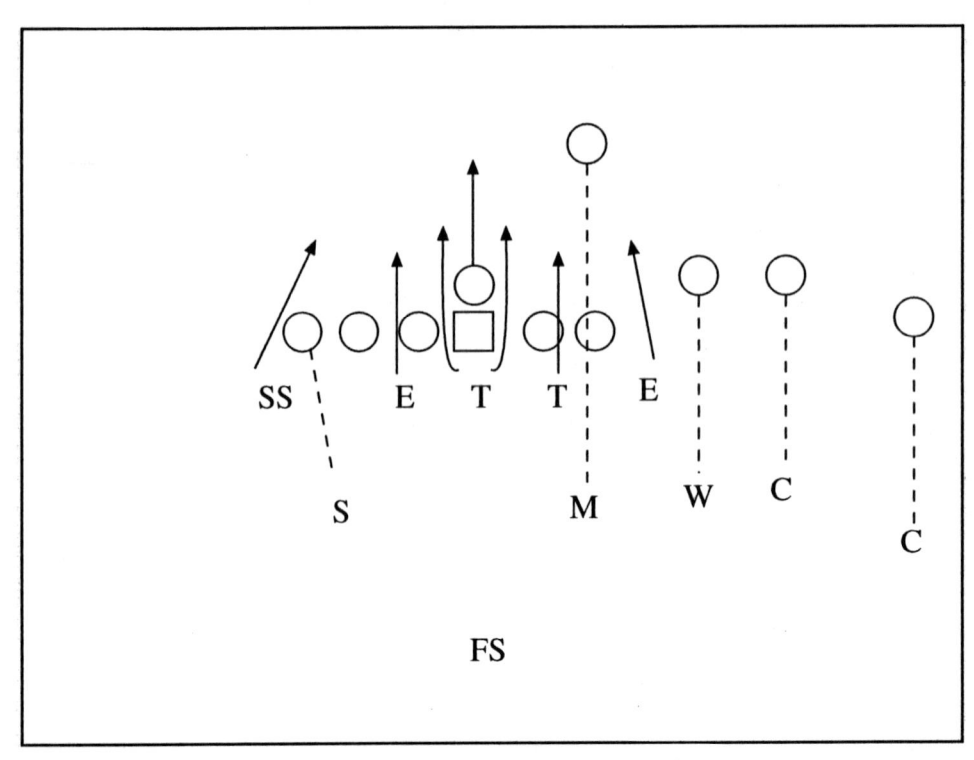

Diagram 9-37: Man-free coverage responsibilities versus an open quads set. The Jayhawk adjustment is also shown.

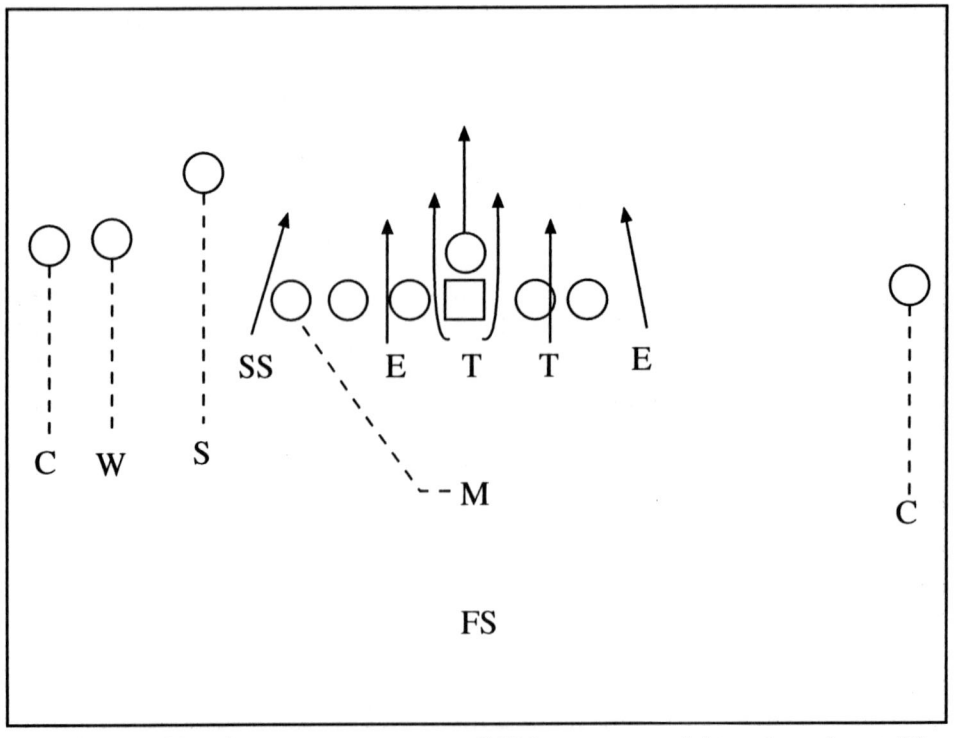

Diagram 9-38: Man-free coverage responsibilities versus a tight end quads set. The Will acts as the adjuster.

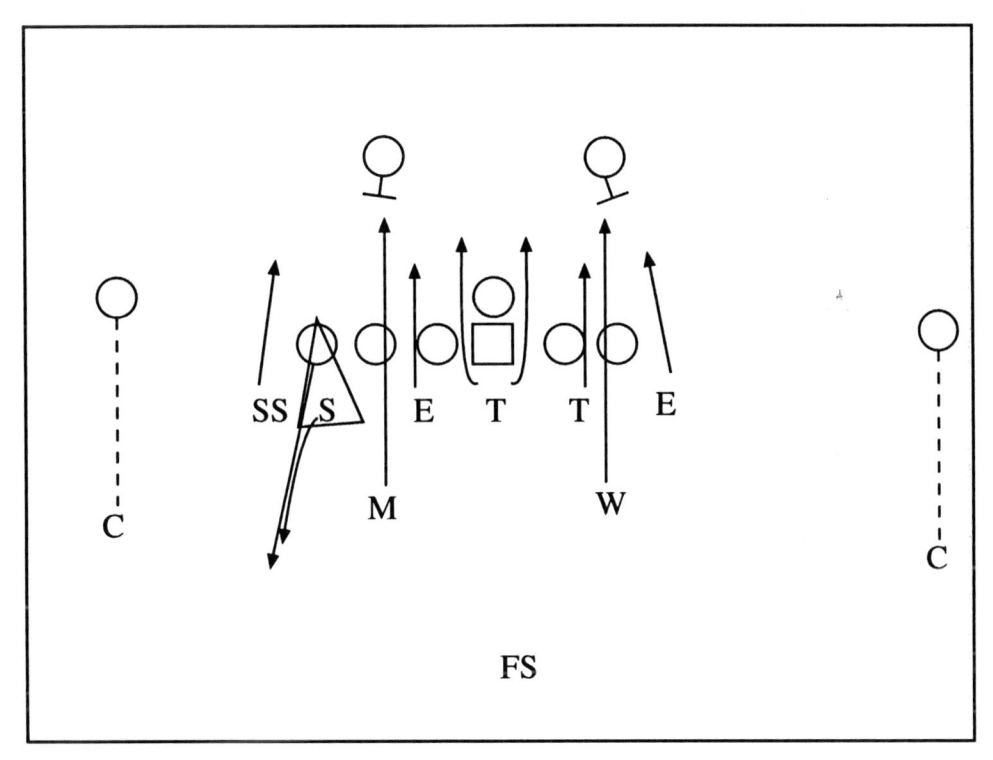

Diagram 9-39: Single-coverage rushers versus both backs blocking results in seven pass rushers against seven blockers.

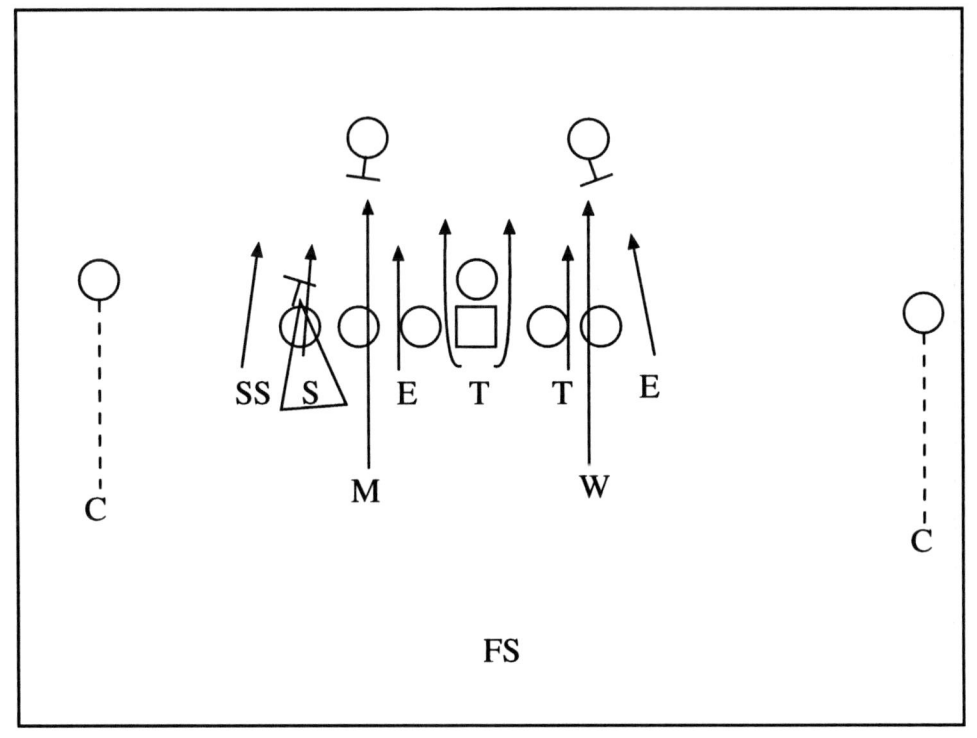

Diagram 9-40: Single-coverage rushers versus both backs and the tight end blocking results in eight pass rushers against eight blockers.

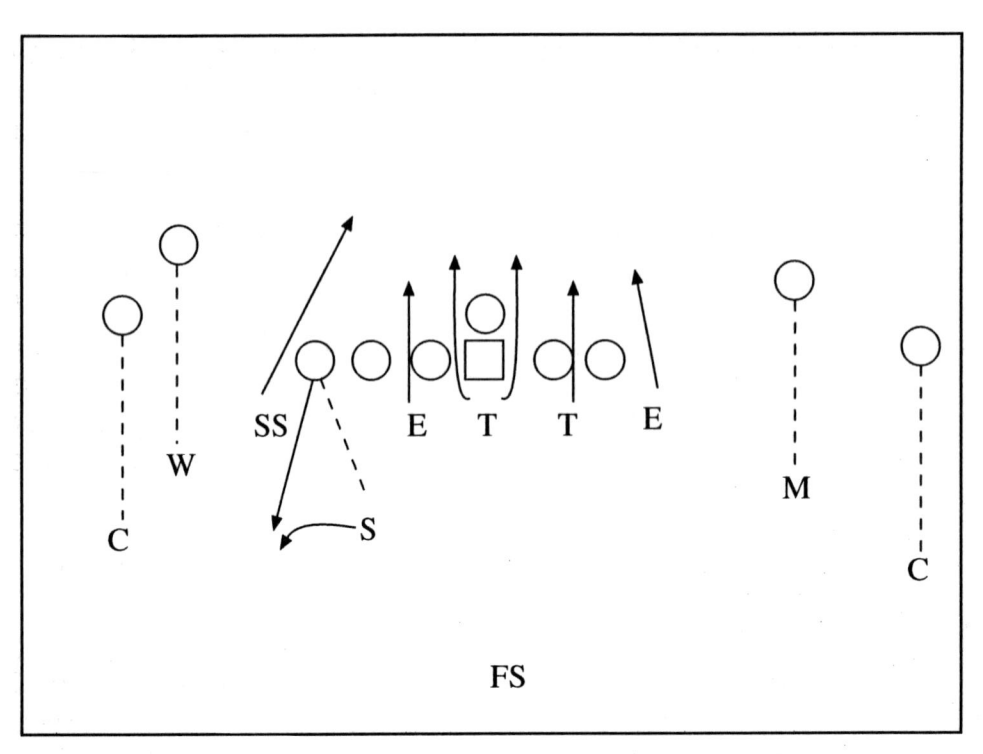

Diagram 9-41: Single-coverage rushers versus a no-back formation results in five pass rushers against five blockers.

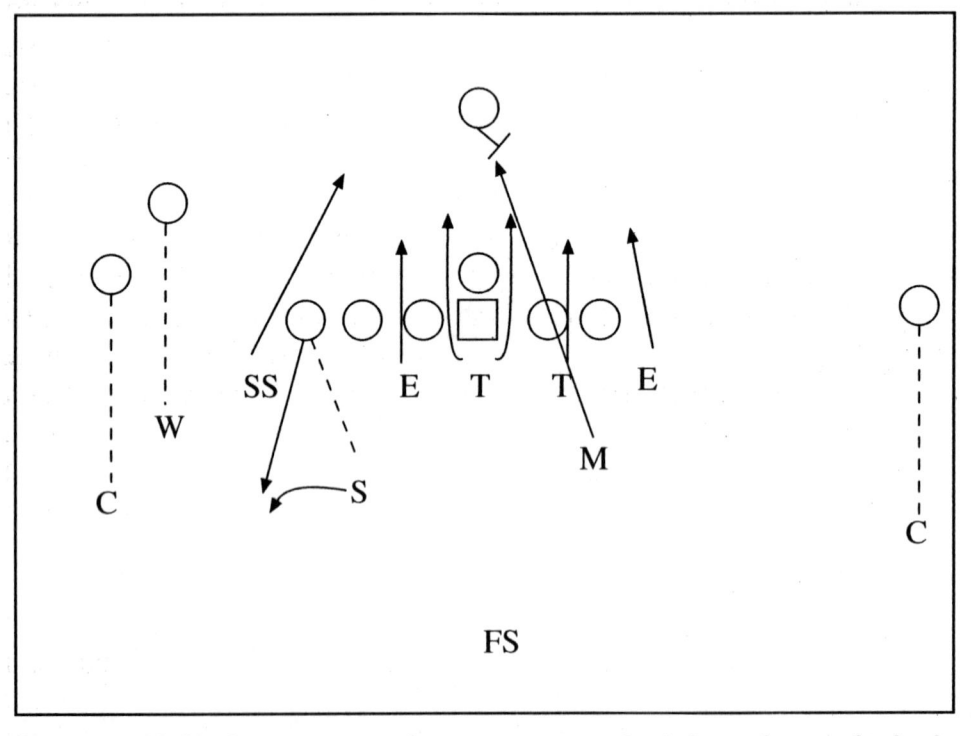

Diagram 9-42: Single-coverage rushers versus a one-back formation results in six pass rushers against six blockers.

previously mentioned, single (i.e., man-free) allows you to provide maximum rush on maximum protection. In fact, single coverage never gives you fewer rushers than the offensive unit has blockers. This is an important fact to remember when considering the tactical advantage of using the man-free coverage.

One principal advantage of playing man-free is the isolation of your pass rushers in a 1-on-1 match up. If you have a dominant pass rusher, the 1-on-1 match ups along the front line give you a significant defensive edge. These 5-on-5, 6-on-6, 7-on-7, or 8-on-8 match ups are created by a simple rule. The rule is: *Whenever the man you are assigned to cover blocks, you should rush and hug him*. Besides the normal 5-on-5 guaranteed by the 46 single call, you could have as many as eight pass rushers, depending on the offensive set and the action of the tight end and backs. Diagrams 9-39 through 9-42 illustrate this concept.

The individual techniques for the single-coverage defenders are as follows:

- Cornerbacks

    The cornerbacks should play a loose man-to-man coverage. The cornerback's alignment is from five to seven yards off the receiver. He shades the outside eye of the defender and places his outside foot forward in a heel-to-toe stagger. Upon the snap of the ball, he shuffles backward in a 3/4 stance turned toward the ball. He should read the quarterback as he feels the receiver. If the quarterback exhibits a low back shoulder in his drop, he is driving to a 5- or 7-step drop. The cornerback should expect an immediate or deep route. If the quarterback demonstrates a high back shoulder as he drops with more of an upright posture, the route will be a shorter 3-step drop pattern. The 7-yard cushion of the cornerback gives him plenty of time to be able to read the quarterback as he shuffles and feels the action of the receiver. If the receiver breaks across the field, the cornerback should stay on top as he mirrors the receiver. The cornerback should attempt to stay on top of the receiver. Any route that is cut short of the cornerback should be played in a conservative manner as the cornerback makes a sure tackle on the receiver. The cornerback should always keep in mind that he has free safety help to the deep inside. If the two cornerbacks are aligned in a corner-over alignment (e.g., versus a twins set), the cornerbacks may exchange their coverage responsibility, depending on the split of the receivers and the subsequent routes of the two receivers. If the split is relatively close and the routes cleanly cross, the cornerbacks may run an exchange (i.e., banjo). On an exchange, the outside cornerback takes the outside break and the inside cornerback takes the inside break. To effectively run an exchange, the cornerbacks must communicate before the snap and again during the play. So that one cornerback doesn't squeeze the route too far over, both cornerbacks should visualize the vertical midline between their alignment as the exchange point. Their primary coverage responsibilities are the X and Y receivers. In our formation recognition rules, the X and Y are designated as dual wideouts (i.e., wide receivers to both sides of the ball). On a two-tight end formation, the weakside tight end is the X receiver. If the X and Y are the sole wideouts and are on the same side of the formation, then the formation is a flop, (i.e., twins) and the cornerbacks align on both sides, as previously mentioned.

- *Mike*

Mike always aligns on the second level (i.e., behind the defensive linemen). His first responsibility is the strongside back of the two-back set. Versus a one-back set, he is responsible for the single back. His no-back coverage rule is 4-strong or 2-weak. This means that against a no-back set with a 3-and-2 balance (i.e., three receivers strong and two receivers weak), he is responsible for the second receiver on the weakside. Versus a quads receiver set, he is responsible for the fourth receiver.

- *Sam*

Sam is man-to-man on the tight end. We designate the primary tight end as the Y receiver. If no tight end is present in a pro type formation (i.e., a formation that is not flopped), then the third receiver to the three-receiver side is the Y receiver. If the one-back set is balanced with two wide receivers to each side, the Y receiver is the second receiver aligned to the strength call.

- *Strong safety*

The strong safety aligns on the tight end side and rushes. If there is no tight end, he simply aligns to the strength call.

- *Will*

Will is the adjuster. While every position must have certain conditions to its base alignment rule in order to cover possible formations from the single scheme, the Will is the primary adjuster. He must be adept at formation recognition. Generally, the Will linebacker aligns to cover the tailback in a two-back set. If the tailback is set wide in a traditional one-back alignment, the Will should move to cover him. The traditional one-back alignment for the tailback is usually designated as a type of receiver position. Common offensive terminology used for this position identifies this position as the R back position, the A back position, or B back position. For our use, we have designated the removed tailback position as the R back position. For those of us concerned with consistency, the R back is plainly identified as the tailback—in a receiver alignment. One reason the Will linebacker is described as an adjuster is because of the multiple positions of common R back alignments. In any alignment where three or more receivers are aligned to the tight end side (i.e., pro side), the R receiver is the second receiver on the strong side. If the formation is a flop (i.e., twins), and three receivers align on the same side, the R receiver is the third receiver. It is important to note that in a two-tight end deuce (one-back) formation, Will covers the weakside tight end—in accordance with his R back coverage against a balanced double slot. Note that the Will's rule is consistent in balanced sets, he covers the second weakside receiver. In the open double slot, the second weakside receiver is the R back; in the two-tight double flanker, the second weakside receiver is the weakside tight end.

- *Free safety*

    The free safety is a middle safety free to help out in a game-planned tactic. This tactic normally includes the middle of the field. However, the free safety can be used to accomplish a number of defensive aims. He can weave to help a cornerback who is isolated in a 1-on-1 coverage on a wide receiver, he can sit on any dig route, he can support the overloaded defenders of the multiple-receiver side, or he can be moved close to the line of scrimmage for run-game support. His alignment may range from 9- to 15-yards deep. He generally stays between the hash marks. His primary movement can be a flat-footed shuffle, a bounce, or a backpedal, depending on the objectives of the free safety.

Charts 9-1 through 9-8 identify the various alignments of the single scheme against twelve different formations. Certainly to cover all formations from any type of coverage involves some adjustments. The adjustments can be simplified in several ways including:

- *Not using the corner-over alignment rule.*

    When the cornerbacks don't flop with the twins formation, the front adjustments are less detailed when considering all possible formations. The trade-off is the resulting distortion of the front against a normal two-back flopped formation (i.e., twins). Remember that the static nature of the front against most *standard* formations is a precept of the 46 concept. The corner-over rule provides this stability of the front. Also by aligning

Chart 9-1:

Pro Formation	
Strong Corner ___	Z receiver
Weak Corner ___	X receiver
Strong Safety ___	Rush
Sam ___	Y receiver
Mike ___	Fullback
Will ___	Tailback

Chart 9-2:

Twins Formation	
Strong Corner ___	Z receiver
Weak Corner ___	X receiver
Strong Safety ___	Rush
Sam ___	Y receiver
Mike ___	Fullback
Will ___	Tailback

Chart 9-3:

One-Back Formation (White)	
Strong Corner ___	Z receiver
Weak Corner ___	X receiver
Strong Safety ___	Rush
Sam ___	Y receiver
Mike ___	Fullback
Will ___	R back (slot)

Chart 9-4:

Tight End Trips Formation	
Strong Corner ___	Z receiver
Weak Corner ___	X receiver
Strong Safety ___	Rush
Sam ___	Y receiver
Mike ___	Fullback
Will ___	R back (2nd receiver)

Chart 9-5:

Open-End Trips Formation	
Strong Corner ___	Z receiver
Weak Corner ___	X receiver
Strong Safety ___	Rush
Sam ___	Y receiver
Mike ___	Fullback
Will ___	R back (3rd receiver)

Chart 9-6:

Open Double-Slot Formation	
Strong Corner ___	Z receiver
Weak Corner ___	X receiver
Strong Safety ___	Rush
Sam ___	Y receiver
Mike ___	Fullback
Will ___	R back (2nd receiver)

Chart 9-7:

Open Quads Formation	
Strong Corner ___	Z receiver
Weak Corner ___	X receiver
Strong Safety ___	Rush
Sam ___	Y receiver
Mike ___	Fullback
Will ___	R back (3rd receiver)

Chart 9-8:

Tight End Quads Formation	
Strong Corner ___	Z receiver
Weak Corner ___	X receiver
Strong Safety ___	Rush
Sam ___	Y receiver
Mike ___	Fullback
Will ___	R back (2nd receiver)

the corners to the same side (flopping) against the twins formation, the cornerbacks continue to do what they do best, cover wide receivers. Remember that against any three-deep or man-free structure, the desire of the opponent is to isolate a talented receiver in the slot against the mismatched linebacker who is squirmed out to cover him. By flopping the corners, the twins formation is now facing a mismatch on both sides. The two best cover personnel are aligned to the side of the two wide receivers, while the strongest run defenders are aligned to the tight end side.

- *Assigning the free safety to a coverage rule.*

For example, putting the fourth receiver strong and second receiver weakside on the no-back would eliminate the exceptions for the Mike linebacker. However, when considering the removal of the free safety from his free middle-of-field technique, you should also understand that you may be playing right into your opponent's hands. Once an offense finds that it can remove your free safety from the middle, it will exploit this adjustment and consequently work to exploit your corrupted man-free concept. Remember, that every coverage defender in the single coverage is coached to expect help from the free safety. If the free safety is consequently unavailable, each defender must also be aware of his unavailability. In the heat of battle, this comprehensive understanding of the free safety's removal is highly unlikely. The ignorance and unmet expectation of just one defender would leave him isolated and extremely vulnerable.

- *Using automatics.*

Any good defensive scheme has automatics versus unusual formations such as the quads formations, double flanker formation, and double slot formation. Through the inclusion of automatics versus such alignments as no-back formations, etc., the conditions of adjustments can be limited to a degree where in fact no adjustments are needed, other than by the adjuster. However, even without automatics, the single scheme adjustments are not excessively complex. Note that Charts 9-1 through 9-5 show no adjustments for any position other than Will, the adjuster. Chart 9-6 illustrates only a nominal adjustment for the Sam linebacker along with the Will. In examining the rest of the alignment charts for the single coverage, you will see a consistency of the remaining adjustments which are easily communicated.

- *Incorporating the strong safety in the coverage scheme.*

    By incorporating the strong safety in the coverage scheme instead of allowing him to rush, the adjustments can be simplified. However, the incorporation of the strong safety would make the defense significantly weaker versus various formations. For example, the tight end trips formation is an excellent running formation. If you remove the strong safety from his pressure role on the edge, the offense will have three blockers on three perimeter defenders. While this ratio is theoretically sufficient from a defensive standpoint of not trading one defender for one blocker, it puts tremendous pressure on the strongside 3 technique to defeat the reach block and work to pursue to the perimeter. Even with effective 3 technique play, the running back would have a very good chance of turning the edge against a "forceless" defense to the tight end side.

Given the need for multiple—yet, simple—adjustments, the man-free scheme is not a soft pass-specific scheme. The man-free scheme can provide you with superior run support, particularly against tight formations exhibited by the wing-T attack, power I, and full-house T offense. In the case of facing tight formations, the man-free coverage scheme gives you far better run support than the chalkboard three-deep zone. The reason for this superior run support from the single scheme is the quicker run key read. The quicker run key results from the standard man coverage technique of the defender focusing on his receiver. If the receiver blocks, the defender gets an immediate run read and is subsequently able to attack the line of scrimmage to provide run support. In a zone coverage scheme, the defender is commonly taught to look in the backfield for the quarterback's action. Against a tight formation, particularly a deceptive wing-T attack, the zone coverage defender's run support is usually slower than the man coverage defender. Not only does the man-free scheme provide better run support against a tight formation, it actually is a more effective pass defense as well. Whenever a defender looks solely at the receiver, instead of the backfield, he avoids the possibility of being mesmerized by the backfield action as a receiver runs free behind him.

Two adjustments are available to you against the weakside of the two-tight end formation. The first adjustment is shown in Diagram 9-43. Diagram 9-43 illustrates the weakside cornerback covering the weakside tight end from an outside alignment. The common alignment varies from five yards off the line of scrimmage and three yards outside the tight end to seven yards off the line of scrimmage and two yards outside the tight end. The position of the cornerback's alignment is normally determined by the preferences and philosophy of the defensive coordinator. As shown in Diagram 9-43, the defensive end will move to a 7 technique (i.e., inside eye on the tight end). In the case of the cornerback's outside alignment on the weakside end, the cornerback becomes the primary force (i.e., run support) to that side.

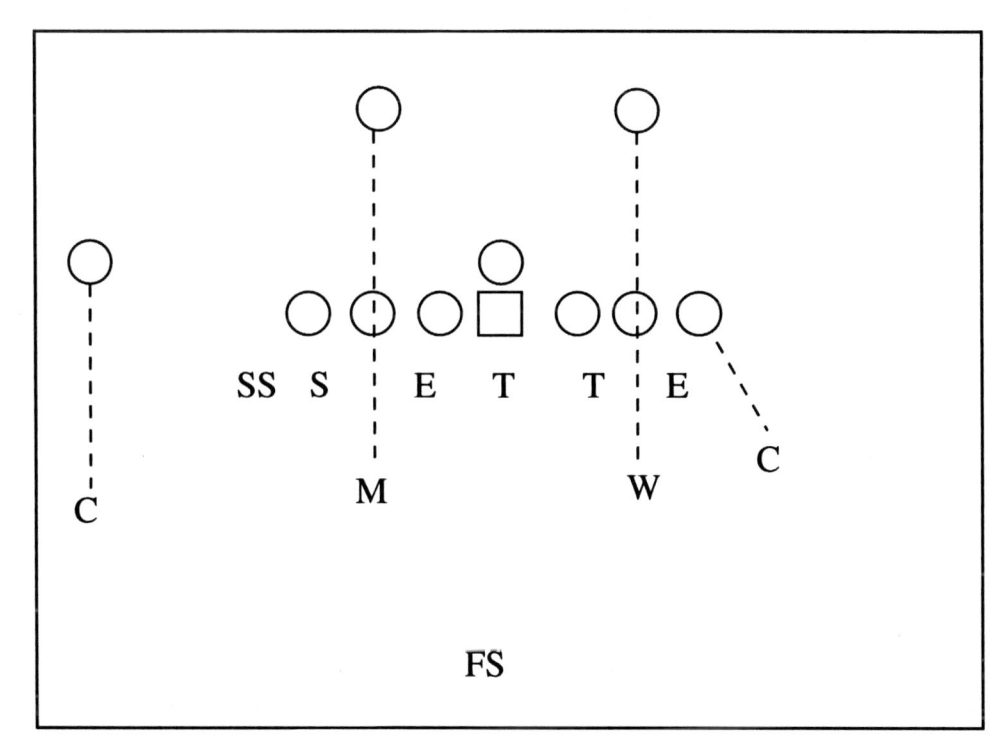

Diagram 9-43: Single coverage versus a two-tight end formation with two backs.

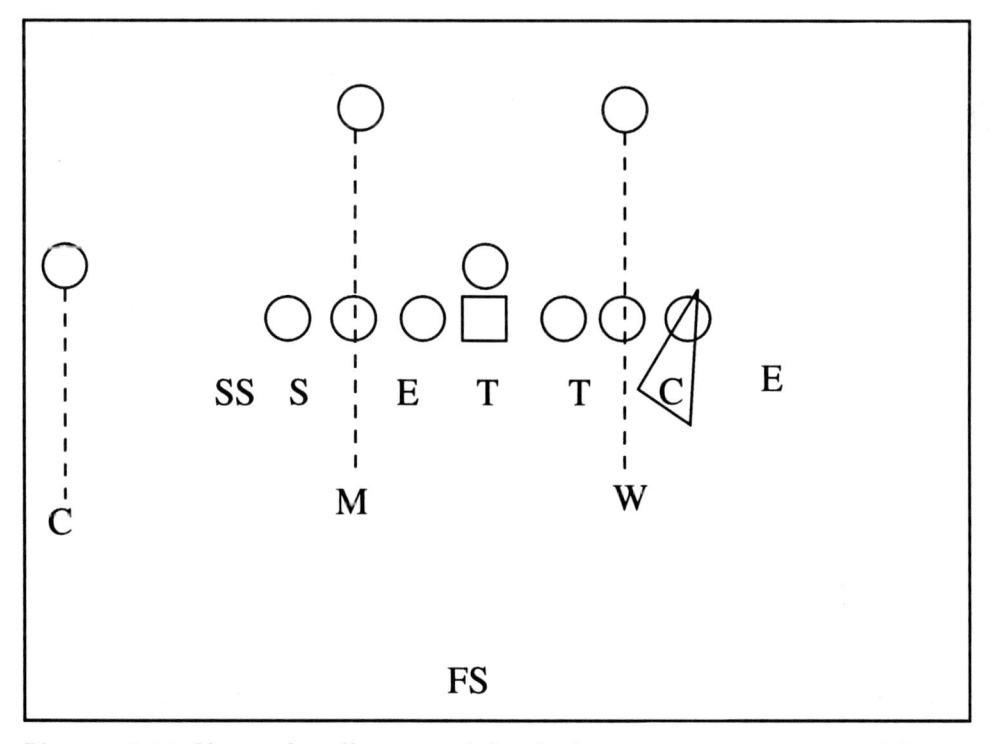

Diagram 9-44: Alternative alignment of the single coverage versus a two-tight end formation with two backs.

129

Diagram 9-44 shows an alternative way to force the weakside of the two-tight end formation. The alternative alignment puts the cornerback on or near the line of scrimmage in a 7 technique alignment. The defensive end, who normally is the primary weakside force, aligns in a loose 9 technique on the weakside end and exercises his normal force technique. This particular adjustment gives you a double 46 perimeter against the two-tight end set. While the weakside cornerback isn't particularly physical or adept at whipping a tight end's block, he can generally hold his own and neutralize any significant size advantage of the weakside tight end on most scrimmage downs. Certainly, having both options available to you is a notable advantage whenever you are facing a down-to-down diet of a two-tight end formation. The coverage assignment for the cornerback doesn't change whenever he aligns in the 7 technique; he simply covers the tight end from a clutch position on the line of scrimmage. His coverage technique is nearly identical to the Sam linebacker on the strongside tight end in that he uses both hands to clutch the tight end and cover him.

For numerous reasons, the single scheme is the flagship coverage of the 46 package. Its simplicity against the standard formations, its availability to provide eight rushers against maximum protection, its guaranteed 1-on-1 match ups of the defensive linemen on the pass blockers, and its excellent run-forcing capacity due to the quicker reads of the man coverage defenders demonstrate why the single-coverage scheme is the preferred coverage of 46 coaches at all levels.

Spy coverage:

The spy coverage is a good change-up from the single coverage. Used against a two-back formation, the spy coverage looks exactly like the single coverage because the alignment is identical. This identical alignment versus the two-back set sets the stage for the biggest advantage of using the spy coverage. While the man-free coverage provides you with the maximum pressure you can get with a free middle safety, the spy coverage gives you the maximum coverage you can get with a free middle safety. Because the coverage is designed for a two-back set, it is extremely simple, yet deceptive.

In the spy coverage, the strong safety and weakside defensive end act in conjunction to provide the spy technique coverage on the two backs. Diagram 9-45 shows the coverage technique of the strong safety and weakside defensive end.

The dynamics of the spy coverage include the weakside defensive end's and strong safety's responsibility to sell the single-coverage look by driving two or three steps upfield and reading the action of the nearback. If the respective nearback swings out on a flare (i.e., swing) route, the strong safety or defensive end covers him. If both backs run a swing route, each defender will cover the back out to his side. If the nearback blocks, the strong safety or defensive end continues to rush the quarterback through the nearback's block.

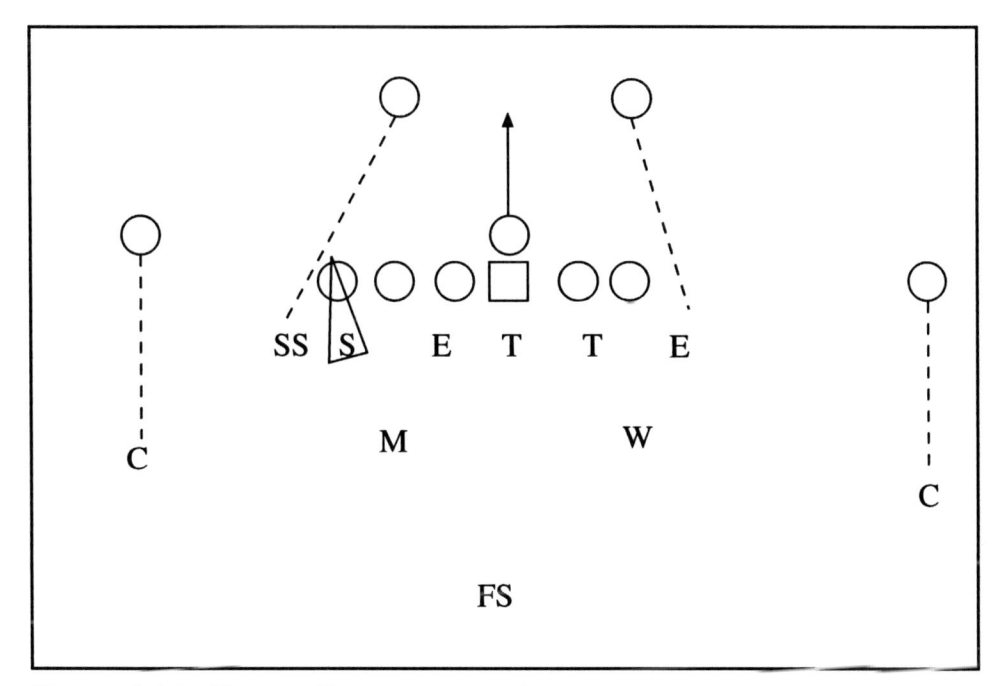

Diagram 9-44a: The spy alignment versus the pro set.

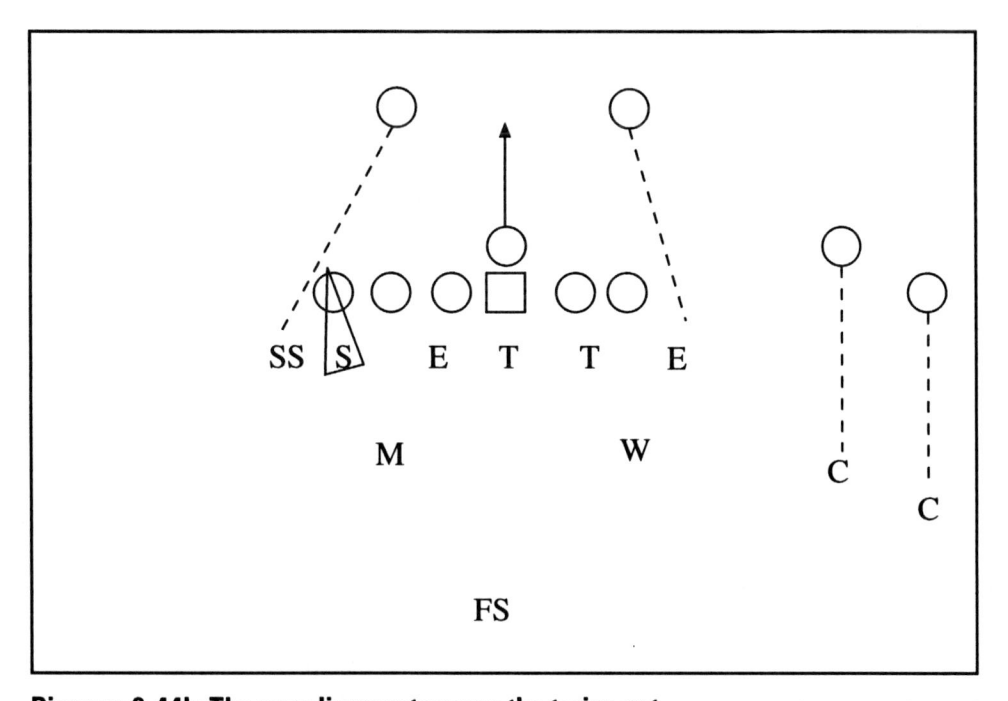

Diagram 9-44b: The spy alignment versus the twins set.

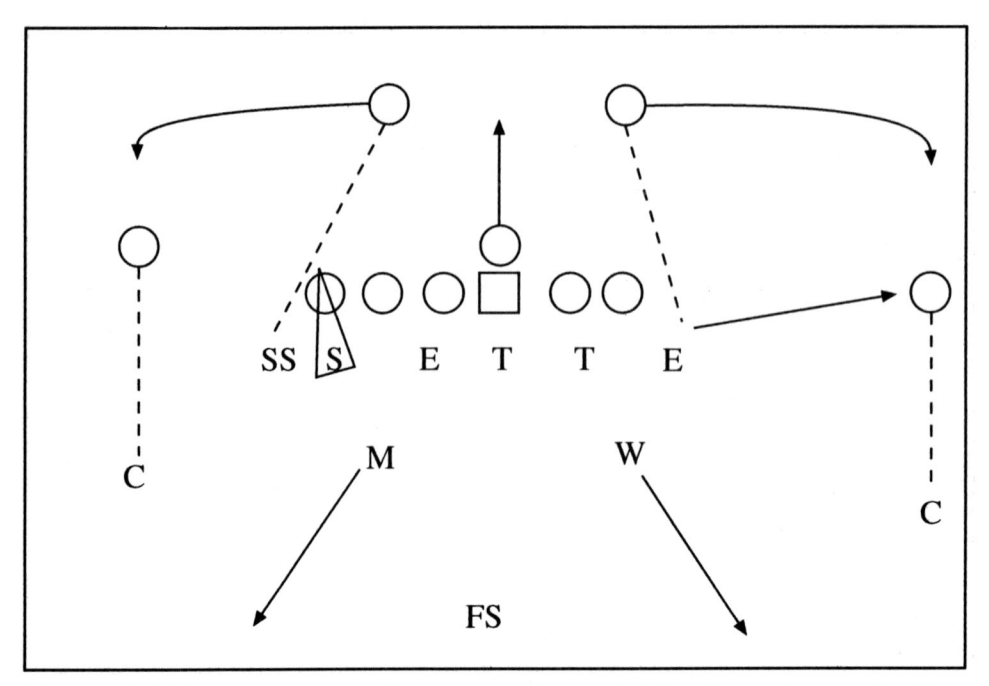

Diagram 9-45: In spy coverage, the strong safety and defensive end cover the flare routes of the running backs.

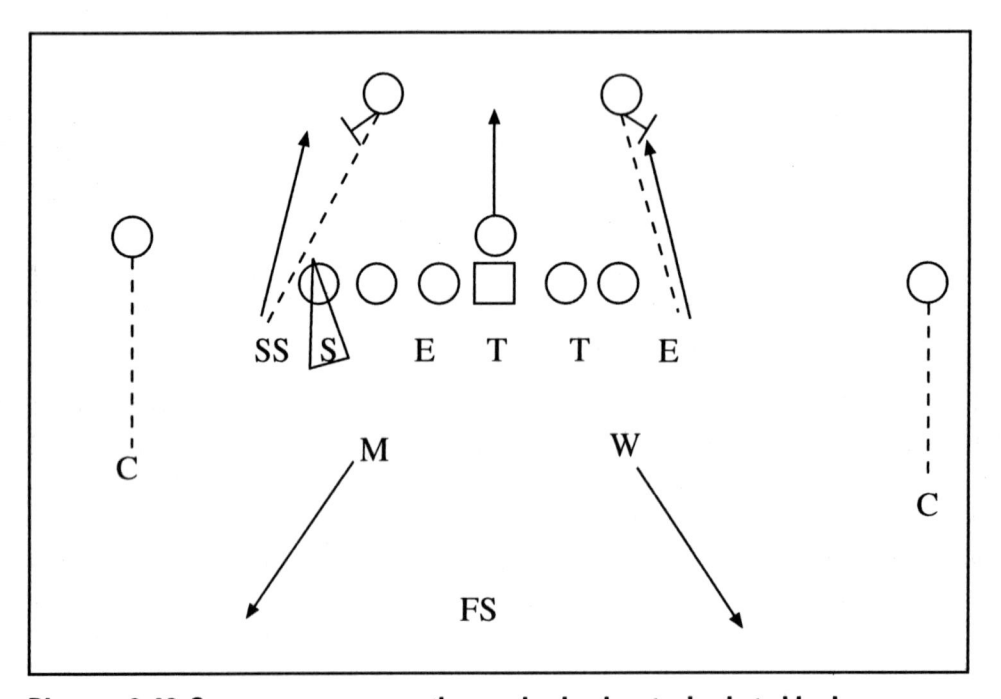

Diagram 9-46: Spy coverage versus the running backs staying in to block.

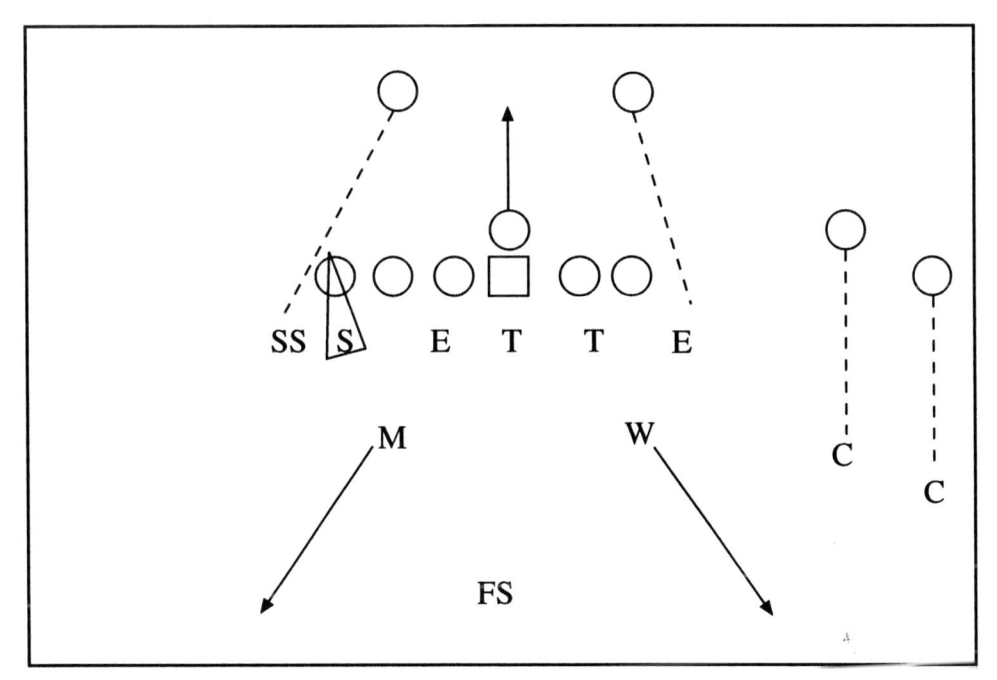

Diagram 9-47: The spy alignment versus the twins set.

The assignment of the nearbacks to the strong safety and defensive end allow the linebackers, Mike and Will, to drop to the numbers. Meanwhile, Sam is locked in on the Y receiver, just as he is in the single coverage.

With the free safety in the hole, the Mike and Will provide zone coverage of the numbers area to each side while the two cornerbacks are locked in man-to-man coverage on the wide receivers, X and Z. One result of the spy scheme is that you get 8 pass defenders versus 5 pass receivers. Against a maximum protection scheme, you get 5 pass defenders versus 2 pass receivers. In Diagrams 9-48 and 9-49, you can see how the spy coverage would easily confuse a quarterback— particularly if he misreads the spy coverage as the single coverage.

Occasionally, you will face a team possessing an especially talented halfback. Against such a halfback it would be prudent to assign the Will linebacker—instead of the weakside defensive end—to the halfback. In this situation, the weakside cornerback would be isolated in his man-to-man coverage of the X if the halfback released into the pattern. The weakside defensive end would then rush the passer without regard to the halfback's action. If the halfback doesn't release into a pattern, the Will linebacker drops to the numbers, providing underneath help to the weakside cornerback.

The numbers drop of the Mike and Will put them underneath any type of deep comeback route by the wide receiver. Mike Singletary was particularly effective in executing this technique. It can be a confusing read for the quarterback.

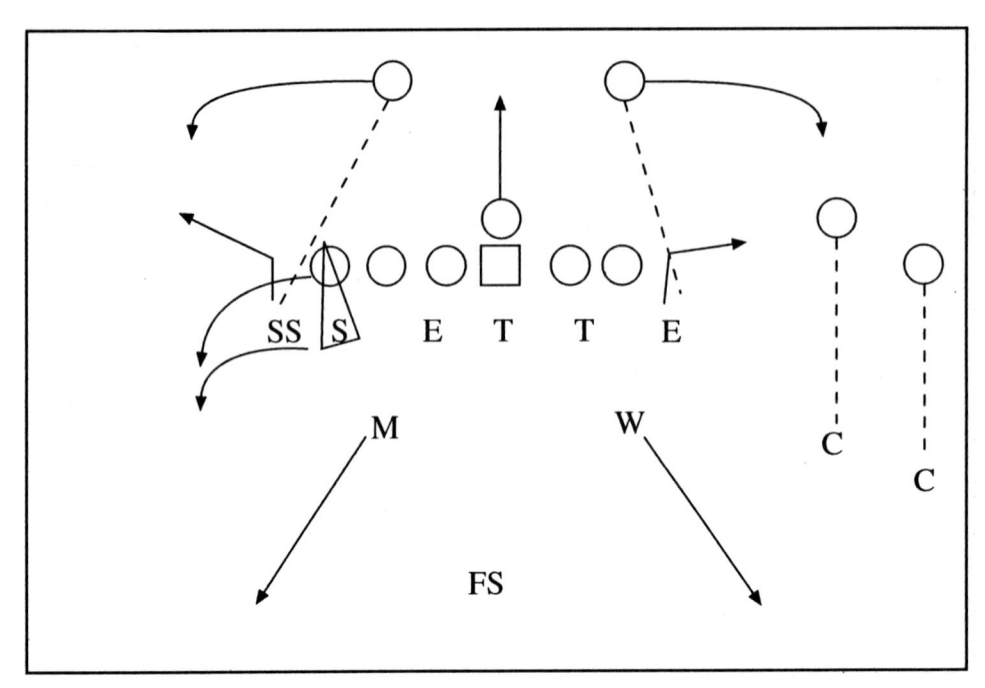

Diagram 9-48: Spy coverage results in eight droppers versus this twins set pattern.

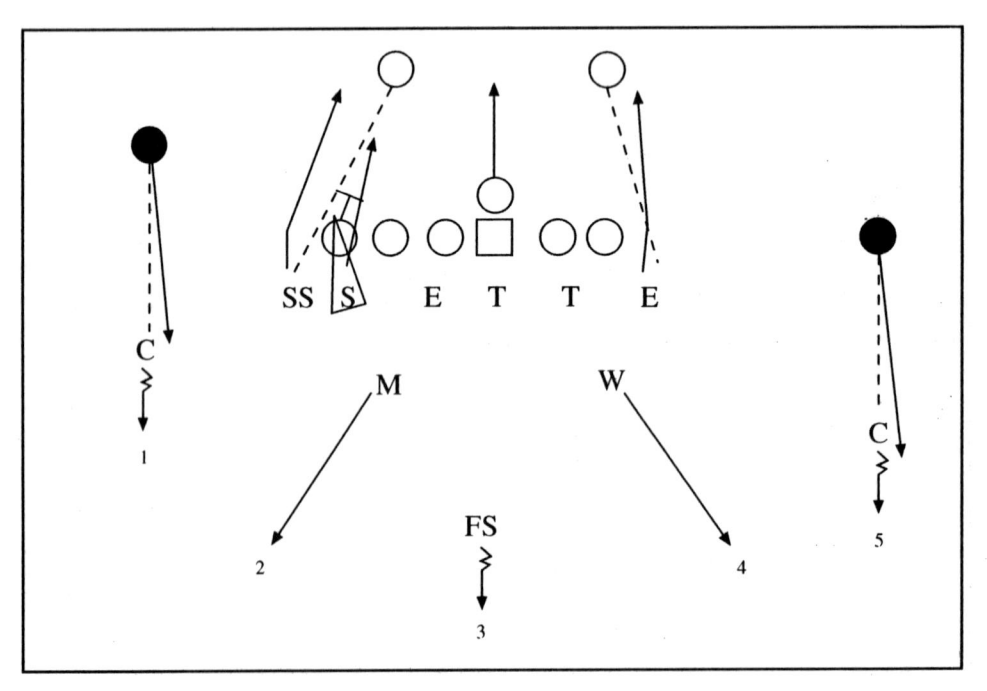

Diagram 9-49: Spy coverage results in five droppers versus this pro set maximum protection scheme.

134

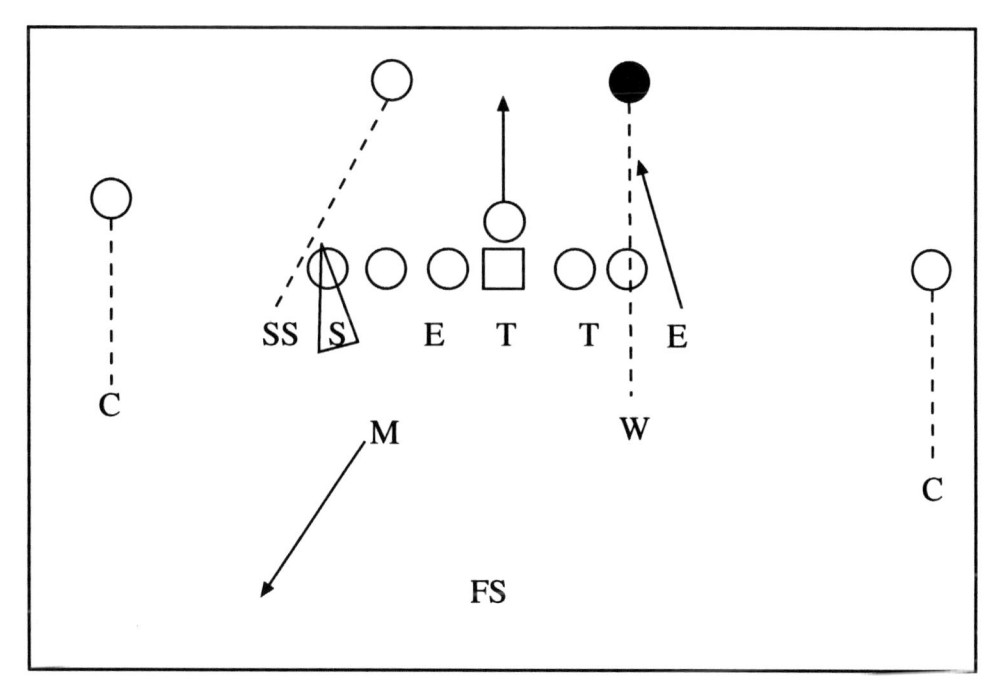

Diagram 9-50: Versus an extraordinarily talented halfback, Will can replace the weakside end in the man-to-man coverage.

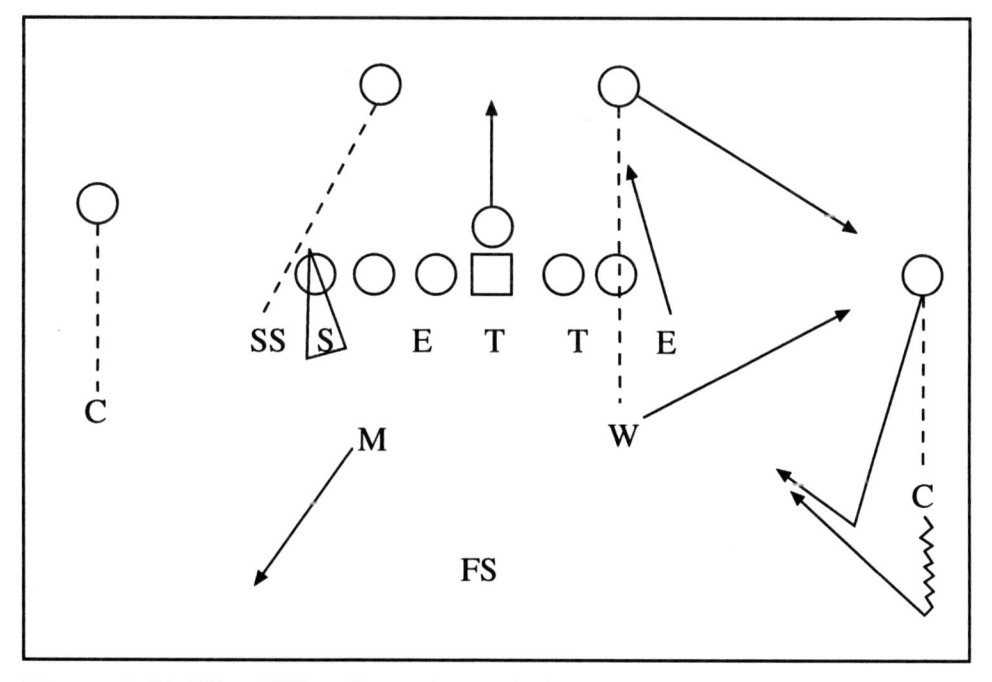

Diagram 9-51: When Will replaces the weakside end in the man-to-man coverage, the weakside cornerback is isolated on the X receiver.

135

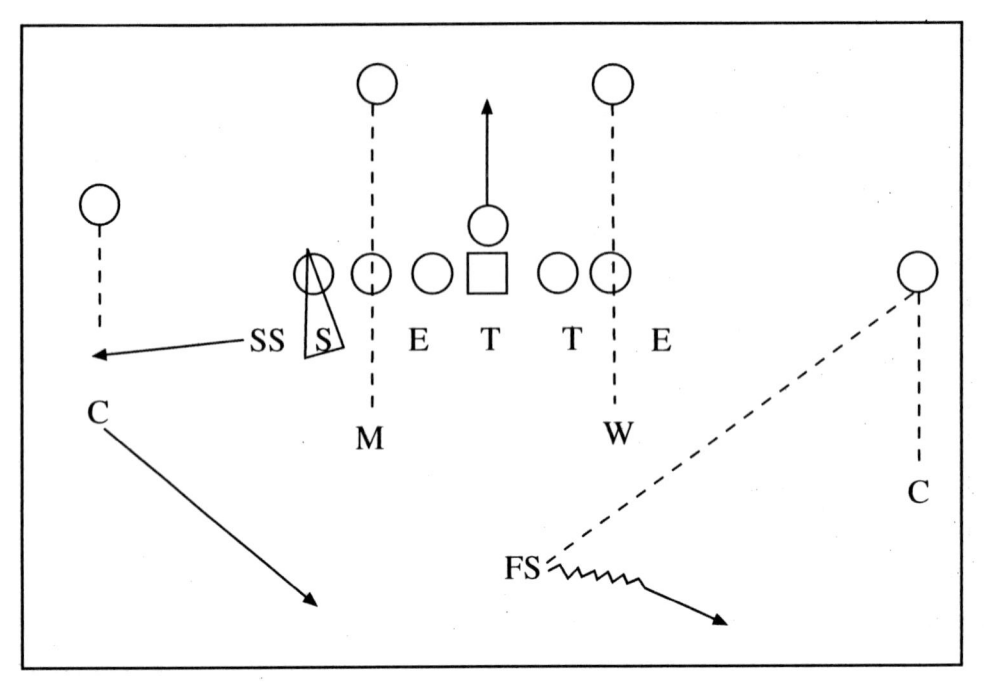

Diagram 9-52: The weakside rotation coverage.

Weakside rotation:

The ability to play the weakside rotation coverage is what separates the true 46 defensive scheme from imitations. The weakside rotation coverage—cover 7 in our terminology—provides for double coverage of the X receiver (i.e., split end) by the cornerback and free safety.

Cover 7 has multiple schemes available for the weakside double coverage of the X receiver. The first technique is the fist technique. Shown in diagram 9-53, the weakside cornerback and the free safety techniques present the X receiver with inside-out press coverage and over-the-top coverage. On the fist call, the weakside corner assumes a bump-and-run alignment and uses both hands to shuck the receiver and prevent a free release. Meanwhile, the free safety cheats to the weak side and covers the X receiver over the top.

The second weakside rotation technique is the thumbs technique. In the thumbs technique, the free safety will move to within 7- to 9-yards of the receiver and align 3 to 4 yards inside the normal split of the X receiver. The cornerback will align at his normal depth and shuffle back on the snap to play over the top of the X receiver. The thumbs technique alignment is shown in Diagram 9-54.

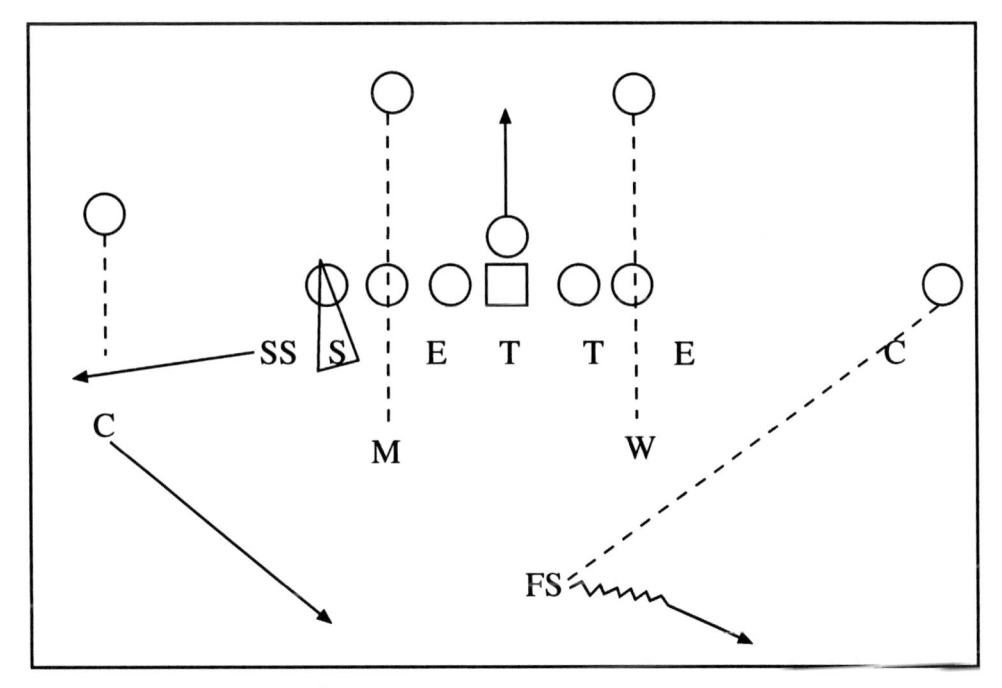

Diagram 9-53: The fist call.

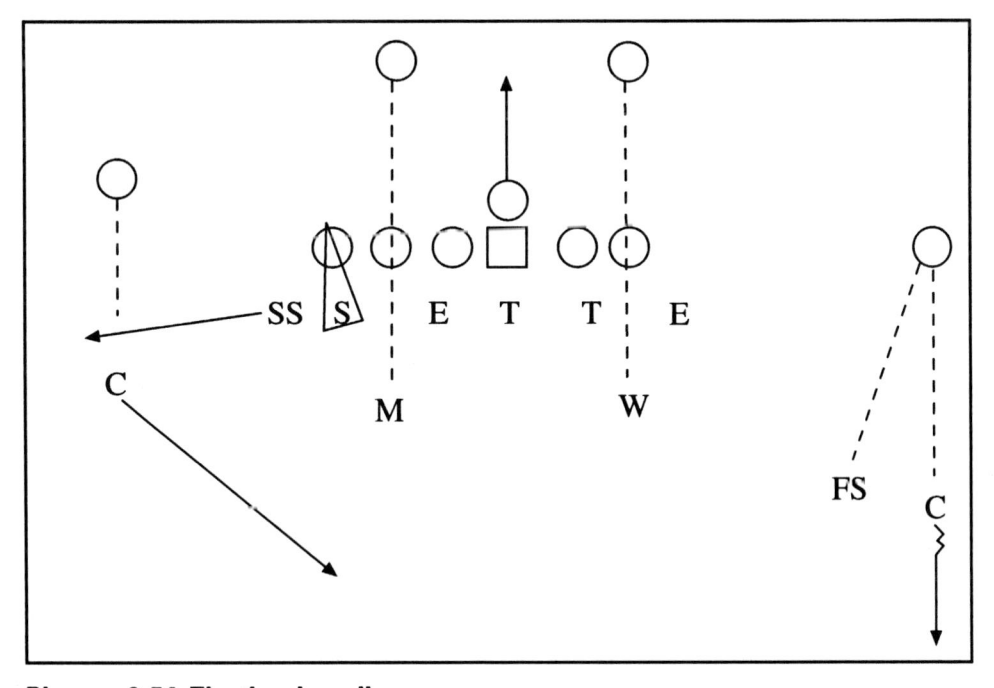

Diagram 9-54: The thumbs call.

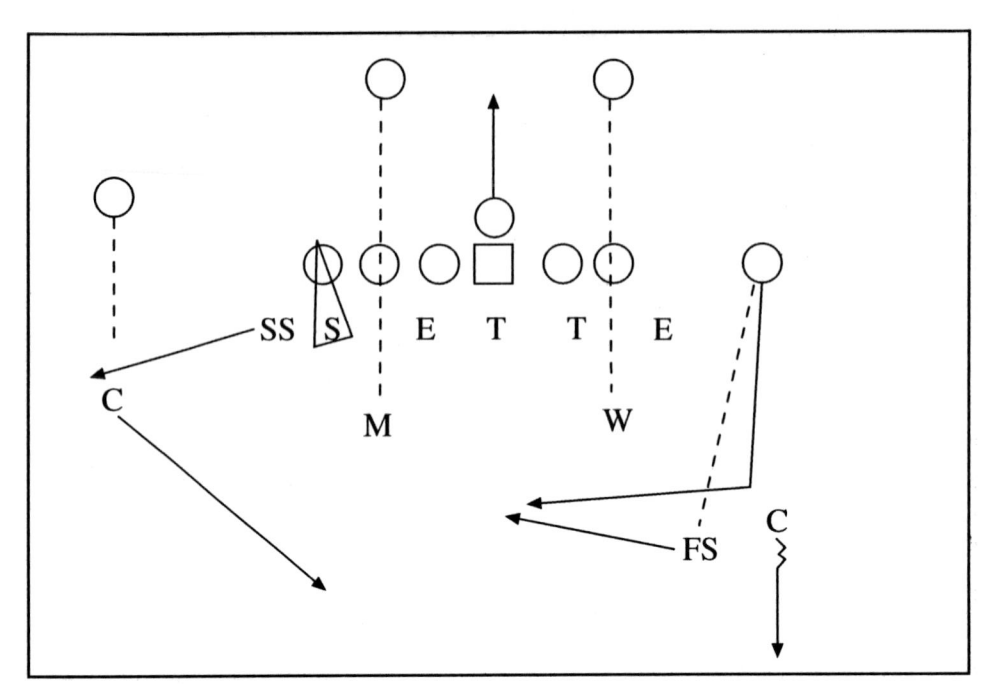

Diagram 9-55: The slice call versus an over route by the X receiver.

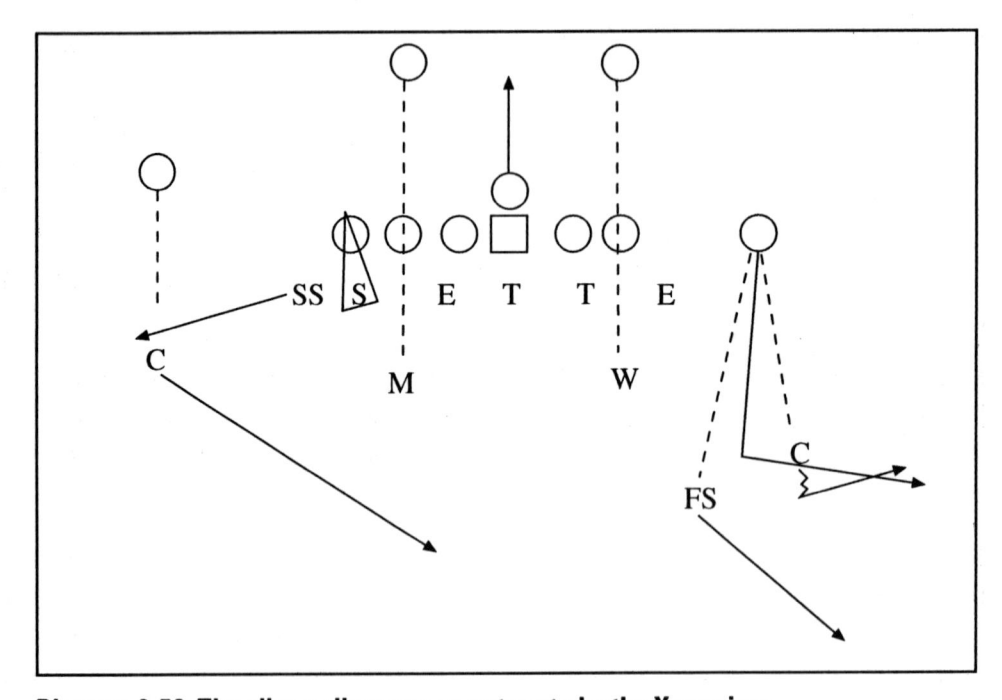

Diagram 9-56: The slice call versus an out route by the X receiver.

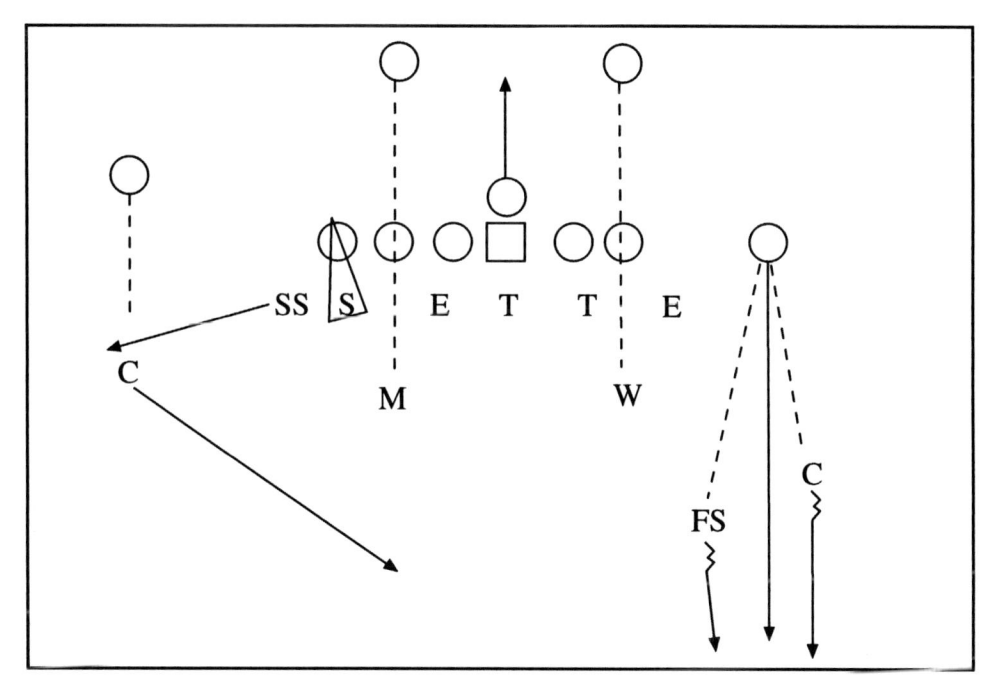

Diagram 9-57: The slice call versus a vertical route by the X receiver.

The third weakside rotation technique is the slice technique. The slice technique—also known as the bracket technique—is used against an undersplit (i.e., unusually tight split) receiver. If the receiver runs an over (i.e., crossing) route, the free safety will drive for the receiver to aggressively challenge the pass. Versus the over route, the cornerback will sink off the over route and look across the field for a deep route from another receiver. Another common combination route with the over route is the wheel route from the backfield. Diagram 9-55 shows the slice technique versus an over route.

If the receiver runs an out route, the cornerback will drive for the out route and challenge the pass. When the receiver runs an out route, the free safety will sink to cover the out-and-up route. Diagram 9-56 shows the slice call versus the out route of the X receiver.

If the receiver runs a vertical route, the slice call will give you a defender on each side of the vertical. If the vertical is broken off into a dig, deep curl, or a skinny post, the free safety will cover the route from inside-out. If the vertical is broken off to an outside comeback route, the cornerback will drive on the route while the free safety plays over the top.

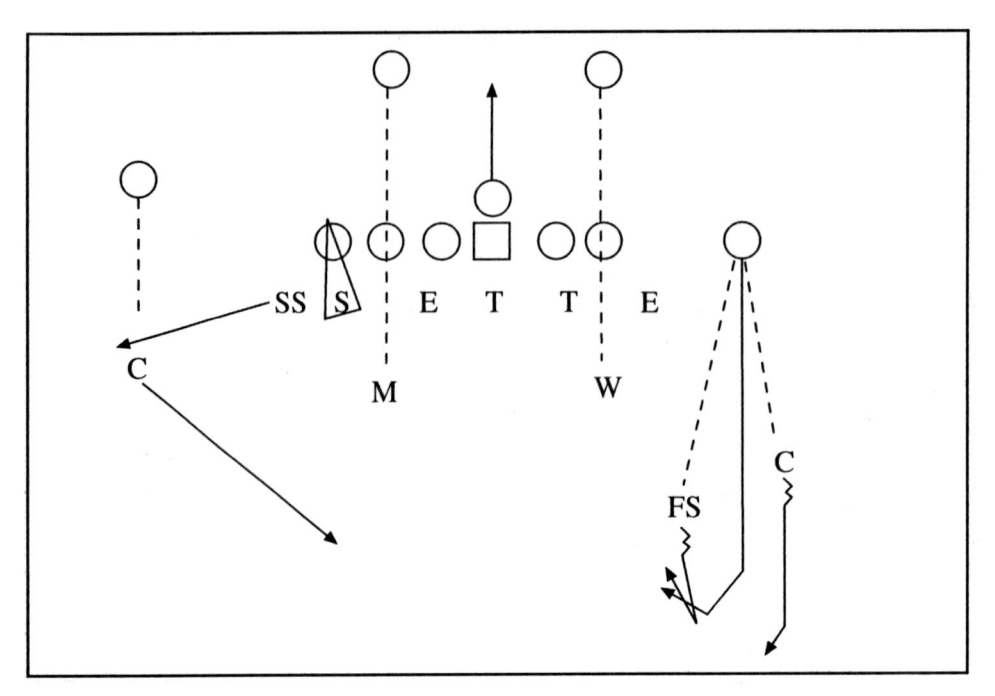

Diagram 9-58: The slice call versus a deep curl route by the X receiver.

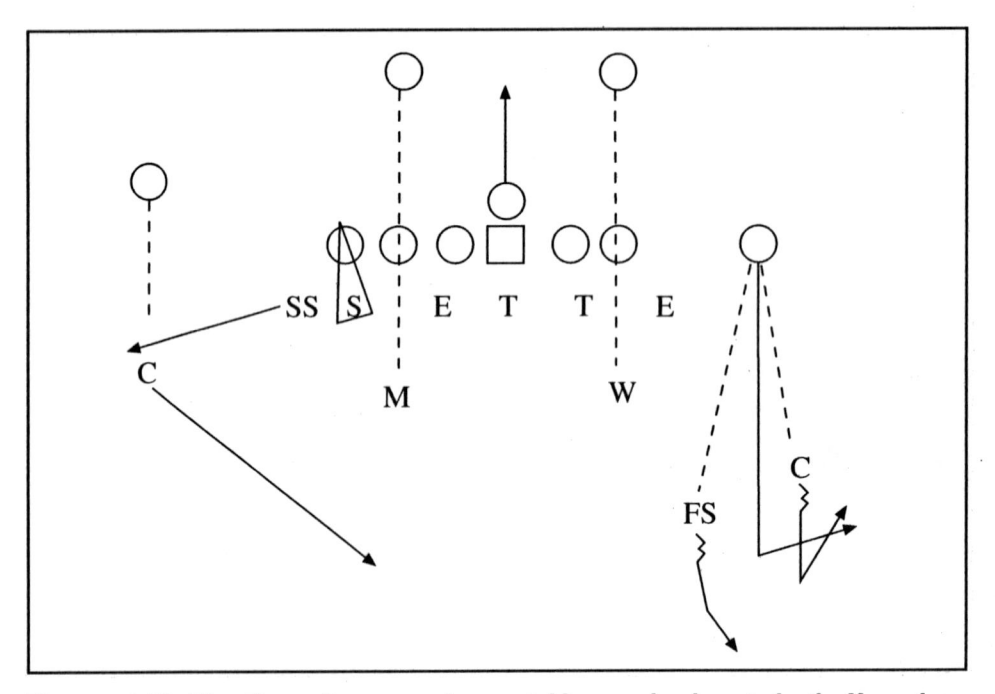

Diagram 9-59: The slice call versus a deep outside comeback route by the X receiver.

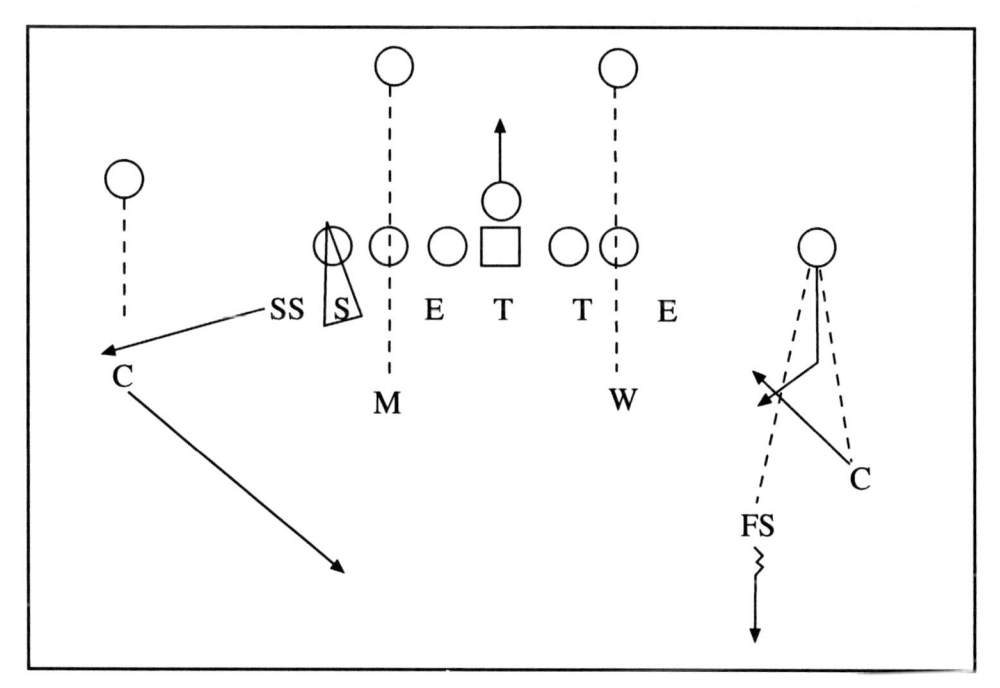

Diagram 9-60: The trap call versus a quick slant route.

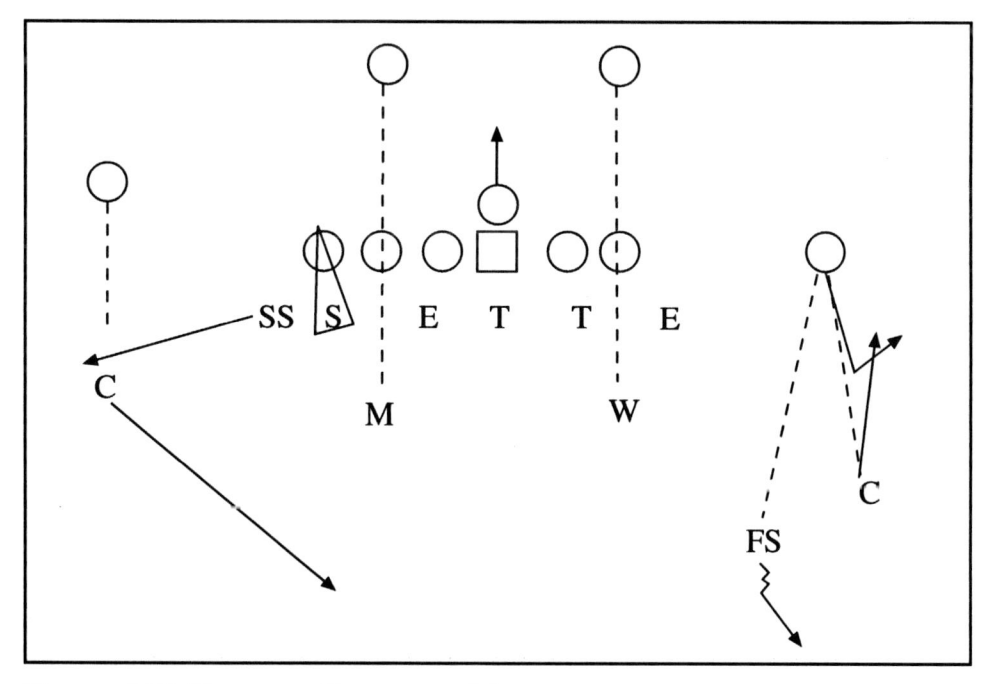

Diagram 9-61: The trap call versus a quick out route.

141

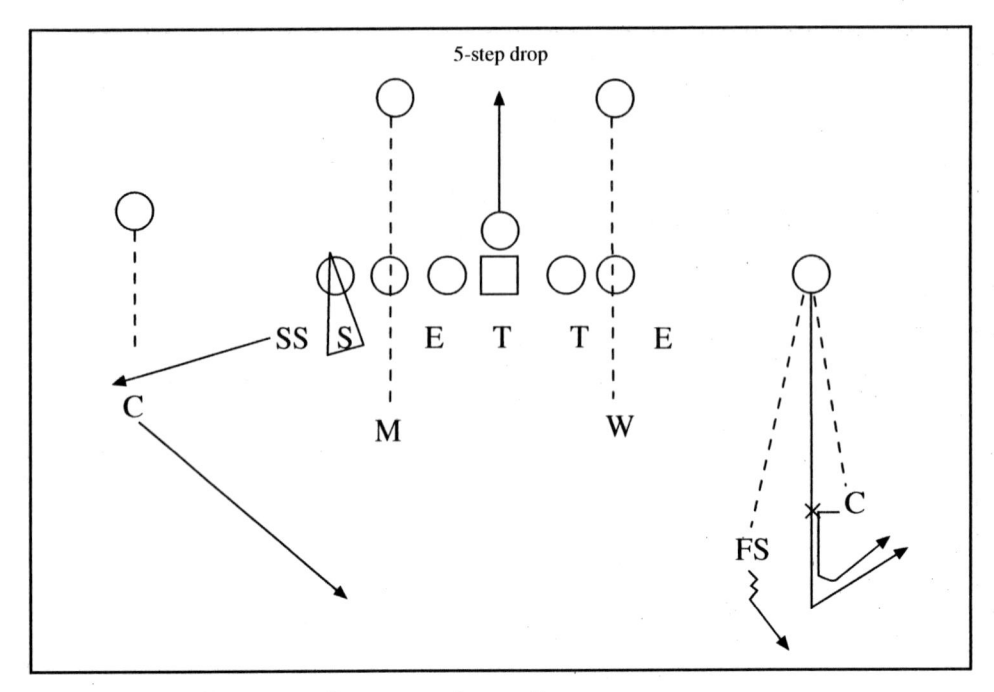

Diagram 9-62: The trap call versus a deeper 5-step route.

The fourth strategy of the cover 7 call is the trap technique. Used as a primary defensive weapon against the short passing game, the trap technique provides a challenging squat type of coverage against a quick slant or quick out route. On a trap technique, the cornerback will sit at his normal alignment and read the 3-step drop. If the quarterback does execute a quick pass drop as expected, the cornerback will drive for the interception, regardless of whether the route is an inside break or an outside break.

If the quarterback continues on a deeper 5- or 7-step drop, the cornerback will settle and jam the receiver as he continues upfield and breaks the cushion. From that point, the cornerback will cover the receiver from an inside-out trail position. Meanwhile, the free safety provides the over-the-top coverage.

In the strong side make up of the coverage, the basic coverage is the swipe technique. The swipe technique requires the outside underneath dropper—the strong safety—to fly out in a man coverage technique directly underneath the number one receiver. Since the tandem efforts of the weakside cornerback and free safety give you at least one deep defender in the weakside 1/2 zone, the cover 7 swipe call is basically a 2-man, 5-under type of coverage.

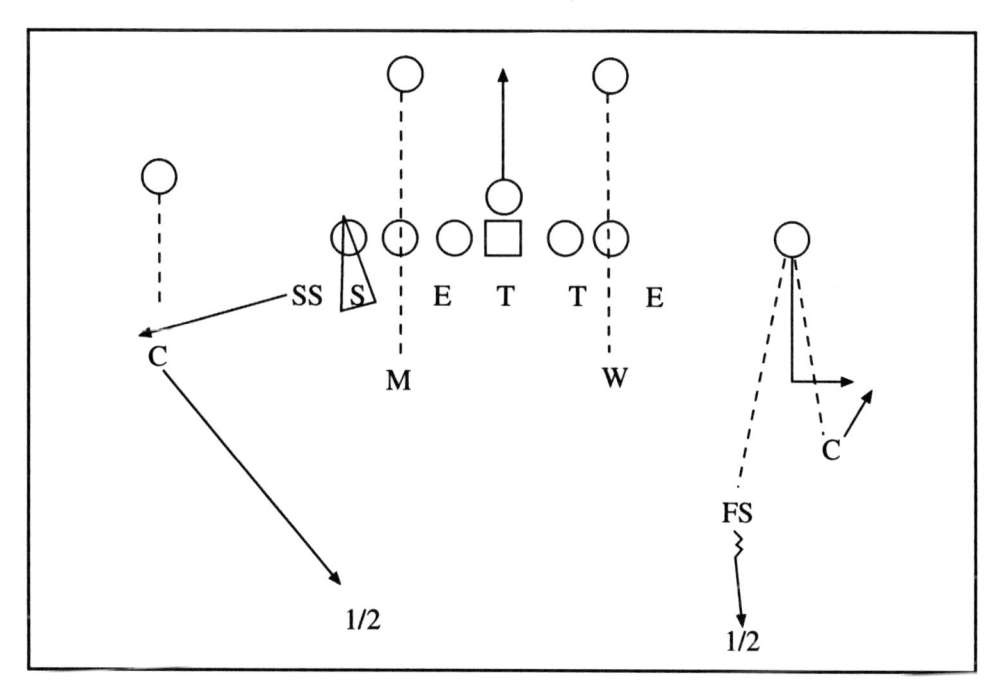

Diagram 9-63: Cover 7 swipe technique gives you a 2-deep and 5-underneath coverage.

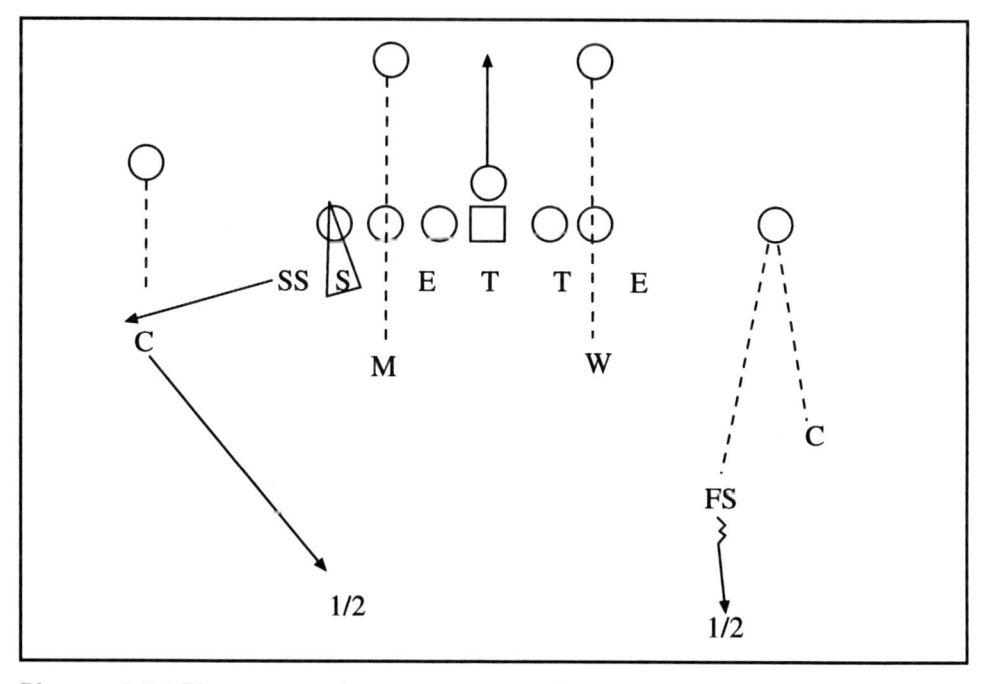

Diagram 9-64: The strong safety executes a swipe technique and sprints underneath the number one receiver.

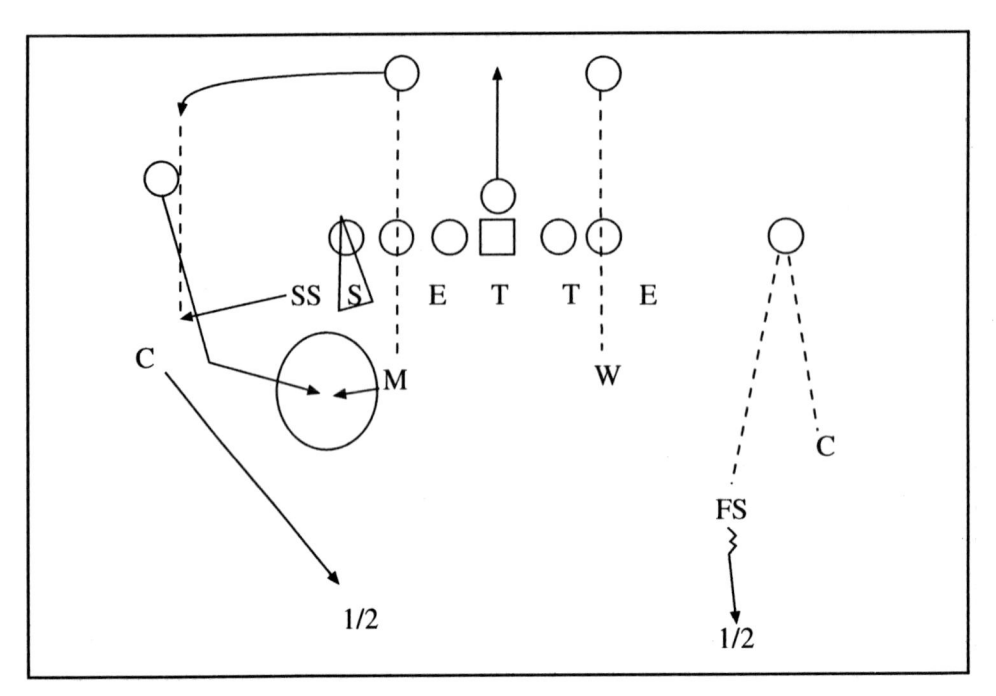

Diagram 9-65: The strong safety executes a push call and sprints underneath the number two receiver.

If the number two strongside receiver is a threat to outflank the Mike linebacker, the Mike linebacker makes a push call to the strong safety. The call can be communicated before the ball is snapped or just as the play develops. On the push call, the strong safety pushes outside to pick up the number two receiver just as the number one receiver runs an over route. With practice, the strong safety and Mike linebacker can easily learn to convert the swipe technique to a push technique versus the combination of a quick over route by the number one receiver and a quick flat route by the number two receiver. The push call results in an exchange between the strong safety and the Mike linebacker.

In the Diagrams 9-66a—9-66c, cover 7 is shown against several basic formations. Keep in mind that in cover 7, the Sam linebacker is locked in man-to-man coverage on the tight end. Cover 7 is an excellent coverage against most types of three-receiver and four-receiver sets. Versus the multiple-receiver side, the defenders have several options. We like to allow our players to make decisions in mixing the type of 3-on-2 coverage. The options available to the three defenders include:

- *Doubling the outside receiver.*

    —The outside cornerback locks in on the wide receiver from a press alignment and the deep safety covers on the top.

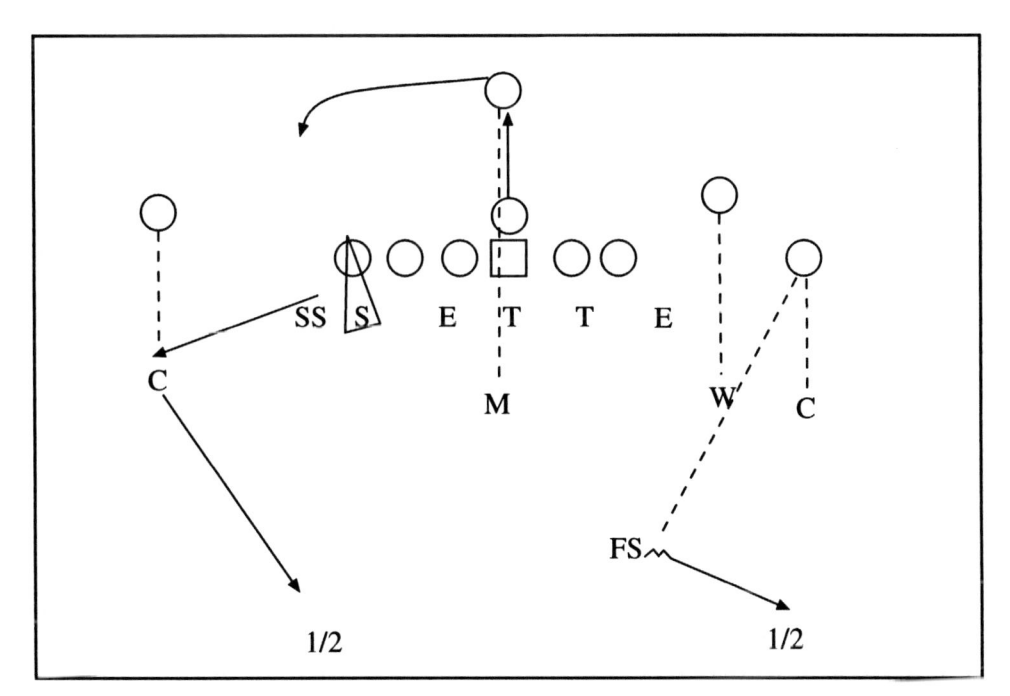

Diagram 9-66a: Cover 7 versus a balanced one-back formation.

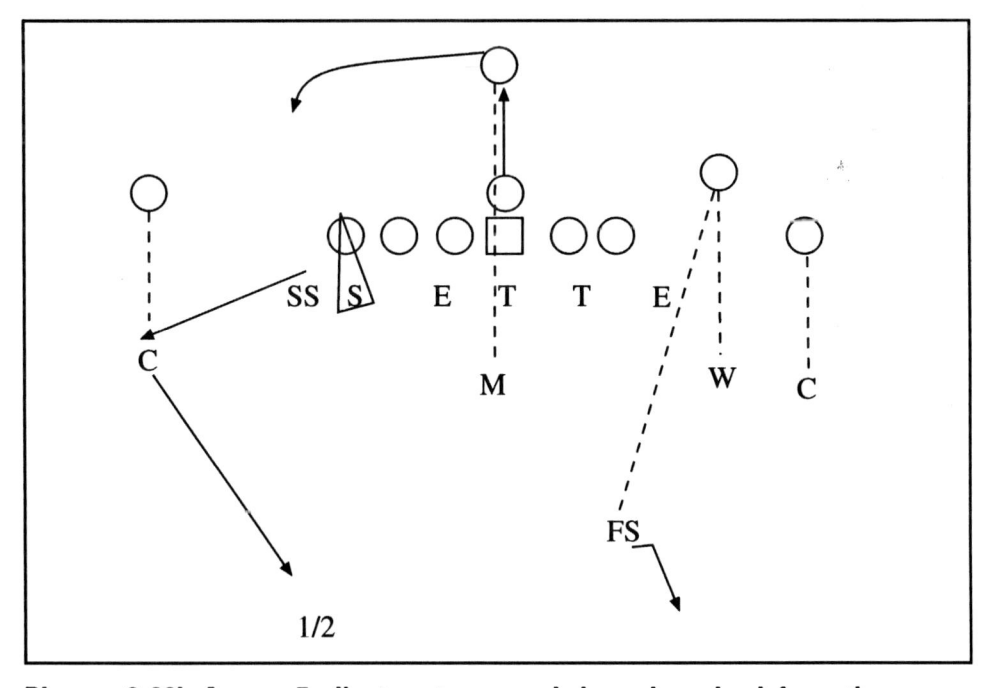

Diagram 9-66b: A cover 7 adjustment versus a balanced one-back formation.

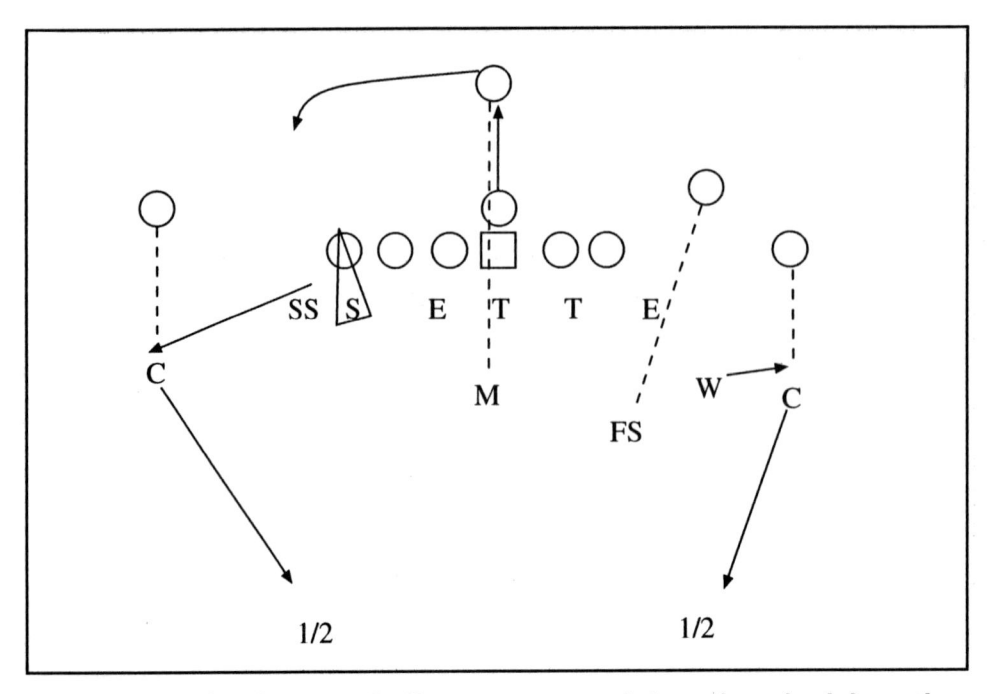

Diagram 9-66c: Another cover 7 adjustment versus a balanced one-back formation.

- *Swiping the outside receiver.*

    —The inside defender swipes to the outside receiver and the corner covers deep. The free safety covers the inside receiver.

- *Doubling the inside receiver.*

    —The inside defender and the free safety double cover the inside receiver while the cornerback locks on the outside receiver.

- *Playing man-to-man underneath with the safety over the top.*

    —The cornerback and inside defender cover from a cushion man-to-man alignment as the free safety covers over the top.

The 6Z weakside rotation:

Earlier, we stated that the thumbs player on the strong side of the cover 7 was the strong safety. The strong safety flew out underneath the number one receiver on the swipe call. In cover 6Z, the first linebacker aligned inside the formation and off the line of scrimmage is the thumbs dropper. Like cover 7, the strongside cornerback will drop to cover the deep 1/2.

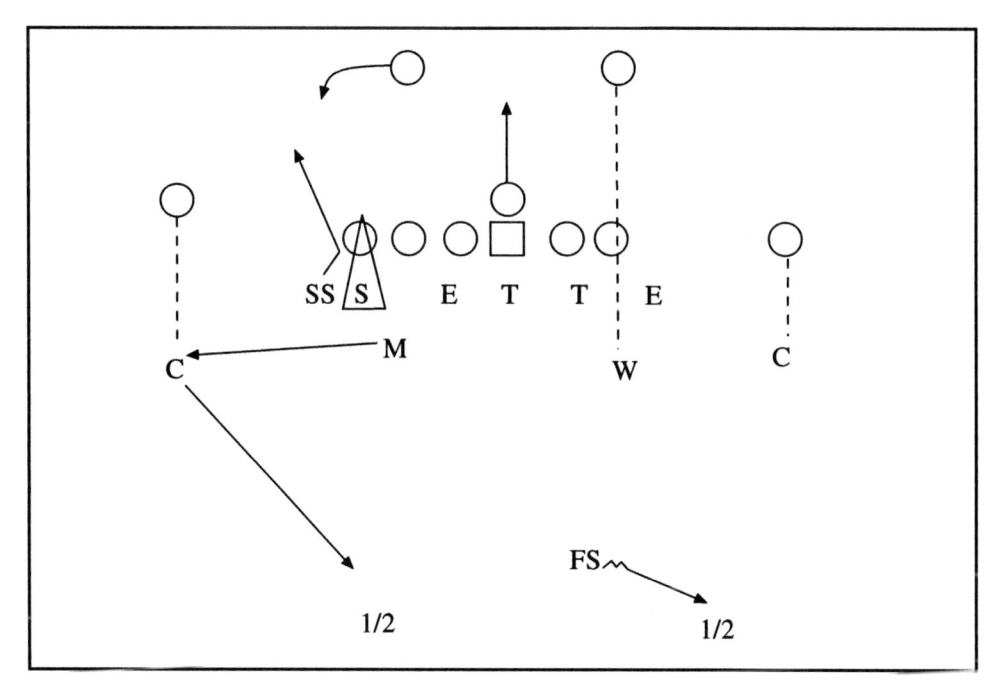

Diagram 9-67: Cover 6Z

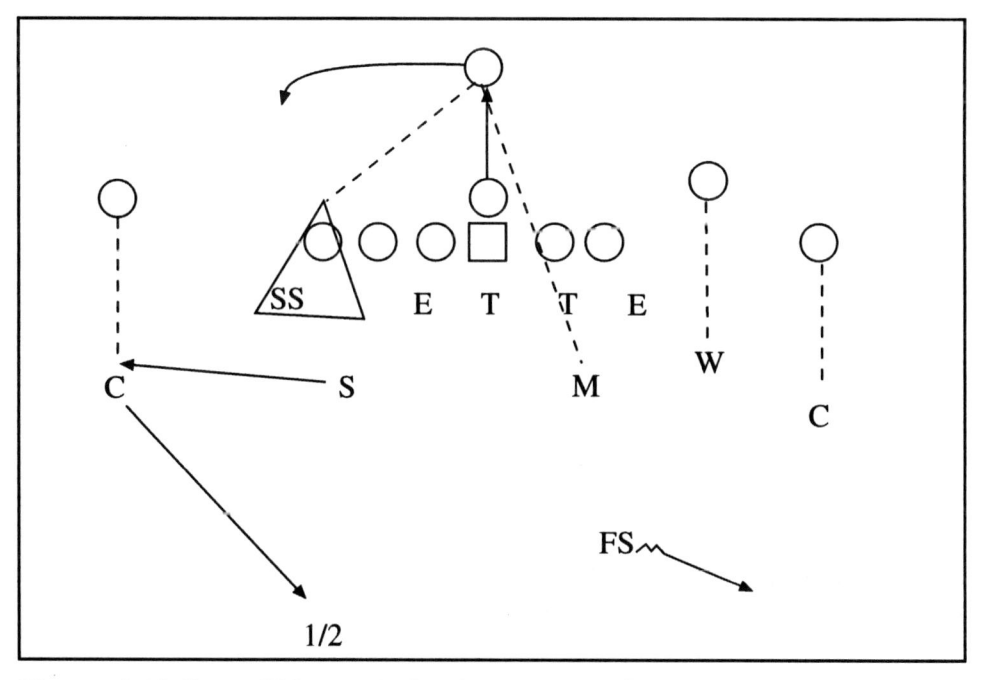

Diagram 9-68: Cover 6Z from a Jayhawk adjustment. Sam and Mike work together to cover the tight end and lone back. Will and the weakside cornerback have an automatic exchange, if necessary.

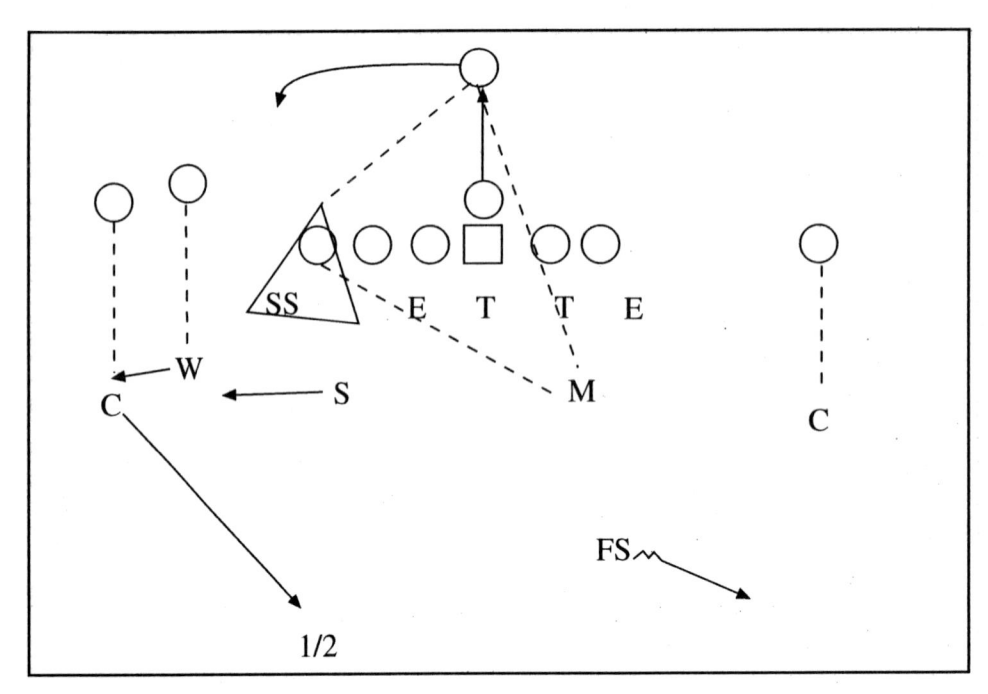

Diagram 9-69: Versus tight end trips, Will (the adjuster) swipes number one and Sam swipes number two.

On the weakside of cover 6Z, the exchange is automatic. Also, the cornerbacks naturally flop with the twins set. Mike will declare the strength to the tight-end side where the strong safety and Sam linebacker will play a banjo on the tight end and nearback. Since there is no wide receiver to the strong side who is not covered in a man-to-man technique, Mike can play over the top of the number one receiver to the strong side. This action fits with the swipe rule of the first strongside linebacker.

The weakside of the 6Z coverage resembles the old cover 2 (i.e., two-deep zone). The weakside cornerback funnels the X receiver to the inside, exactly in the same manner as the hard corner position in cover 2. The weakside corner stays on the outside shoulder of the receiver as he releases inside. If the receiver continues inside on a crossing pattern with the number two receiver, the Will linebacker picks up the coverage of the wide receiver, and the cornerback pushes off to cover the flat break of the number two receiver. We generally see a lot of 3-step routes which attempt to find an open receiver coming off a crossing route. The most common combination is the quick slant (i.e., pick) route and swing route. Remember, if the running back converts his swing route into a wheel route, the cornerback will cover him from an inside-out position. This conversion route often comes off of a deeper 5-step drop, particularly with a 3-step pump fake. Even though the cornerback has deep help by the free safety in the weakside deep 1/2 zone, he should carry the number two

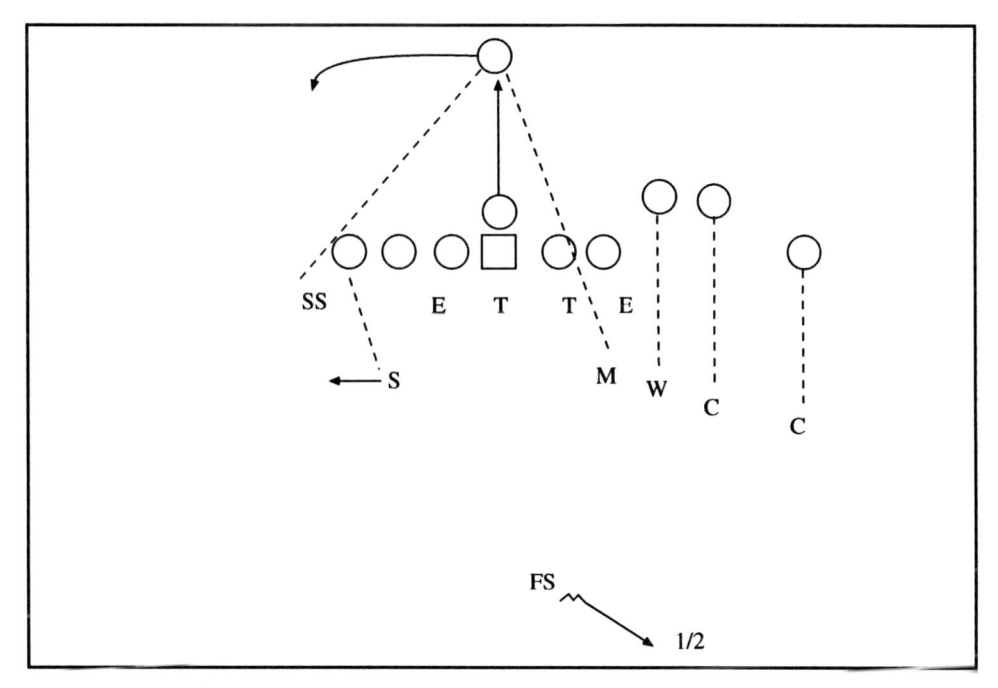

Diagram 9-70: Cover 6Z versus an open end trips.

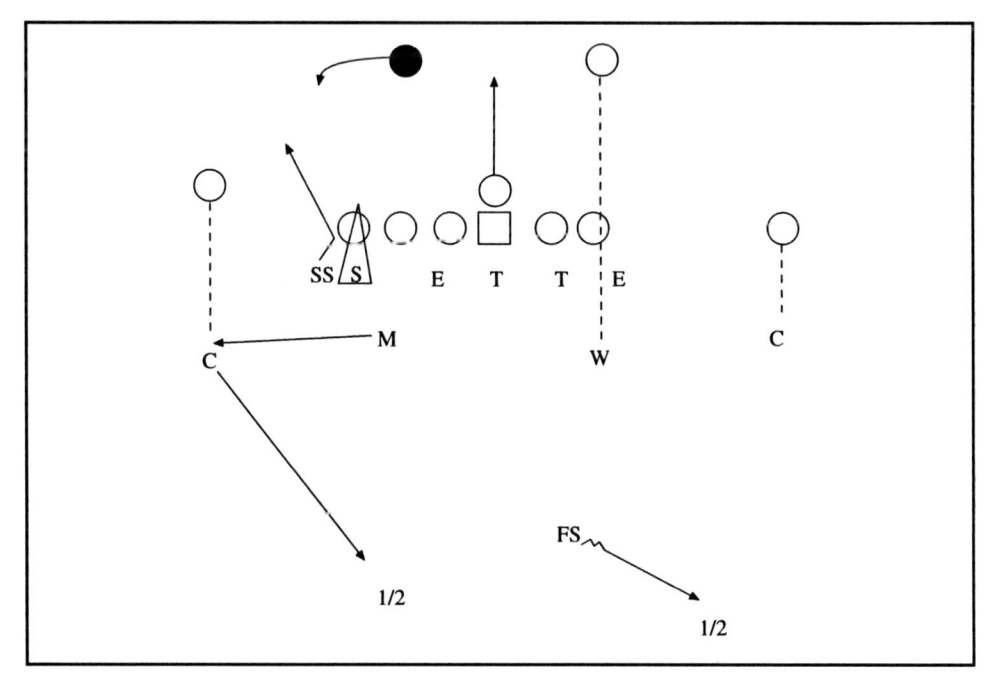

Diagram 9-71: Cover 6Z versus a back set to the strongside.

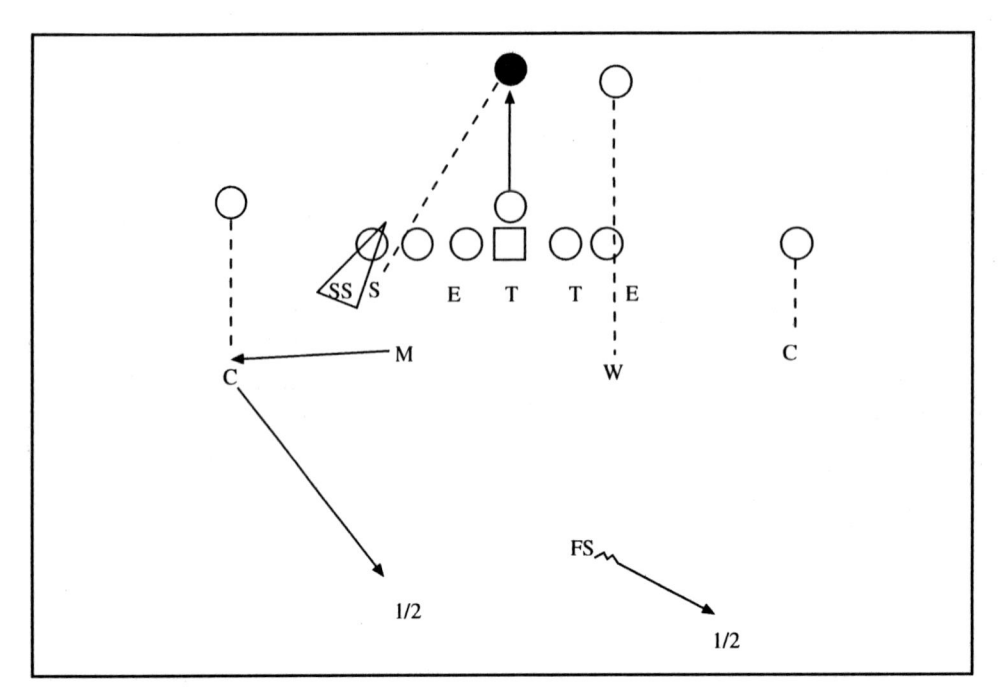

Diagram 9-72: Cover 6Z versus a back set to the weakside.

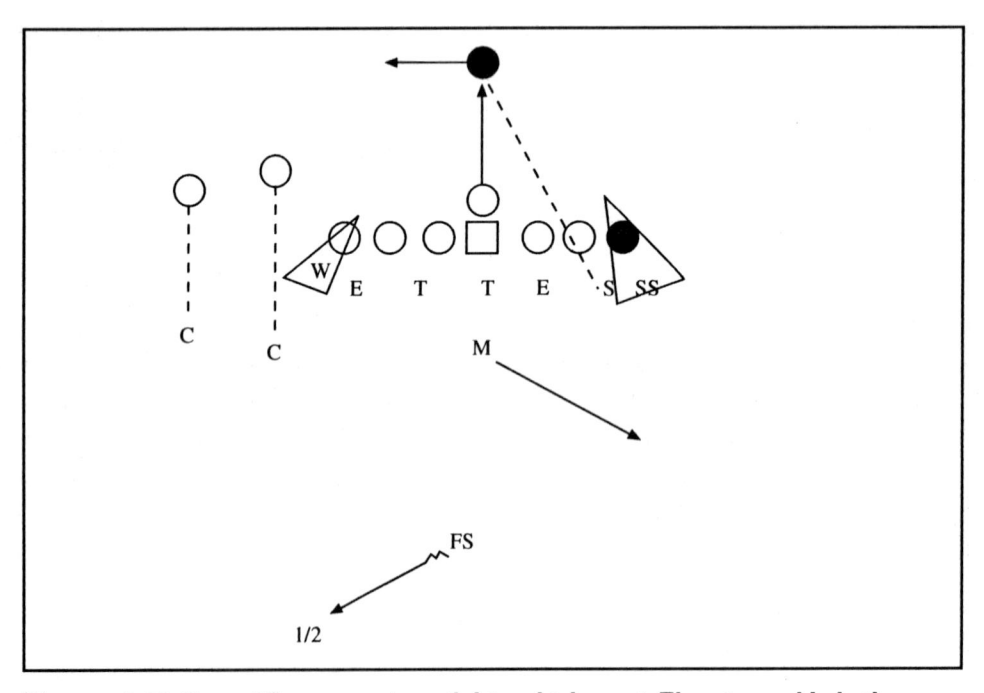

Diagram 9-73: Cover 6Z versus a two-tight end trips set. The strongside is the single-receiver side.

receiver through the zone on the exchange. While the cornerback funnels the X receiver inside, the Will linebacker is funneling the second receiver outside. The combined technique of the weakside cornerback and the Will linebacker makes for a smooth exchange, if needed.

Meanwhile, on the strong side of the coverage, the Sam linebacker will align in his normal alignment unless a Jayhawk adjustment is made. With one exception, Sam will then cover the tight end man-to-man. The strong safety will collision the tight end and cover the strongside back. The combined efforts of the Sam and strong safety depend on the type of offensive set. If the backfield set is a weak set (i.e., set away from the tight end), the strong safety will cover the tight end, while Sam, from his inside-eye alignment on the tight end, covers the back. If the set is a strong set (i.e., set to the tight end), the strong safety will jam the tight end, as already noted, and cover the nearback; Sam will cover the tight end.

The primary difference between cover 7 and cover 6Z is the responsibility of the inside linebacker to push all the way out underneath the number one receiver in cover 6Z. In cover 7, the inside linebacker was an underneath coverage dropper looking for a push call. In cover 6Z, he must push himself out without the benefit of making a push call and exchanging responsibilities with the strong safety.

6Z was a favorite coverage of the Chicago Bears during their dominance of the 1980s. Personnel-wise, the Bears had a strongside cornerback who was capable of challenging the Z receiver from a press alignment. The cornerback would lock on the Z receiver, while Mike Singletary would drop from his linebacker position to cover the strongside deep 1/2. If you happen to have a Mike Singletary on your team, along with a superior man-coverage cornerback, this option is available to you in cover 6Z. Diagram 9-75 shows this particular coverage scheme.

The 6Z coverage is an excellent coverage against one-back teams. Against one-back teams, we will normally play the Jayhawk adjustment. The Jayhawk adjustment is identical in structure to the old double eagle defense. In the Jayhawk adjustment, the Sam linebacker is the first linebacker inside and off the line of scrimmage. In this case, he is the thumbs player in cover 6Z. Against a balanced one-back formation, as shown in the previous diagrams, the strong safety and Mike linebacker will work a banjo on the lone setback. Diagrams 9-68 through 9-70 show the 6Z coverage from a Jayhawk coverage.

It should be noted the schematic difference between cover 6Z from a Jayhawk adjustment and a static 46 front alignment. In the Jayhawk adjustment, the Sam linebacker is the thumbs player, while from the static 46 alignment, the thumbs player is the Mike linebacker. Diagrams 9-71 through 9-73 show cover 6Z from a static 46 alignment on the tight end side.

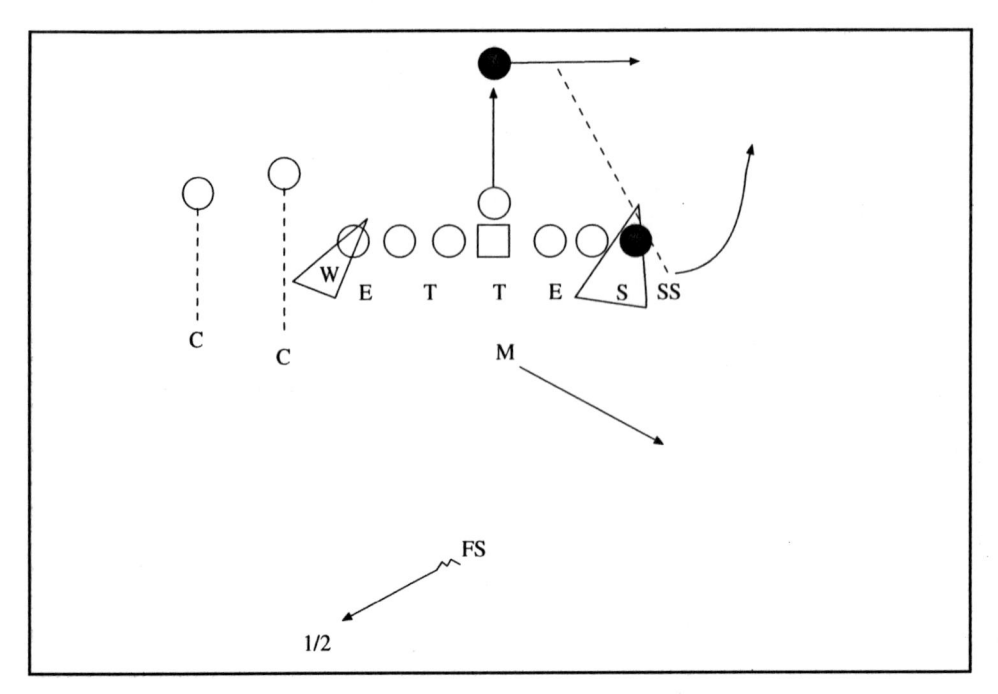

Diagram 9-74: Cover 6Z versus a two-tight end trips set. Sam and the strong safety work a banjo on the tight end and lone back.

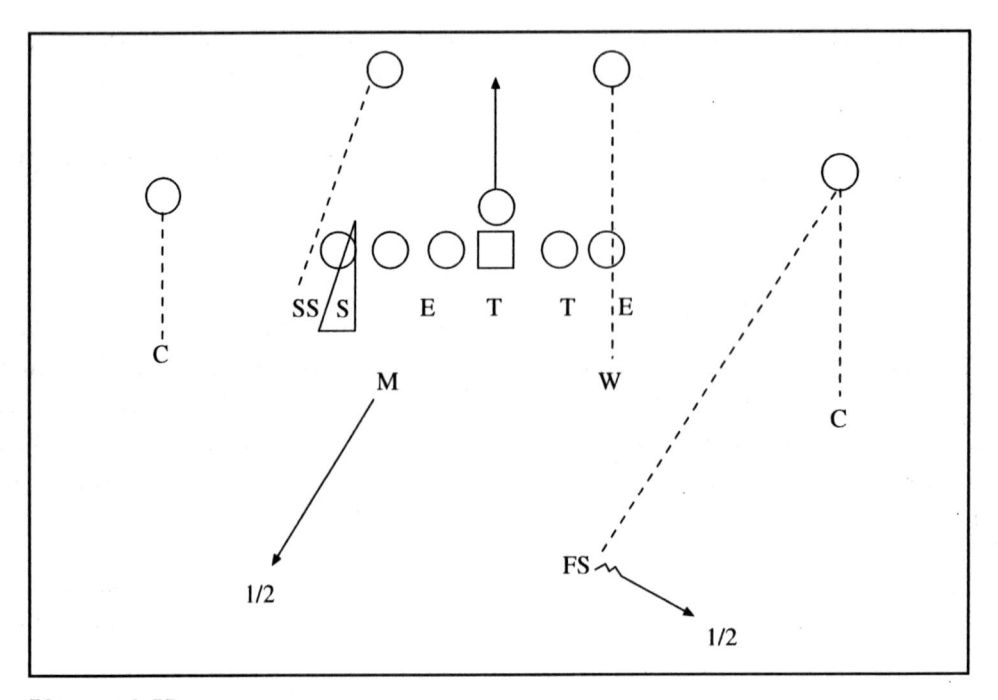

Diagram 9-75.

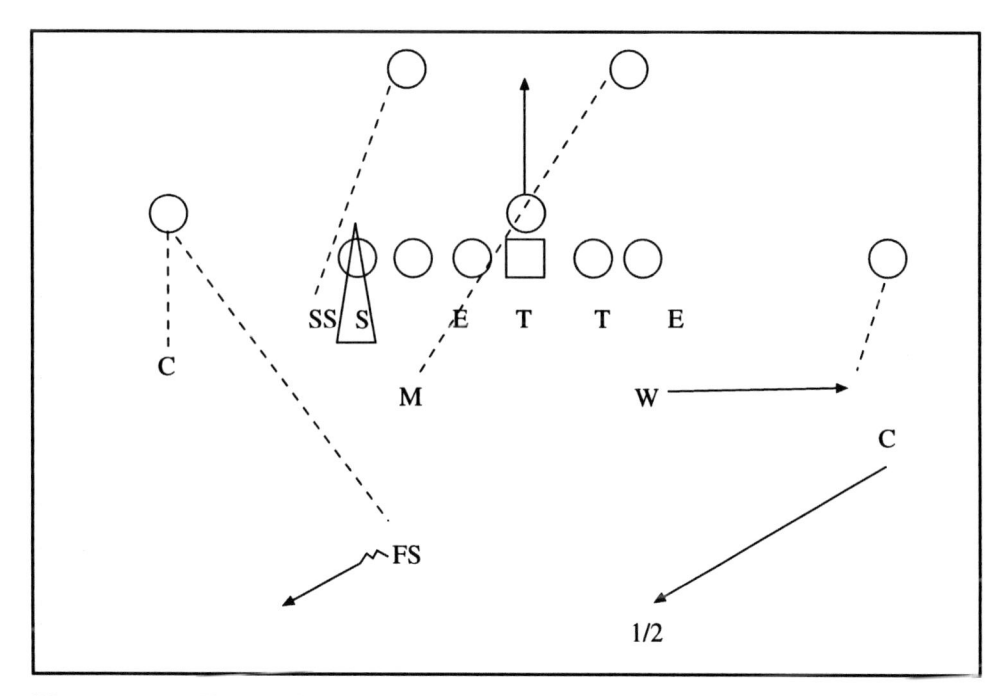

Diagram 9-76: The combo coverage.

Meanwhile, the Will linebacker (the adjuster) and the weakside cornerback will work an automatic exchange on the weak side. In considering a Jayhawk adjustment against a tight end trips, the Will linebacker will swipe out to the number one receiver, and the Sam linebacker will swipe out to the number two receiver. As you can imagine, 6Z is a fully comprehensive coverage versus the one-back passing sets.

The combo coverage:

A great complement to the weakside rotation is the strongside rotation coverage, what we call the combo coverage. In the combo coverage, we double cover the number one receiver to the strongside. It is a mirror coverage of the weakside rotation (6Z) in that we are rotating the coverage to the strong side instead of the weakside. As in cover 6Z, we have a swipe technique in effect away from the coverage roll. In the combo coverage, the swipe technique is to the weakside.

The weakside cornerback will play the deep 1/2 zone as the Will linebacker swipes underneath the X receiver. Against a single receiver to the weakside, the cornerback can favor the deep coverage quite a bit.

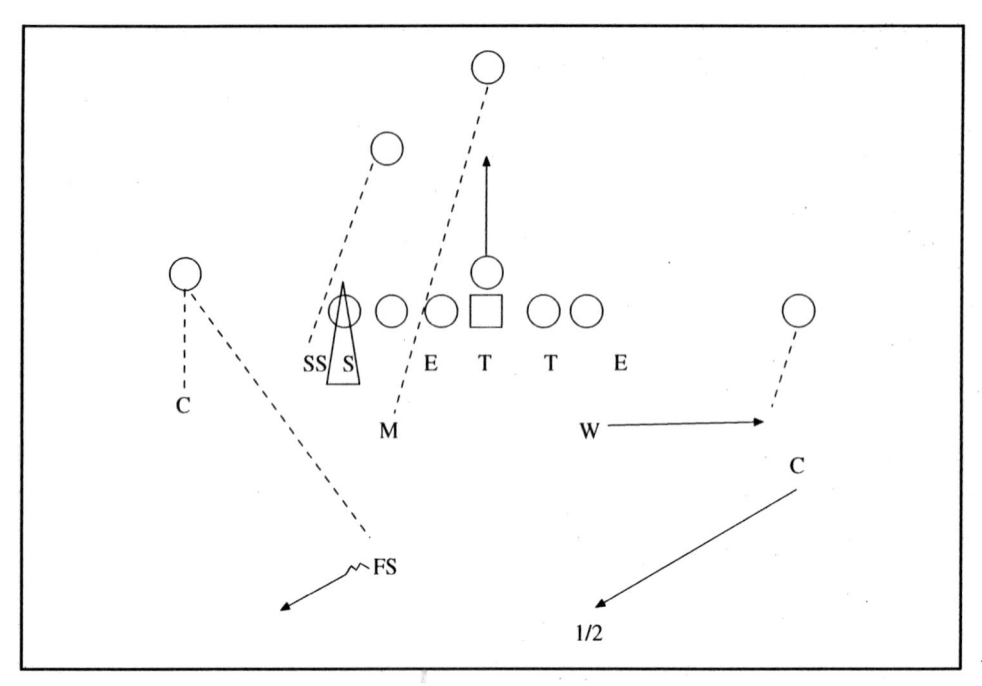

Diagram 9-77: Versus a single receiver to the weakside, the cornerback can favor his deep coverage assignment.

If two receivers are aligned to the weakside, Will should swipe to the number one receiver as the Mike linebacker swipes to the number two receiver. If the Mike linebacker feels that he is going to be outflanked by the number two receiver, he can make a hit call to the weakside defensive end.

The hit call tells the weakside end to make sure the nearback (i.e., the number two receiver) releases inside of him. If the weakside end forces the nearback to release inside of him, the Mike linebacker can cover him. However, if the nearback releases outside the defensive end, the defensive end must cover him. The essence of the hit call is: If the nearback releases inside the defensive end, the Mike linebacker should cover him; if the nearback releases outside the defensive end, the defensive end must cover him. We prefer the defensive end to force the nearback inside to the Mike; however, if he makes it outside, the defensive end must drop off in coverage.

Just as with the weakside of cover 6Z, we have at least three options of several types of double teams on the strongside. We can use a fist technique with the cornerback playing in a press technique on the inside and the safety on top. We can also use a slice technique with the inside and outside double team by the free safety and cornerback, respectively. Our third option is the trap. On the trap technique, the cornerback will drive the 3-step drop, look for a quick ball and go for the interception, as the safety is over the top.

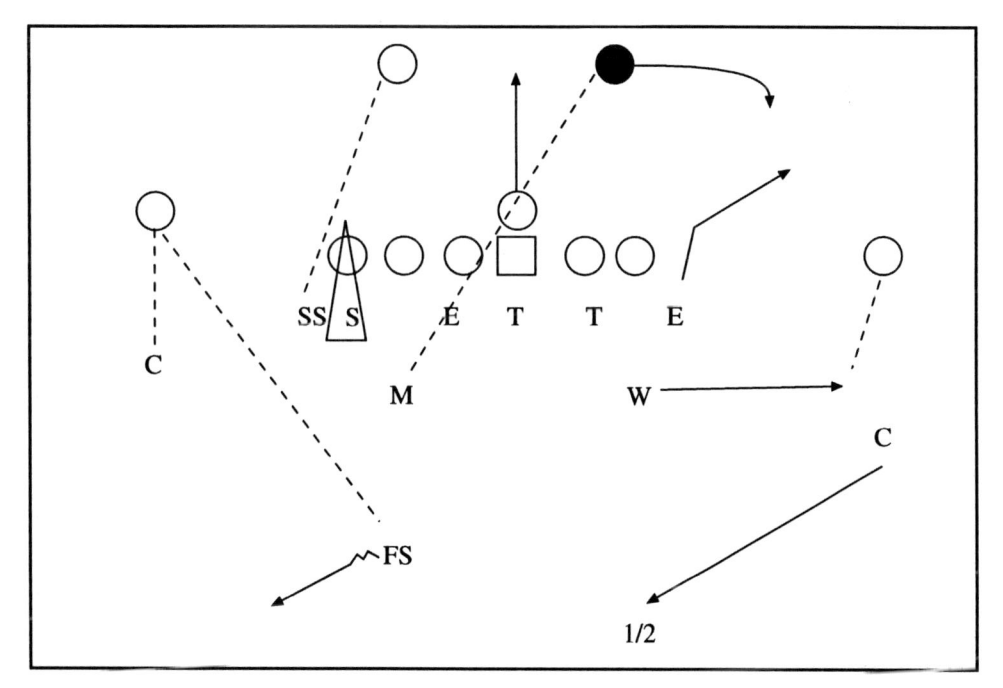

Diagram 9-78: The hit call to the weakside defensive end.

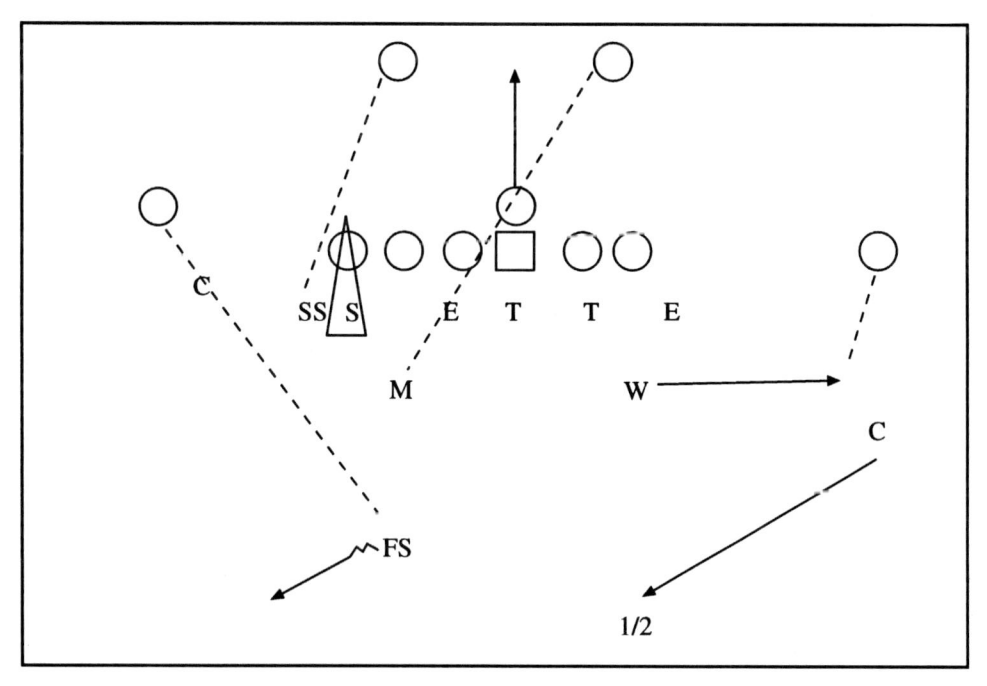

Diagram 9-79: The fist call to the strongside.

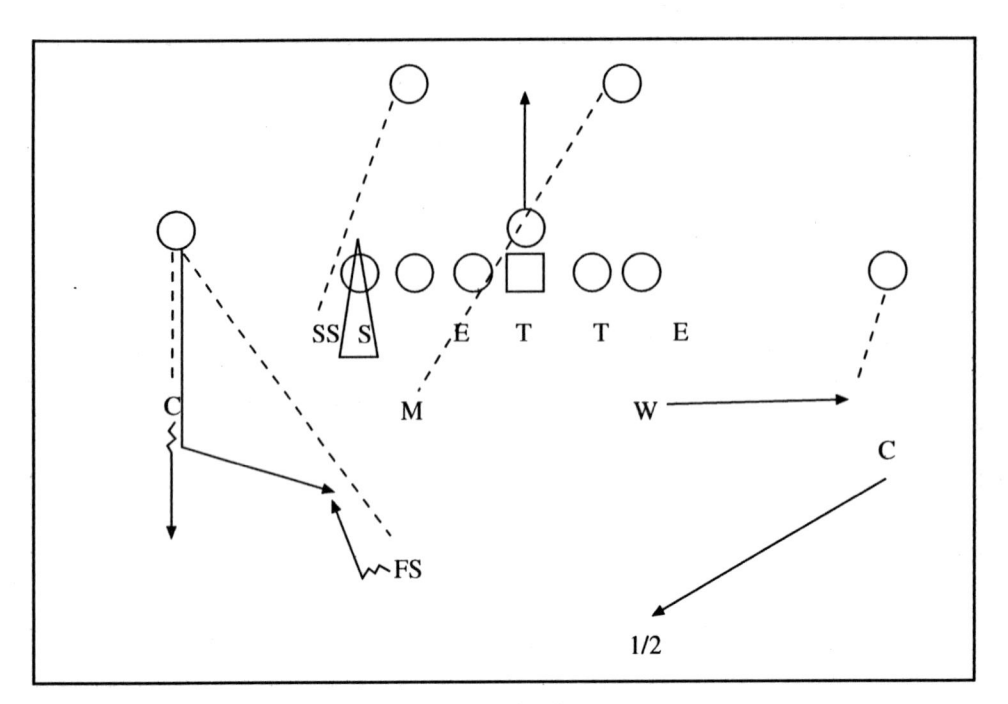

Diagram 9-80: The slice technique versus the Z receiver.

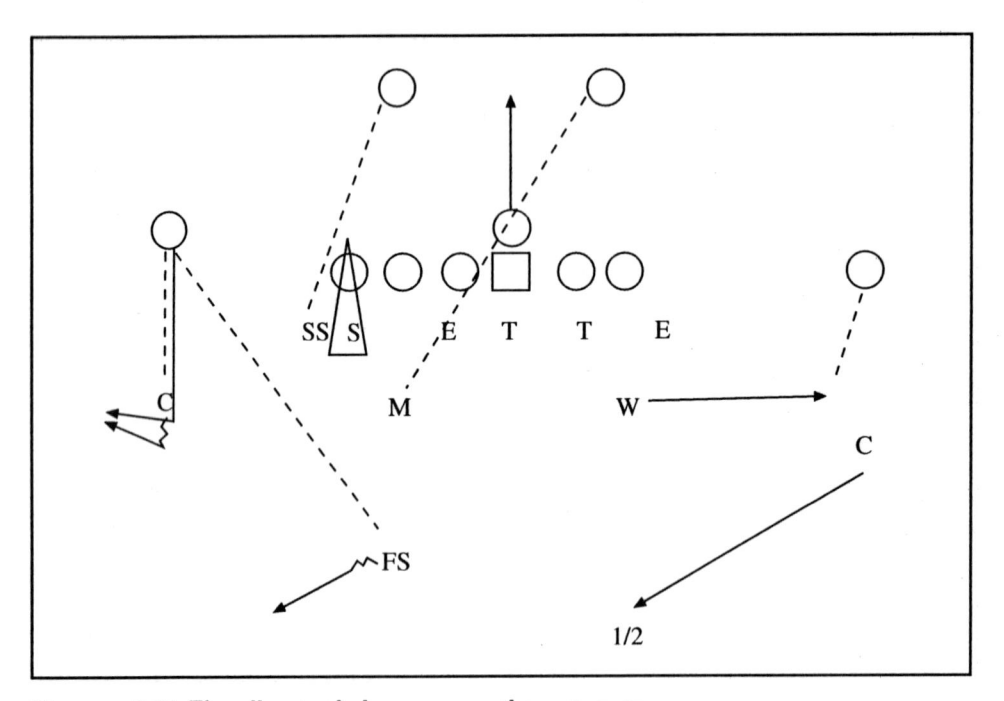

Diagram 9-81: The slice technique versus the out route.

156

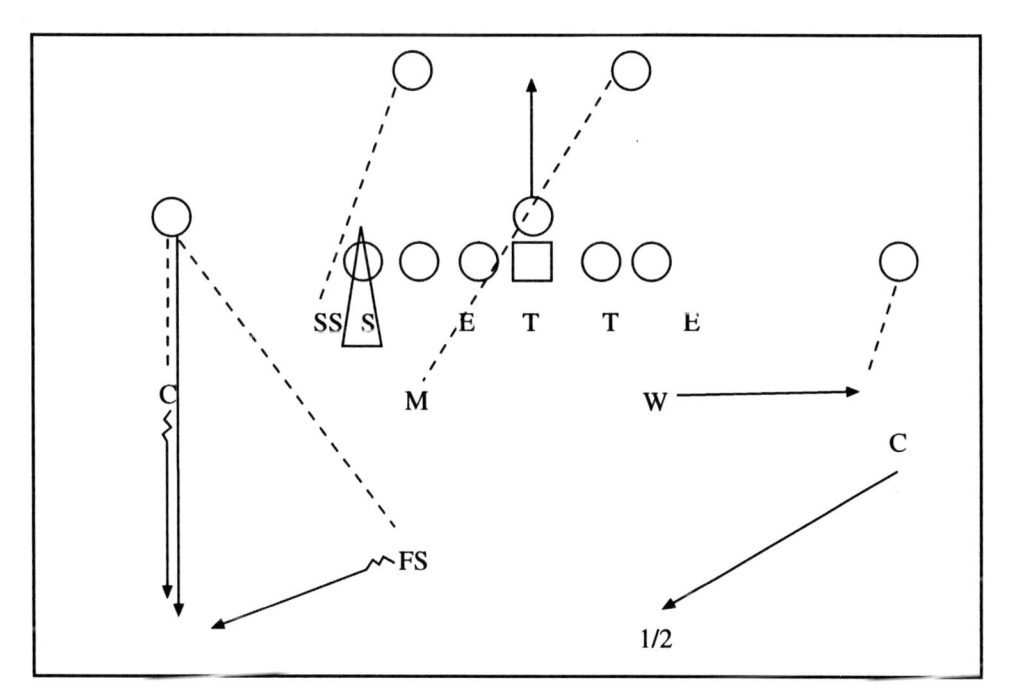

Diagram 9-82: The slice technique versus the vertical route.

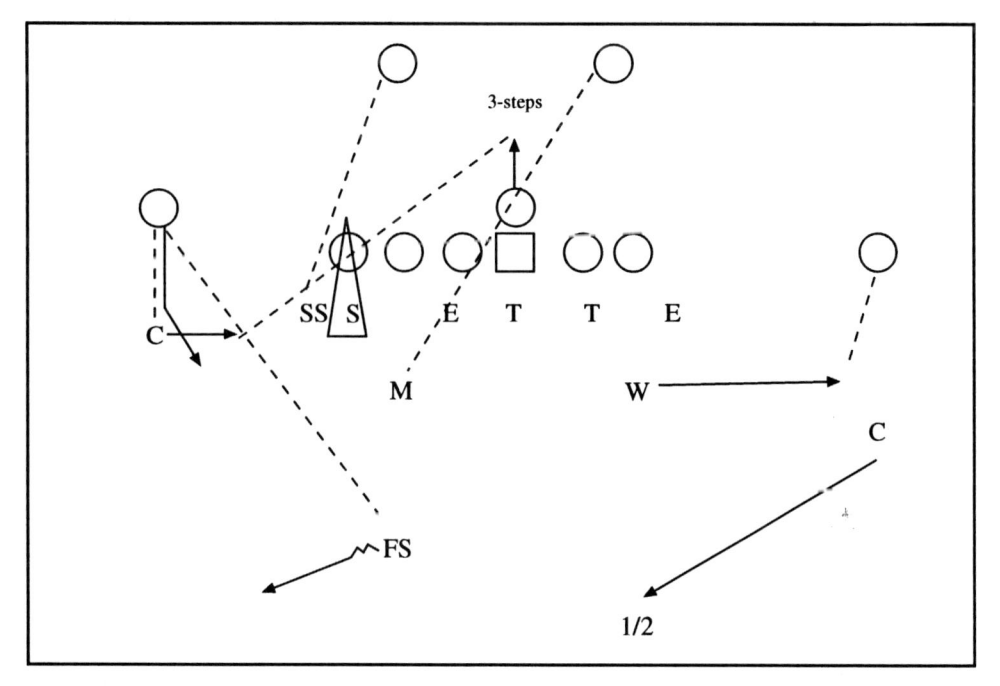

Diagram 9-83: The trap technique on the Z receiver.

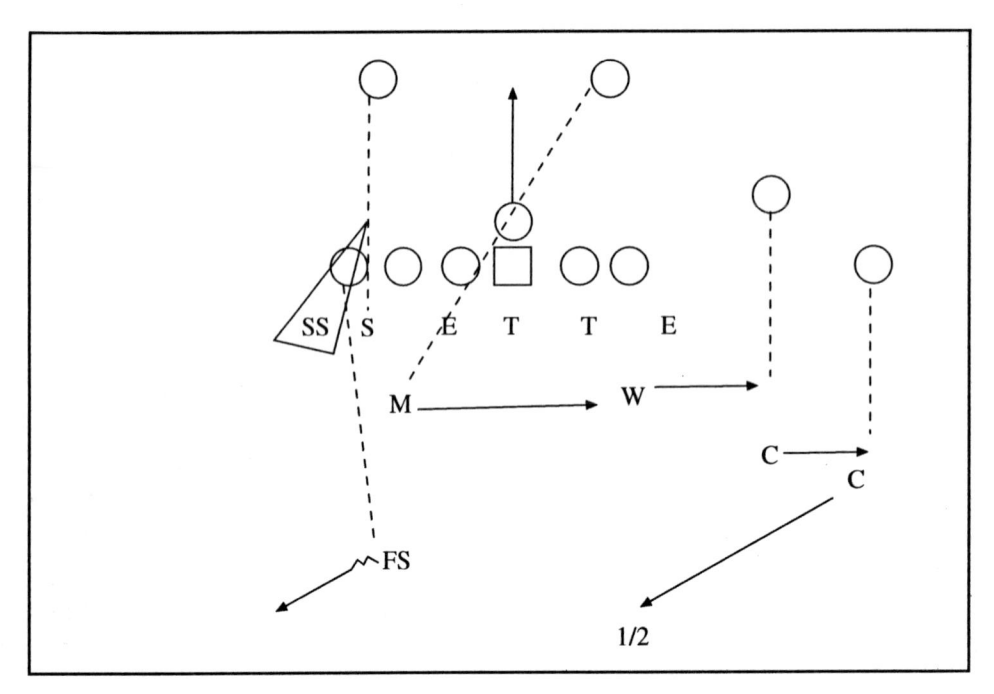

Diagram 9-84: The combo coverage versus the twins formation.

The strongside rotation is a favorite of ours against the flop (i.e., twins) formation. In the flop formation, the tight end is the number one receiver to the strongside. The strong safety is going to slice the tight end with the free safety in a double team. The slice is a particularly effective technique in this case because the strong safety is in an excellent position to play the tight end from an outside-in position, while the free safety's alignment is conducive to playing the tight end on the inside route. The Sam and Mike linebackers will cover the remaining two backs as the Will linebacker swipes out under the Z receiver (i.e., number two). The inside cornerback will swipe outside to the number one receiver.

CHAPTER 10

46 STUNTS AND BLITZES

In keeping with the spirit of pressure defense—playing the run when they are going to run, and rushing the passer when they are going to pass—the 46 alignment and scheme offers an opportunity for incorporating a devastating blitz package. Sound man-to-man coverages, disguised blitz and stunt alignments, and overloaded flanks will destroy the timing and confidence of any passing game—at any level. The theme of the 46 blitz philosophy is based upon one fact: *A receiver is open only when the quarterback can deliver the ball to him.* If the 46 defensive package offers one constant, it is that the proper installation and practice of the 46 blitz package severely limits the availability of *open* receivers.

The core of the 46 blitz package is supported by the man-free coverage scheme. We prefer to give our free safety the opportunity to play freely in the middle of the field and read the quarterback's eyes. Although the free safety is normally assigned to cover a particular receiver, the receiver who is assigned to the free safety is commonly a check receiver (i.e., a receiver who will check the blitz and stay in to block versus maximum pressure). Because the free safety's man is generally the check receiver, the free safety is often free to roam the middle of the field for the interception as the check receiver stays in for maximum protection. Ironically, keeping the check receiver (e.g., tight end, tailback) in to block for maximum protection is exactly the strategy we want the opponent to use.

Single:

The generic base blitz of the 46 package is "single." The single blitz is supported by a man-free coverage scheme (Cover 1). Shown in Diagram 10-1, the single-blitz scheme is also discussed extensively in Chapter 9.

Single provides maximum pressure versus maximum protection. As detailed in Chapter 9, regardless of the number of receivers set into the pattern, the maximum pass rush pressure will isolate the blockers in 1-on-1 match ups. Because single is the staple blitz of the 46 package, most of the following blitzes are best disguised to resemble single. One important point to remember, however—in the disguising of blitzes, you should never sacrifice pressure for trickery. A blitz should be disguised only if the disguising of the blitz doesn't deter from its effectiveness.

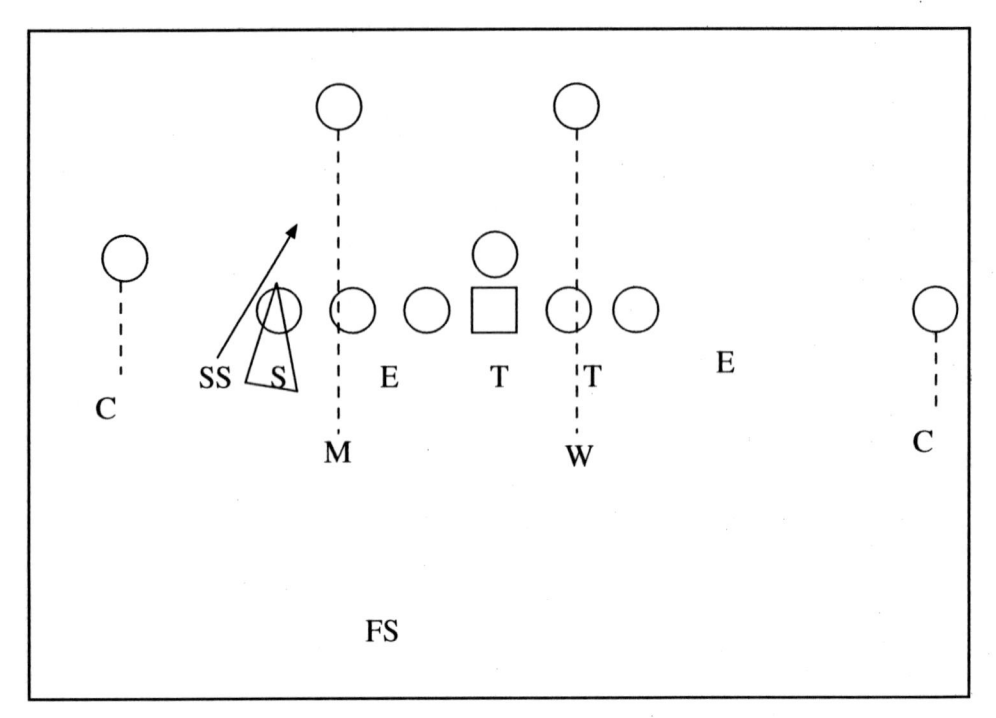

Diagram 10-1: Single.

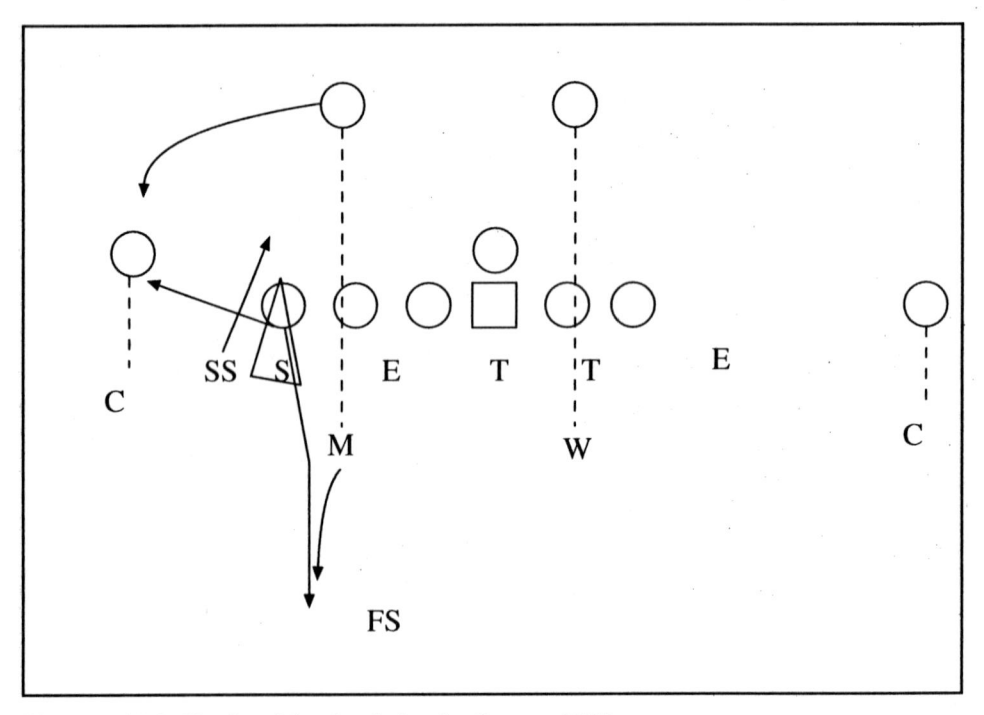

Diagram 10-2: Single with a banjo by the Sam and Mike.

160

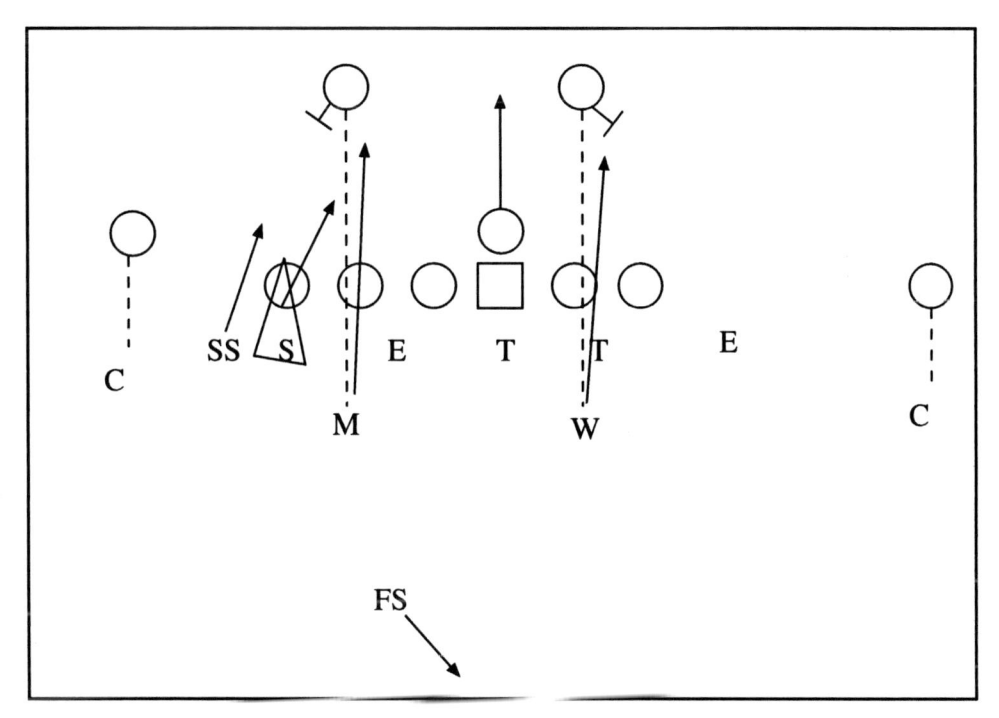

Diagram 10-3: Single versus maximum protection.

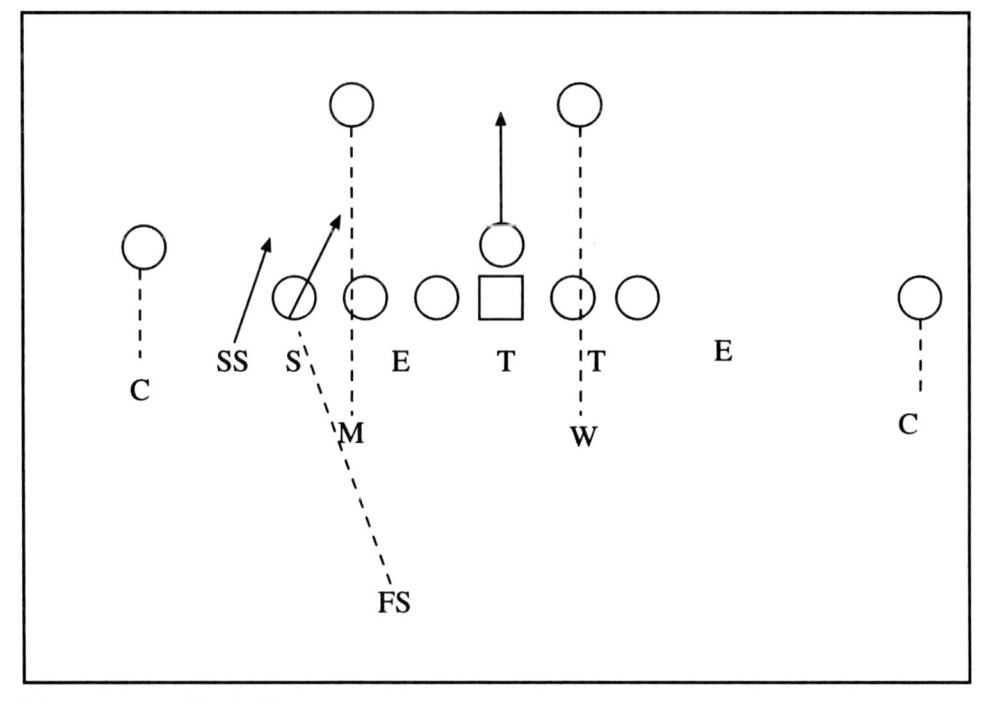

Diagram 10-4: Single Sam.

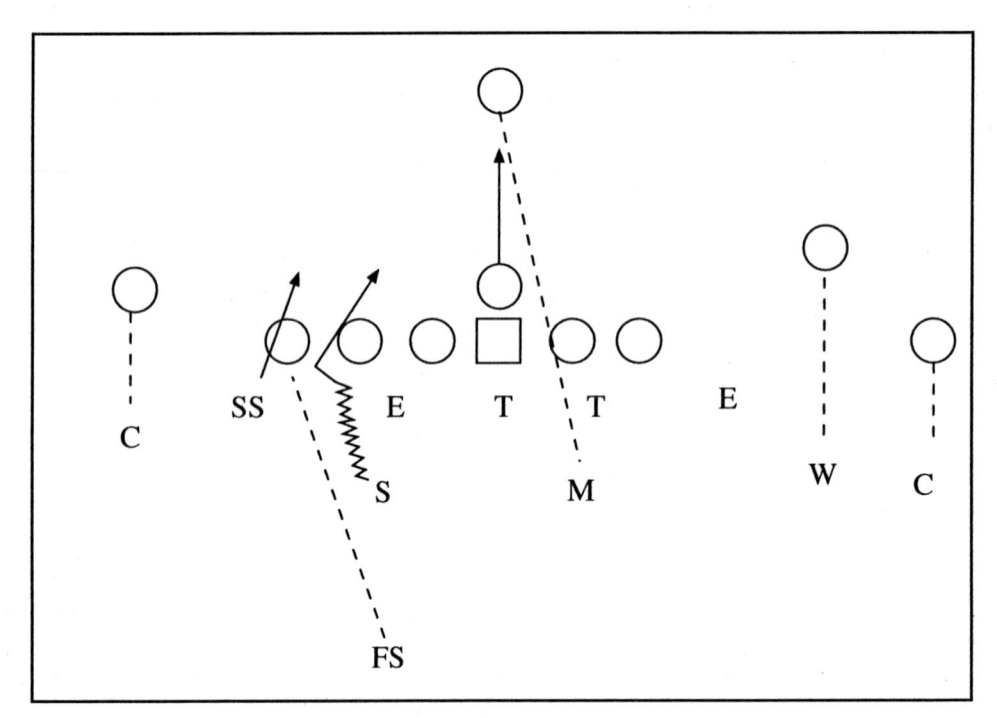

Diagram 10-5: Single Sam from a Jayhawk adjustment and stem.

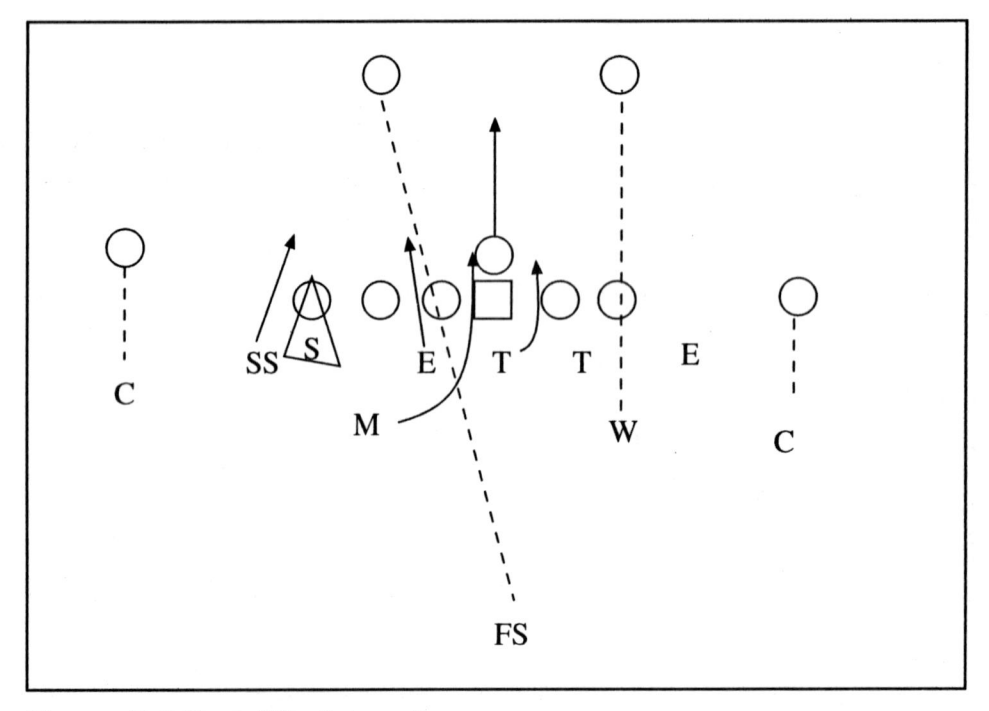

Diagram 10-6: Single Mike "strong."

Single Sam (Hamburger)

Single Sam, also known as Hamburger, is the fundamental single blitz. The addition of the name Sam informs the free safety who he is replacing in coverage. By calling Single Sam, the coach gets the single coverage with the Sam blitzing. The free safety replaces the Sam linebacker in the coverage scheme. Against the pro set shown in the following diagram, Sam blitzes through the "C" gap while the free safety covers the tight end. If the tight end blocks, the free safety goes back to his middle-of-the-field free safety technique. The Single Sam blitz is an excellent blitz versus a weakside slide protection. It can also be run with a stem from the Jayhawk alignment. Hamburger is an excellent run blitz. It is especially effective as a means to force teams to cut their passing game down to a 3-step attack. Furthermore, whenever you make a team depend on its 3-step game to move the ball, it won't beat you via the throwing game.

Single Mike:

Single Mike is the second blitz of the hamburger genre. In the Single Mike blitz, the Mike linebacker alerts the defensive linemen as to where he will blitz. If Mike wants to blitz through the strongside A gap, he calls out "strong." If Mike wants to blitz through the weakside A gap, he calls out "weak." The weak call is especially effective versus the big-on-big protection where the offensive linemen block the defensive linemen in one-on-one matchups. If Mike wants to blitz through the B gap, he calls out "shoot." When Mike calls out "up," he is alerting the defensive linemen that he is blitzing through the C gap. In each of these four blitz calls, the defensive linemen take the appropriate action to open up the Mike's pass rush lane.

As with the Single Sam blitz, the free safety is the adjustor. The free safety will replace the Mike in coverage. If Mike's man stays in to block—which he likely will— the free safety will then be free to read the quarterback's eyes. One important coaching point for the free safety to remember when breaking off his man coverage responsibility is to keep the primary receiver in his line of sight. The opponent may try to sneak Mike's man out into a delay pattern. In this particular case, the free safety would cover the delay route.

Single Will:

Single Will is the mirror blitz to the Single Mike blitz. Will alerts the defensive linemen as to where he will blitz through the use of one of four calls made at the line of scrimmage. If Will wants to blitz through the strongside A gap, he calls out "strong." If Will wants to blitz through the weakside A gap, he calls out "weak." The weak call is especially effective versus the big-on-big protection where the offensive linemen block the defensive linemen in one-on-one matchups. If Will wants to blitz through the B gap, he calls out "shoot." When Will calls out "up," he is alerting the defensive linemen that he is blitzing through the C gap. In each of these four blitz calls, the defensive linemen take the appropriate action to open up the Will's pass rush lane.

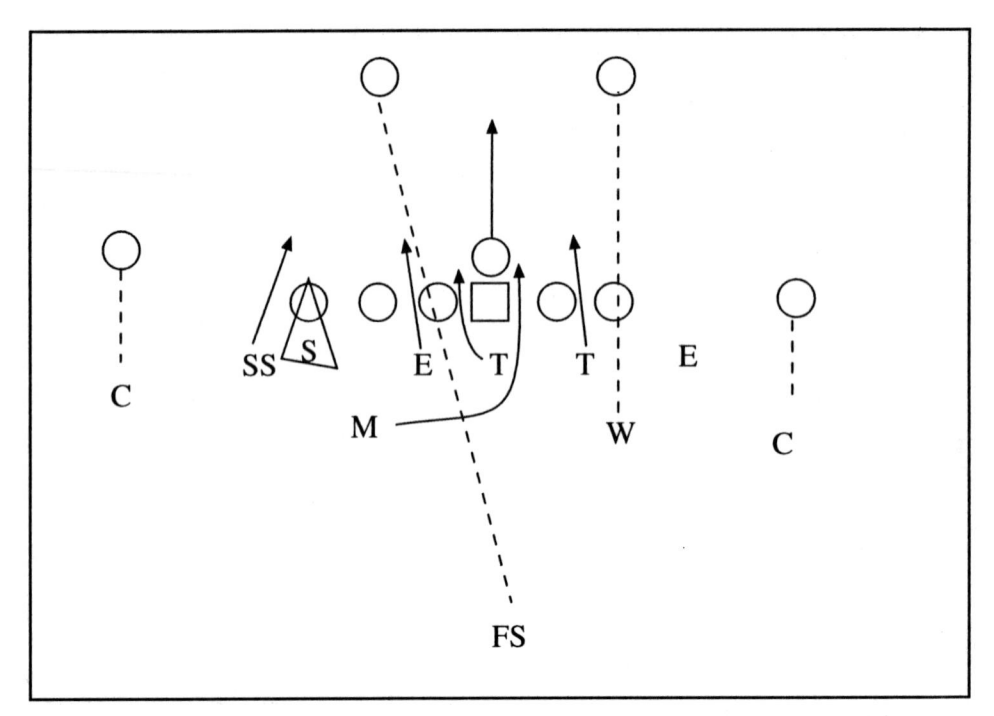

Diagram 10-7: Single Mike "weak."

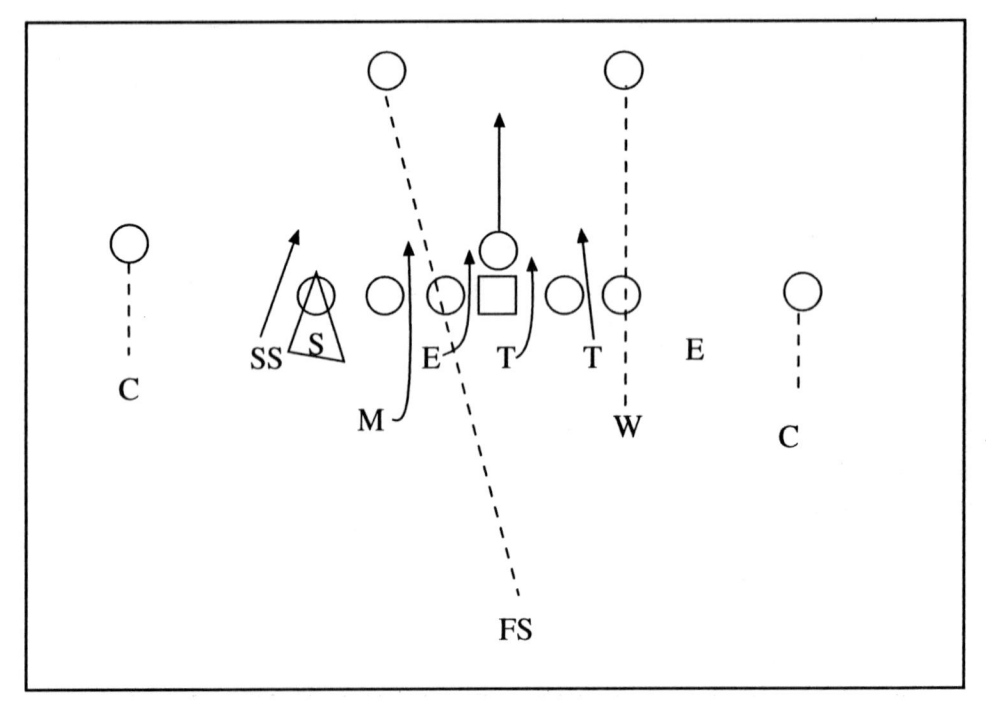

Diagram 10-8: Single Mike "shoot."

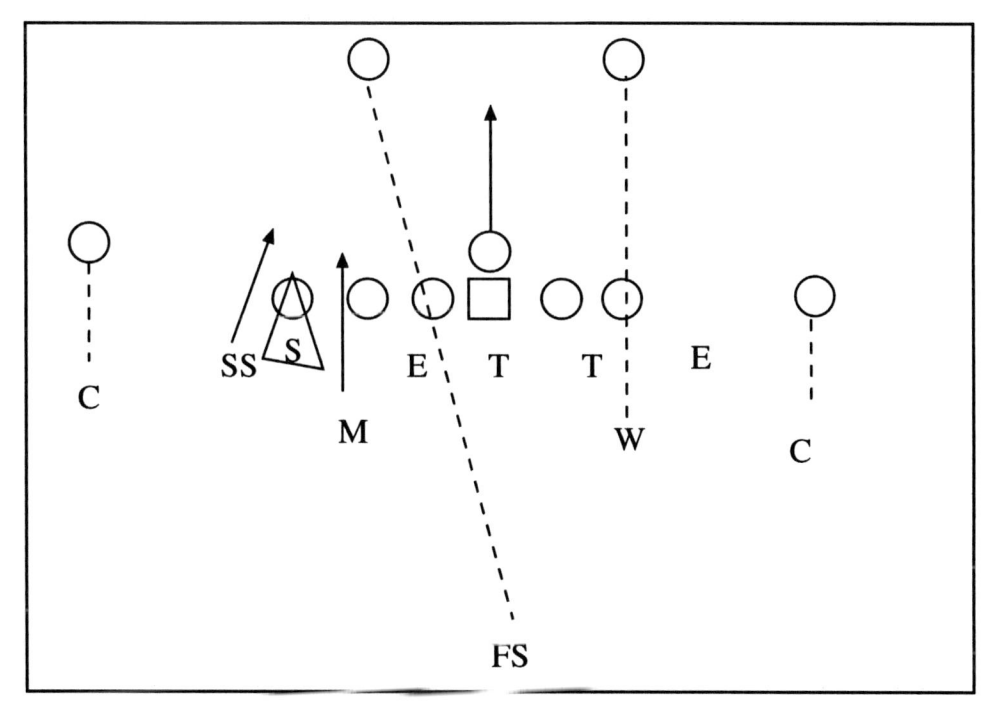

Diagram 10-9: Single Mike "up."

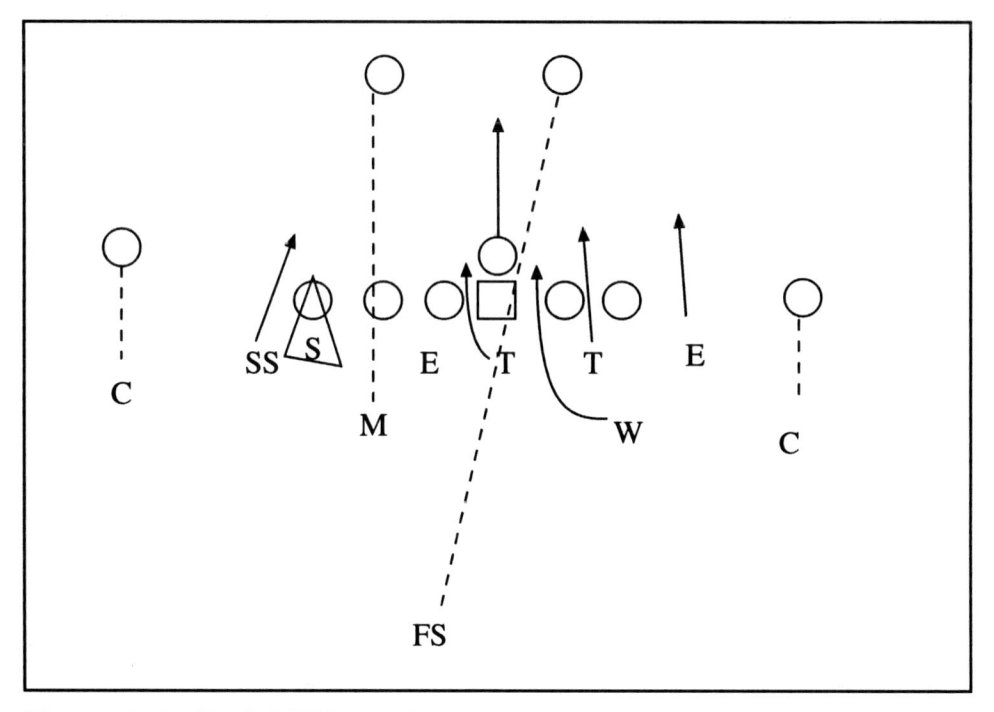

Diagram 10-10: Single Will "weak."

165

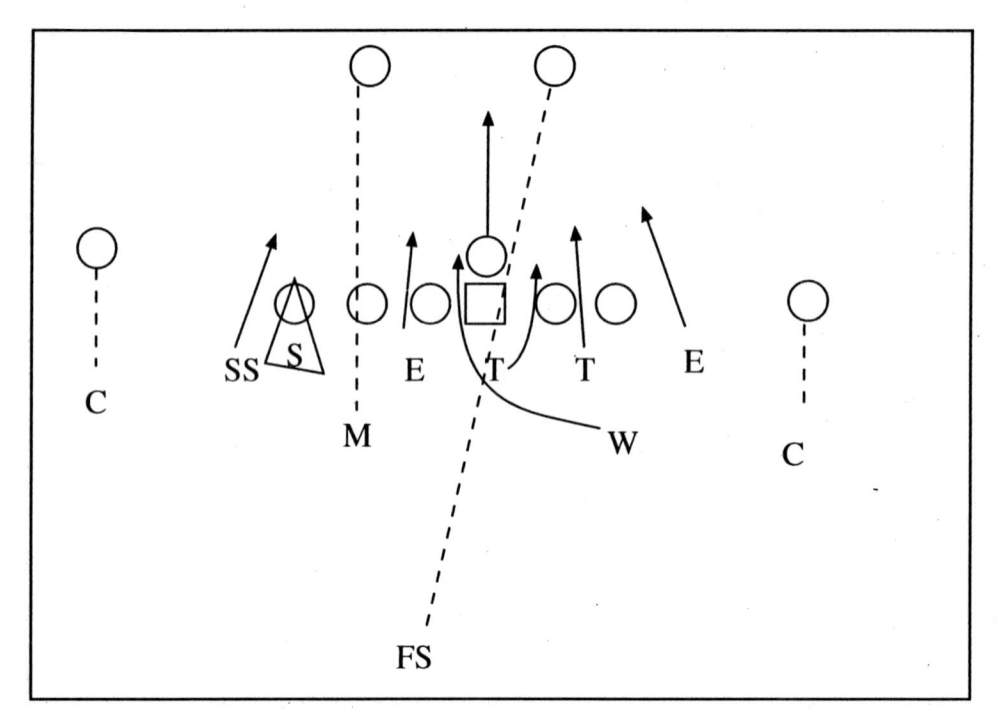

Diagram 10-11: Single Will "strong."

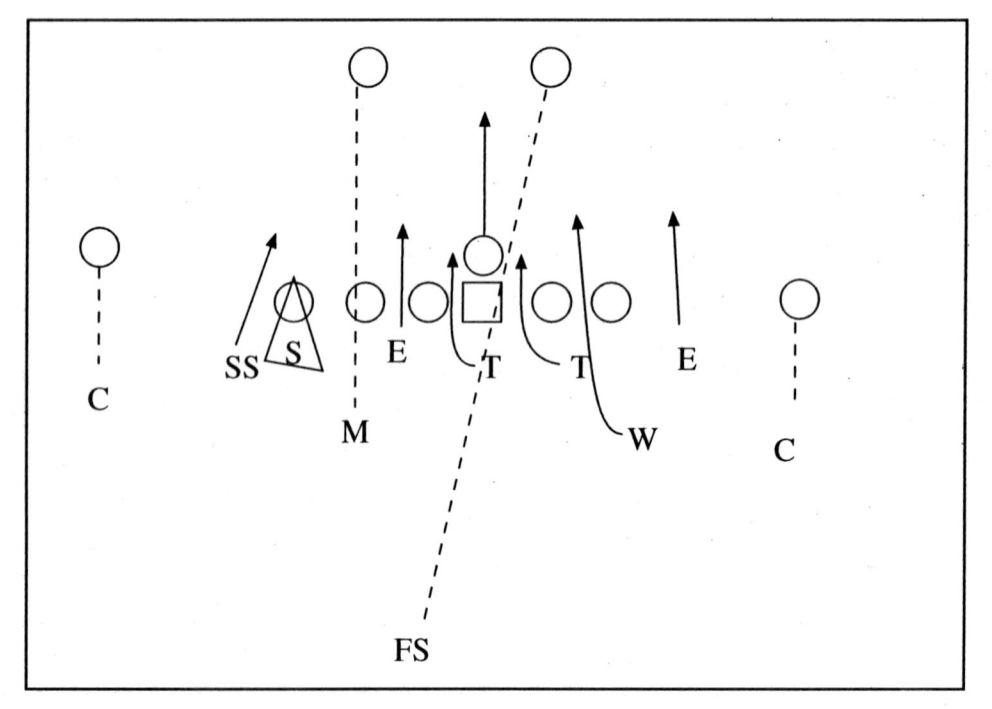

Diagram 10-12: Single Will "shoot."

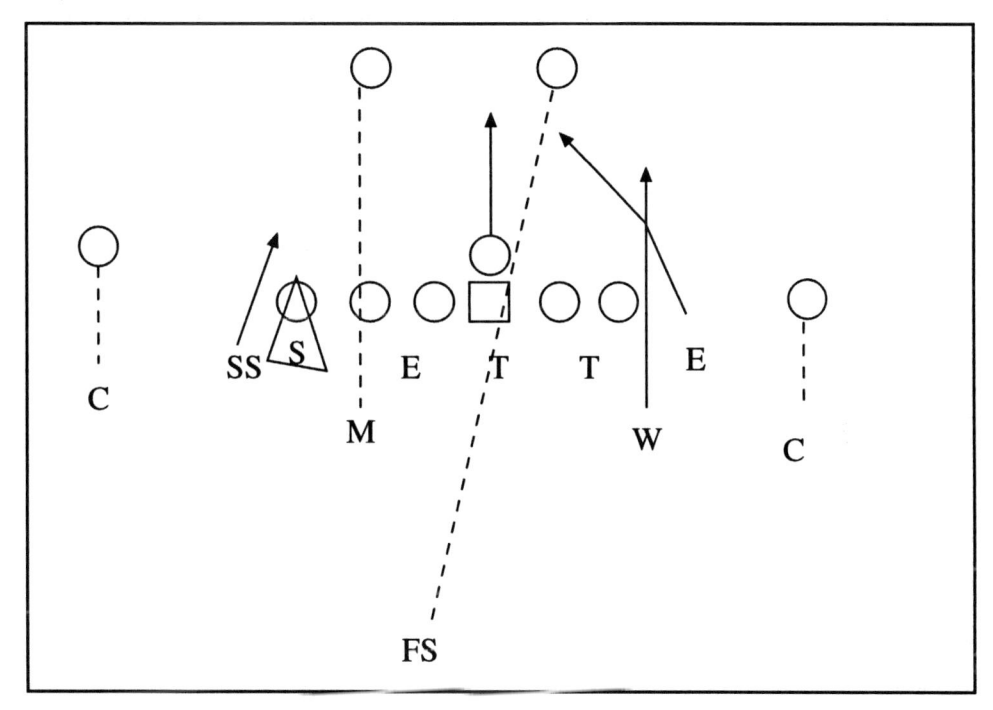

Diagram 10-13: Single Will "up."

Spy Blitz:

Spy Blitz is an excellent blitz versus the split-back alignment. Most beneficial as a complement to the single blitz, the spy blitz resembles single but provides the maximum amount of inside pressure between the tackles. The spy blitz is also discussed in more detail in Chapter 9.

The stunt is a good weakside stunt. As a weakside stunt, it involves the weakside defensive end dropping off into man-to-man pass coverage versus a delayed pattern out of the weakside nearback. If the weakside nearback drives into the pattern immediately on the snap, the defensive end replaces the Will linebacker in the pass rush lane. When the defensive end replaces the Will linebacker as a pass rusher, the Will linebacker drops into man-to-man coverage on the releasing back. Anytime the nearback is aligned wide (e.g., outside the tackle, wide slot, etc.), the Will linebacker must take him. The defensive end cannot be expected to cover a wide-set slotback.

The Mike and Will linebackers read their backs. If either one or both of the backs block, the linebacker blitzes through his respective A gap. In general, the Will linebacker should attempt to beat his back's block to the outside, while Mike should attempt to beat his man to the inside. If one or both backs release hot, the linebackers cover their respective backs.

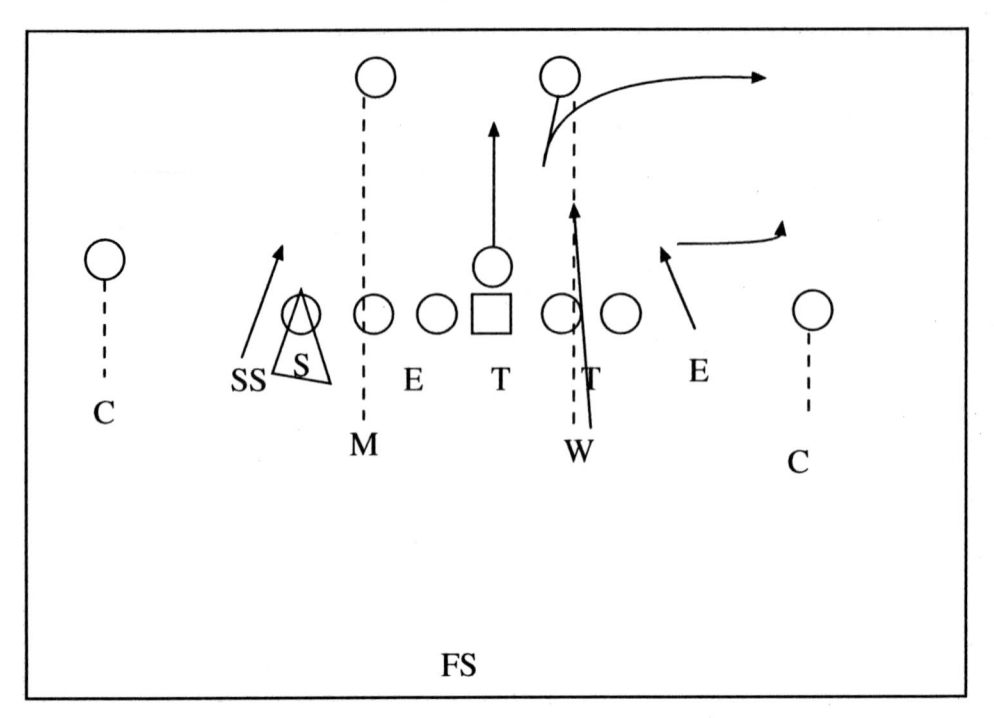

Diagram 10-13a: The weakside back delay releasing versus the spy blitz.

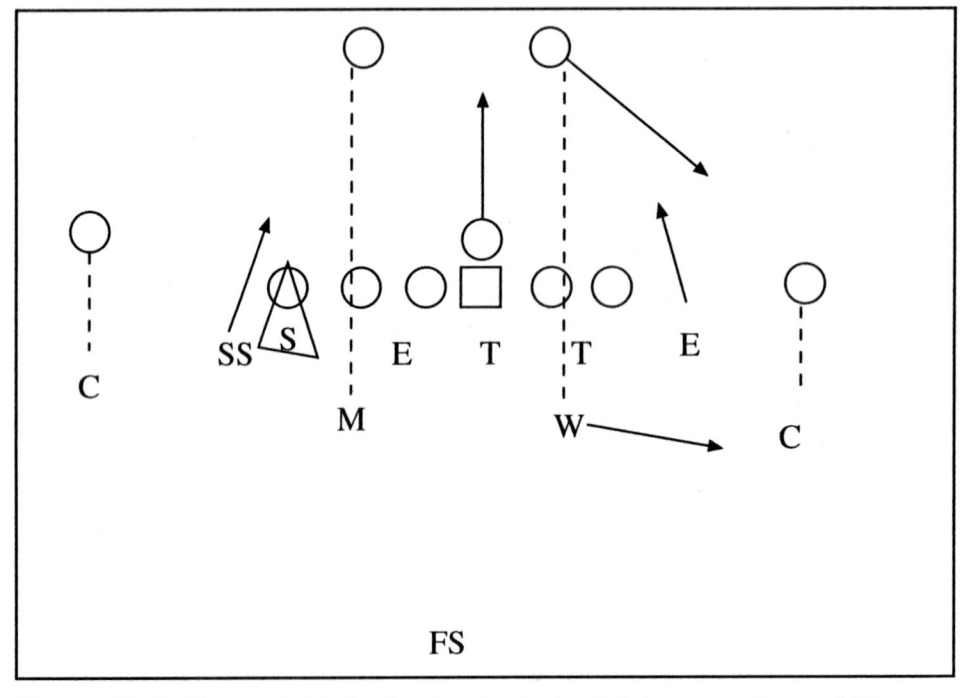

Diagram 10-14: The weakside back releasing immediately versus the spy blitz.

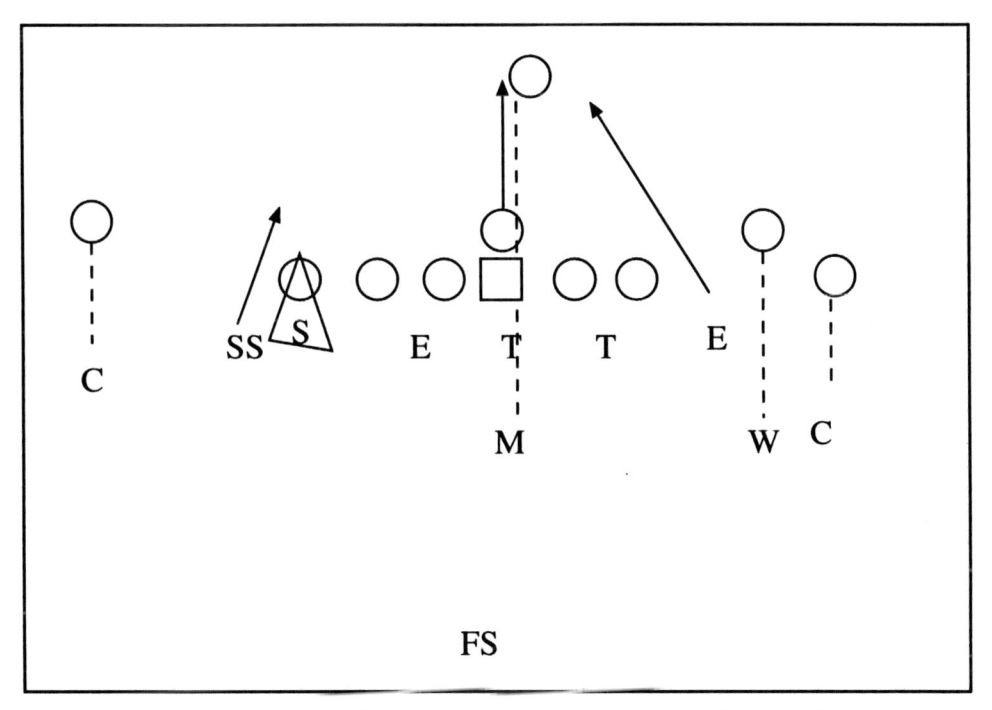

Diagram 10-15: The weakside back set in a wide slot versus the spy blitz.

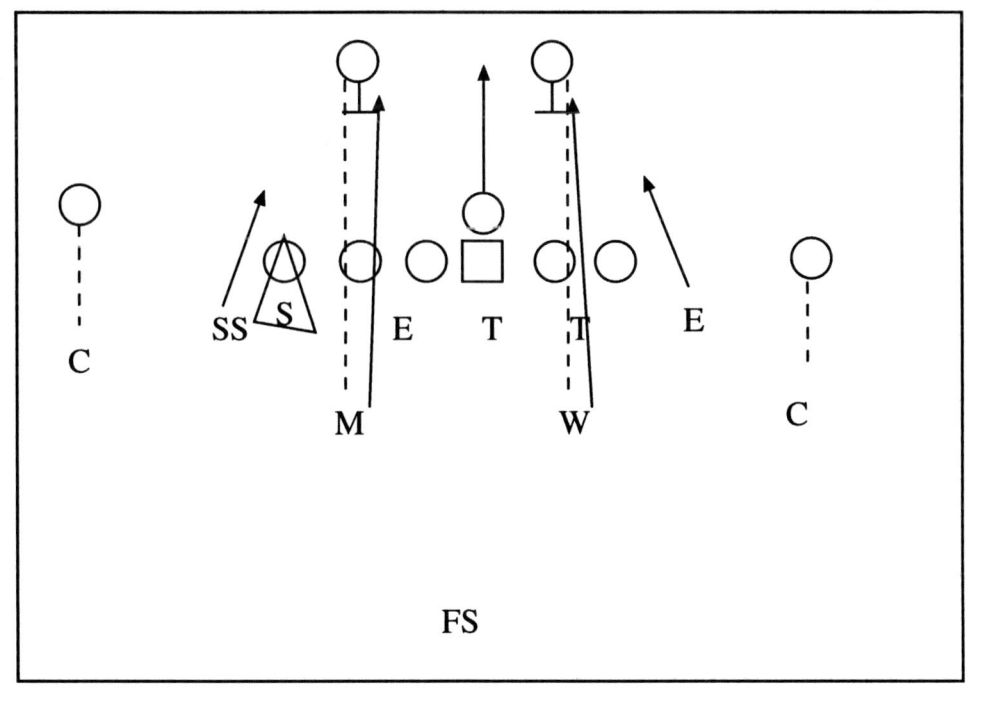

Diagram 10-16: Both backs blocking versus the spy blitz.

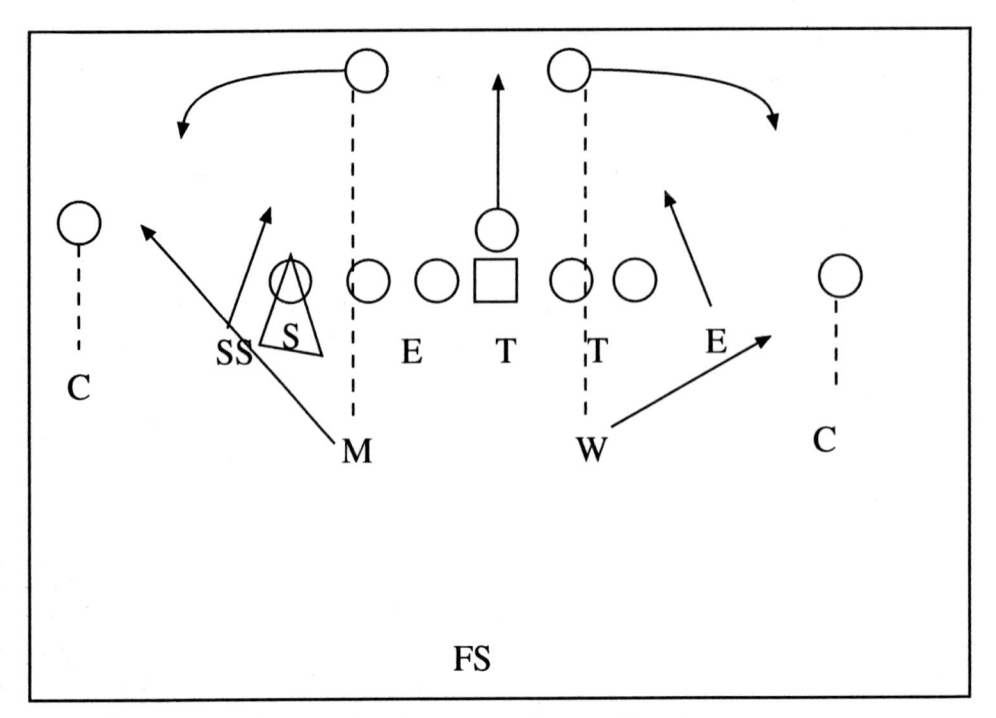

Diagram 10-17: Both backs releasing versus the spy blitz.

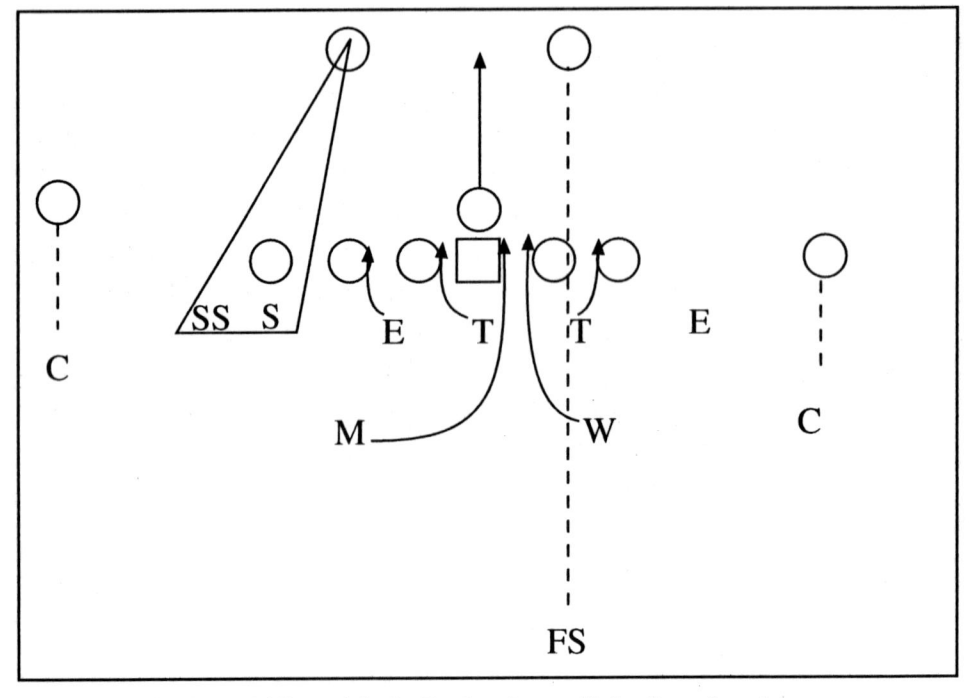

Diagram 10-18: The 50 blitz with the linebackers off the line of scrimmage.

While it is not the most effective blitz versus teams that spread the field with multiple wide formations, the spy blitz is exceptionally productive versus teams that prefer slide protection schemes.

The 50 Blitz:

An inside pressure blitz, the 50 blitz is characterized by an up-the-gut charge by the Mike and Will linebackers. The free safety replaces the Will linebacker in the coverage scheme. If teams like to spread the field, the 50 blitz is a particularly useful blitz. It can be run from the two-linebacker Jayhawk adjustment or from the 46 look. If the number two receiver aligned to the weak side is in the wide slot, the Will linebacker can still run the blitz. Remember, it is better to get the jump on the blockers and break from the disguised alignment prematurely, rather than be late and be ineffective on providing pressure.

Will 6Z:

A major variation from the aforementioned single coverage supported blitzes, the Will 6Z blitz is supported by the loaded zone concept of the 6Z coverage. Described in Chapter 9, the 6Z coverage concept is founded upon the free safety rotating over to cover the deep 1/2 of the field while the backside cornerback locks in man-to-man on the Z receiver. The weakside rotation and man underneath scheme of the 6Z coverage is a superior counter to the weakside formations, especially those of the sight reading three-receiver offenses. Against such attacks as the run-and-shoot (i.e., chuck and duck), the Will 6Z stunt is a showstopper.

Shown in Diagram 10-21, the 6Z blitz allows for an exchange between the weakside cornerback and Mike linebacker. If the number one receiver weakside breaks inward, the Mike will pick him up. More importantly, as the number one receiver breaks inside, the cornerback looks through the receiver to the inside route. Once the inside route is determined to be breaking through the zone, the cornerback releases the wide receiver to the Mike linebacker and covers the out-breaking inside receiver. Meanwhile, both the Mike and the cornerback are supported by a deep 1/2 zone rotation of the free safety.

Clearly, the Will's showing of the blitz from a position over the slot receiver baits the sight-reading quarterback to attempt to throw to the weak side. This reaction is precisely the objective of the Will 6Z blitz. As Diagram 10-21 shows, whenever the quarterback throws weakside versus the Will 6Z blitz, he is throwing into the teeth of the coverage. The trap is set weakside—and even the most skilled veteran quarterback has fallen prey to the Will 6Z blitz.

The blitz can be enhanced by a "cowboy" call, as well as other stunts. The cowboy call sends the weakside end to the inside and further baits the quarterback into throwing weak with the on-the-line-of-scrimmage alignment of the Will linebacker.

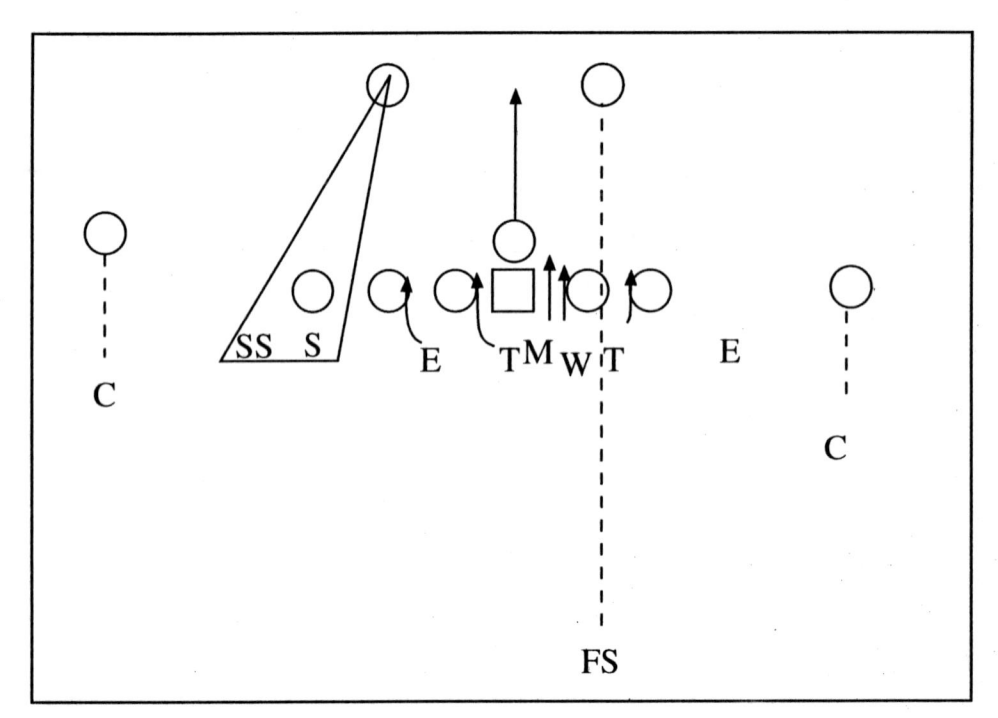

Diagram 10-19: The 50 blitz with the linebackers on the line of scrimmage.

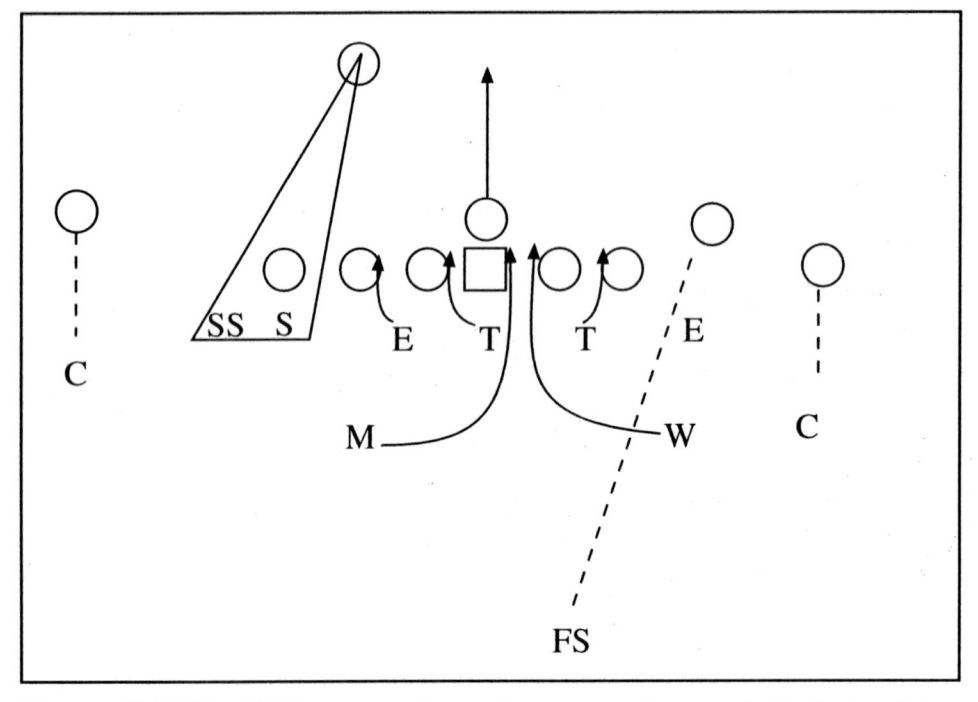

Diagram 10-20: The 50 blitz versus the number two receiver weakside in the slot.

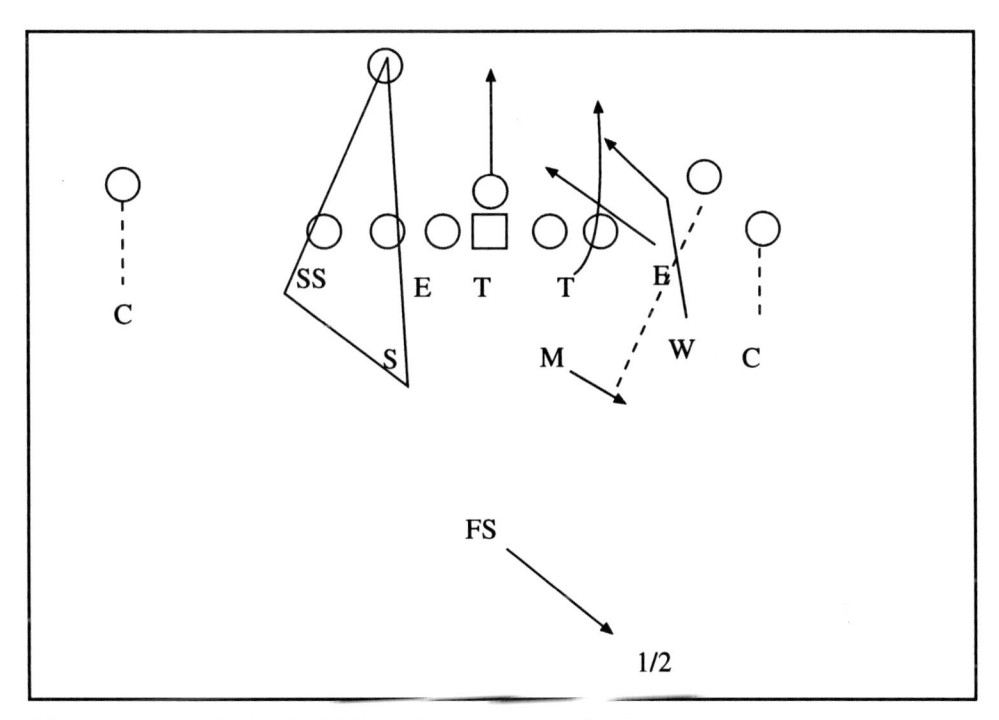

Diagram 10-21: The Will 6Z blitz—from a Jayhawk adjustment.

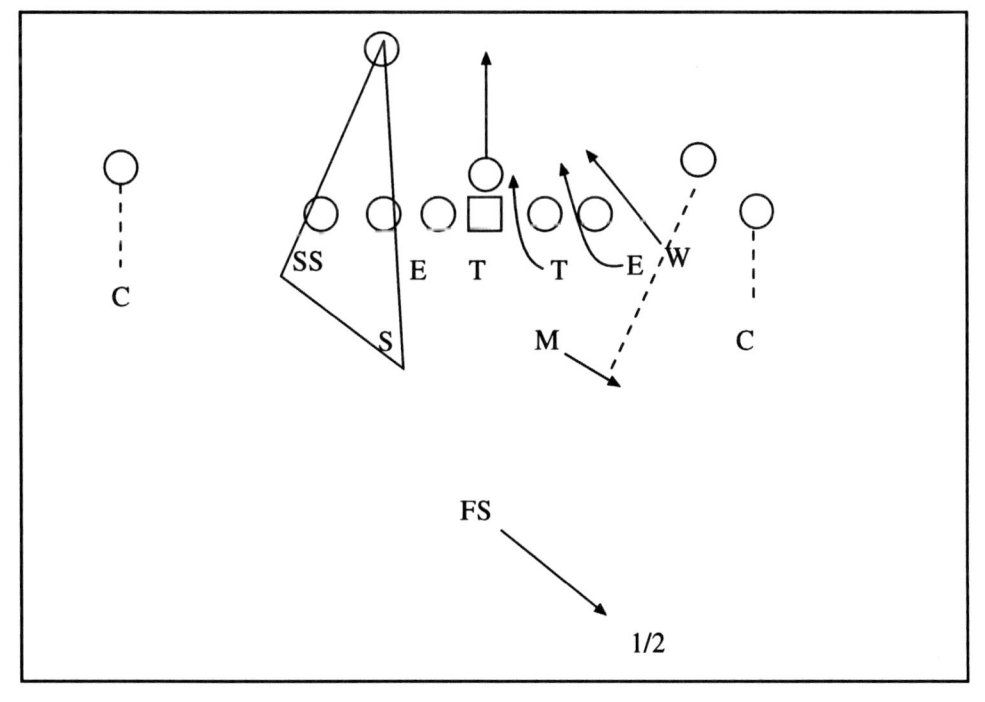

Diagram 10-22: The Will 6Z blitz with a cowboy call—from a Jayhawk adjustment.

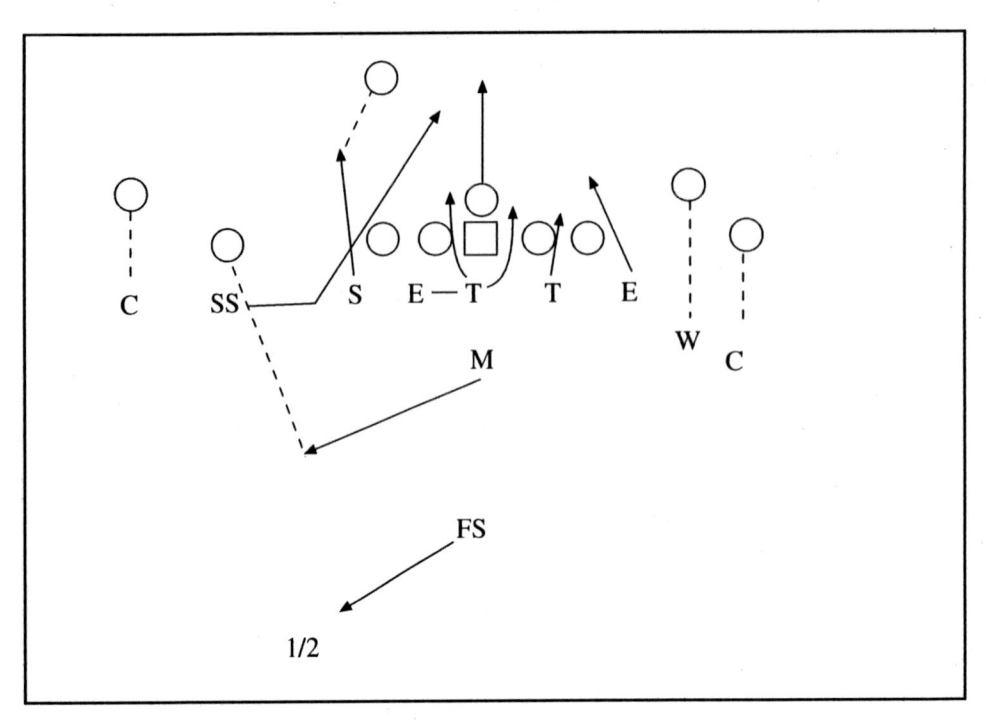

Diagram 10-23: The Giant blitz shown with a "nut" stunt.

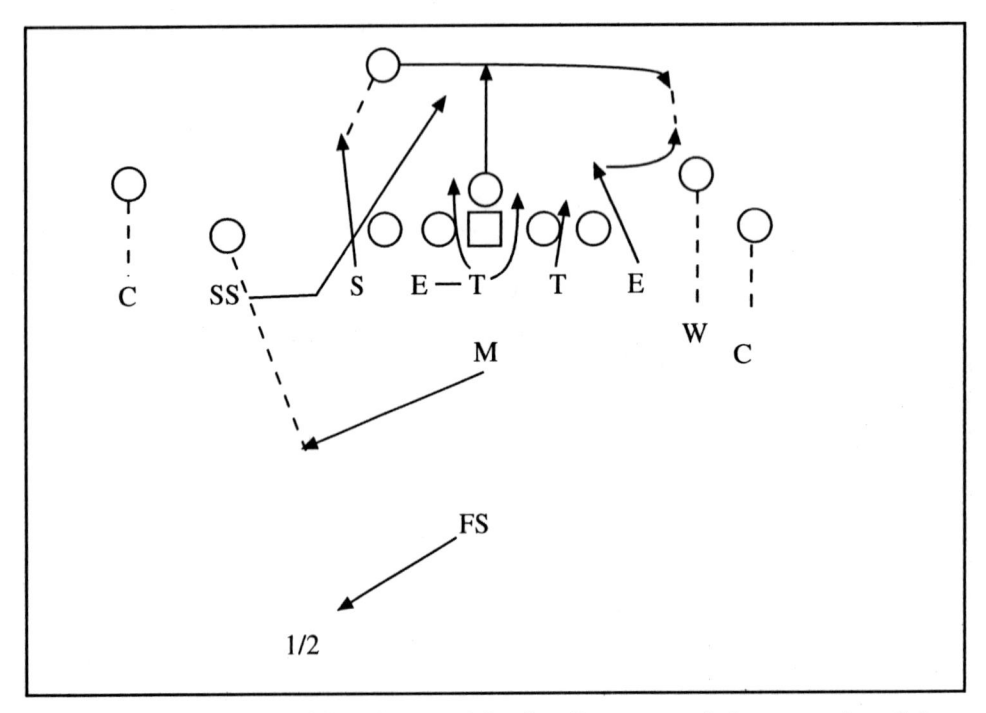

Diagram 10-24: The giant blitz shown with a "nut" stunt—and the execution of the train call.

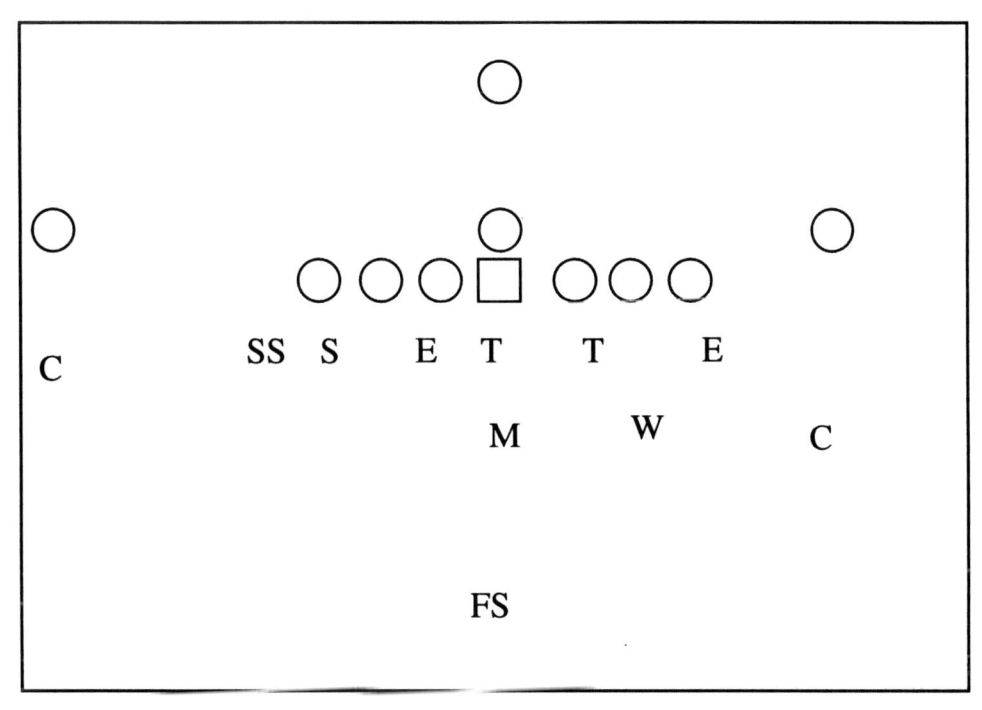

Diagram 10-25: The 46 alignment versus a one-back, two-tight end set.

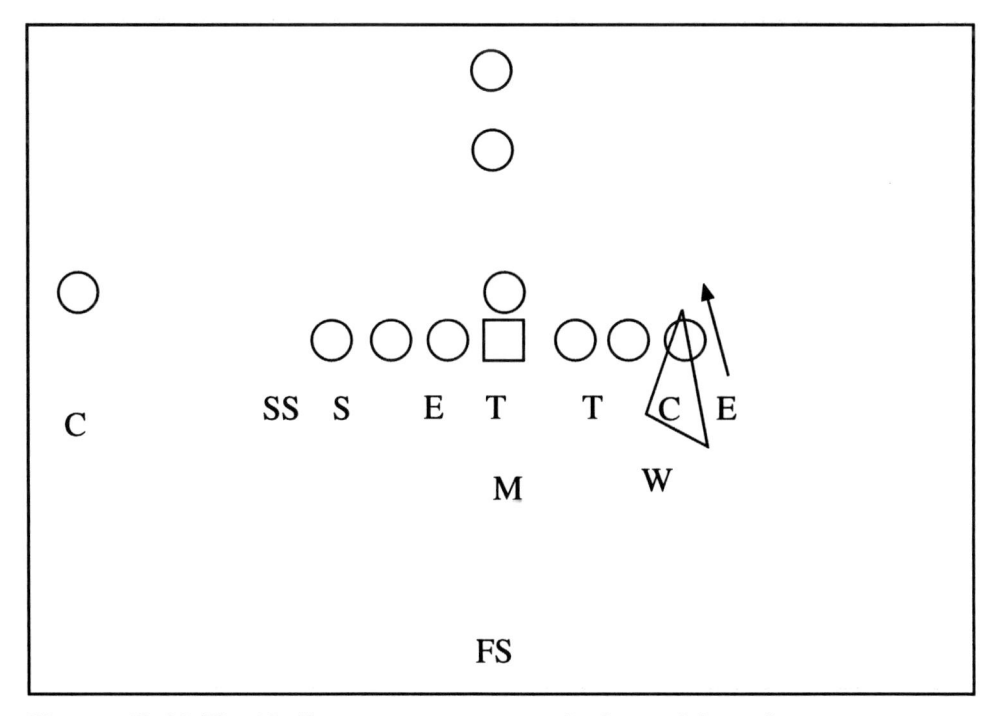

Diagram 10-26: The 46 alignment versus a standard two-tight end set.

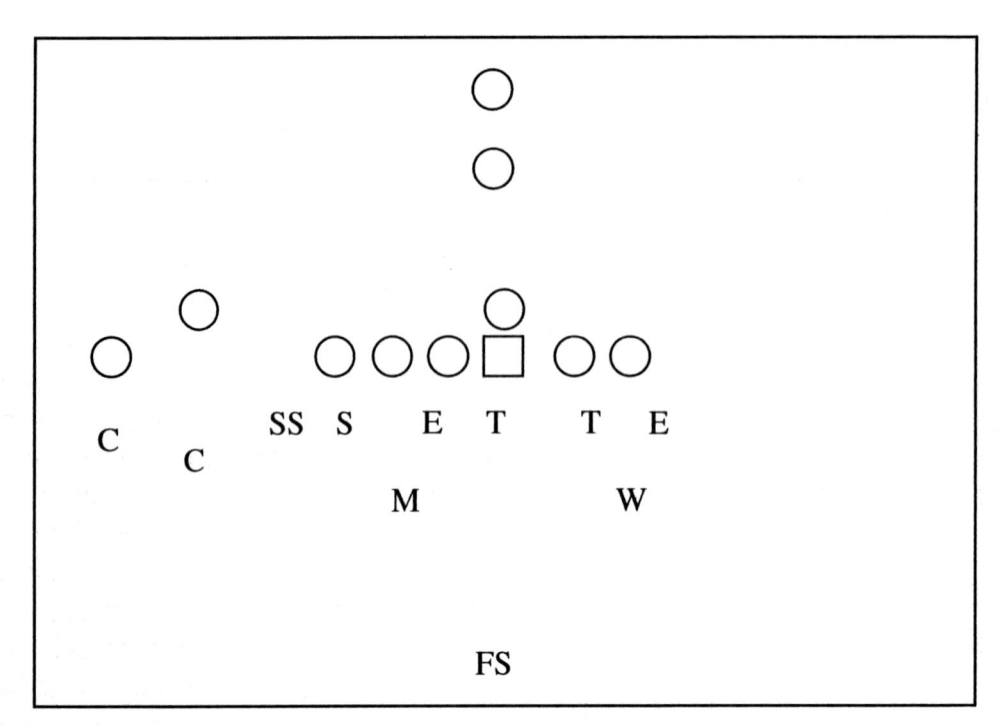

Diagram 10-27: The 46 alignment versus an end-over formation.

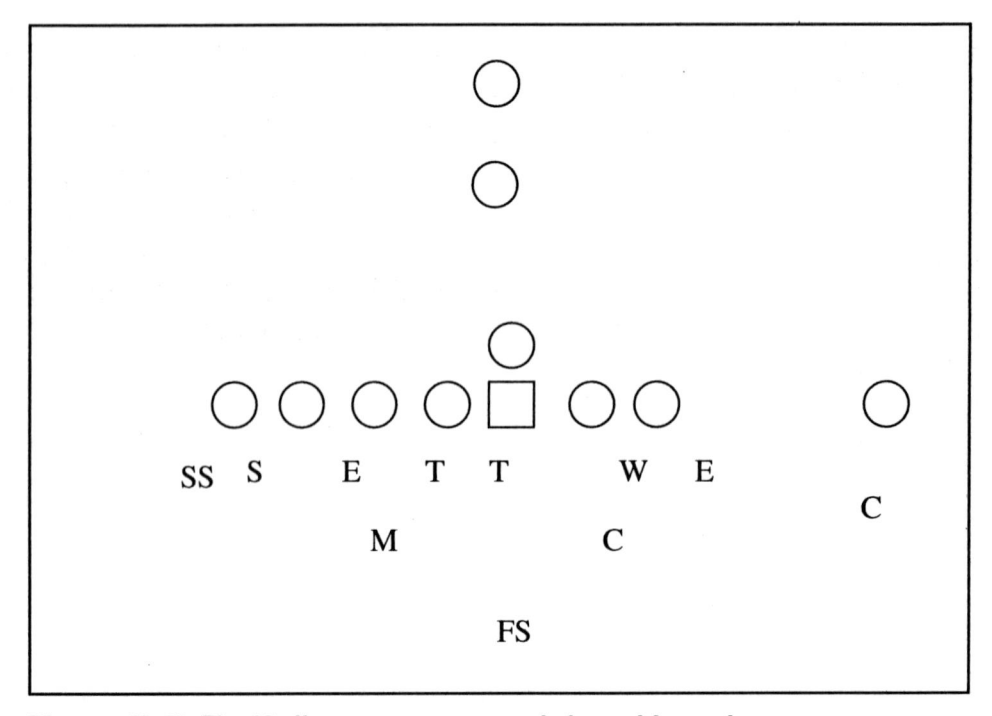

Diagram 10-28: The 46 alignment versus an unbalanced formation.

The Giant Blitz:

The mirror of the Will 6Z blitz is the giant blitz. It is designed for maximum efficiency against strong trips (i.e., three receivers aligned to the tight end side) or four wide receivers. Basically a Will 6Z blitz to the strong side, the giant blitz requires the Sam linebacker to play the peel coverage technique. The peel coverage technique is a technique that the Sam—or other linebacker—uses when he rushes the passer. If a back crosses his face in an attempt to release into a pattern, the linebacker peels off to cover him.

Another important blitz technique which we have not previously discussed is the train technique. Again, this technique involves the perimeter player who is rushing the passer. The train call is made whenever an outside linebacker, such as the Sam linebacker or strong safety, is required to cover a back set to his side. Theoretically, as long as the set back releases toward the covering linebacker, that linebacker is in good shape to peel and cover him. However, if the set back crosses over the formation as the ball is snapped, it would be unsound to expect the linebacker to cover him from the opposite side of the formation. This is where the train technique comes in. Whenever a back is a threat to release across the formation, the responsible perimeter player makes a train call to the opposite perimeter rusher. This alerts the opposite defender to pick up the back, should he cross the formation. Indeed, with practice and refinement, many of the train calls can be understood to be unsaid and a natural defensive response.

46 Adjustments:

One common question about the 46 adjustments is the two-tight end dilemma. The answer is simple. Diagram 10-25 shows the one effective alignment versus two tight ends. Another, more unusual, but also effective adjustment is shown in Diagram 10-26.

Diagram 10-27 shows one good alignment versus a typical end-over set with the Y receiver on the two-man side. And while diagram 10-28 shows an unusual alignment with the cornerback up, the alignment shown against the typical tackle-over type of unbalanced formation allows for flexibility in adjusting to backfield motion. The free cornerback is capable of taking the running back motion out to either side of the ball.

ABOUT THE AUTHORS

Rex Ryan is the defensive line coach of the NFL's Baltimore Ravens. Prior to assuming his present position in 1999, he served as the defensive coordinator at the University of Oklahoma, where his Sooners' defense ranked sixth nationally in total defense, second overall in the Big 12. Before that, as defensive coordinator at the University of Cincinnati (1996-97), Ryan helped lead the Bearcats' defense to the No. 13 ranking in the nation. In 1994-95, Ryan was the defensive line coach for the Arizona Cardinals, whose defensive front was considered the dominant force in the trenches of the NFL during that period. From 1990 to 1993, Ryan coached Morehead State's nationally ranked defense, which set school records in quarterback sacks and interceptions. He also coached at New Mexico Highlands University in 1989.

Jeff Walker possesses a master of education degree from Schreiner College and a bachelor of arts degree from Northeast Louisiana University. A high school coach with over 14 years' experience, Walker has contributed numerous articles to *Scholastic Coach* and *Athletic Director* magazines and is the author of the book, *Coaching Football's 40 Nickel Defense*. Walker resides in Kerrville, Texas, with his wife, Paula, and son, Gabe.

FOUR EXCEPTIONAL VIDEOS
ON
FOOTBALL'S 46 DEFENSE
by Rex Ryan

- **FOOTBALL'S 46 DEFENSE: THE BASE PLAN**
  1998 • 56 minutes • ISBN 1-58518-605-8 • $40.00

- **FOOTBALL'S 46 DEFENSE: BLITZES**
  1998 • 102 minutes • ISBN 1-57167-229-X • $40.00

- **FOOTBALL'S 46 DEFENSE: FUNDAMENTALS OF MAN FREE AND ROTATION COVERAGES**
  1998 • 82 minutes • ISBN 1-57167-228-1 • $40.00

- **FOOTBALL'S 46 DEFENSE: FUNDAMENTALS OF THE THREE-DEEP ZONE**
  1998 • 47 minutes • ISBN 1-57167-231-1 • $40.00

TO PLACE YOUR ORDER:
CALL TOLL FREE: (888) 229-5745
MAIL: COACHES CHOICE
       P.O. Box 1828, Monterey, CA 93942
FAX: (831) 372-6075
ONLINE: www.coacheschoice.com

ADDITIONAL FOOTBALL RESOURCES FROM COACHES CHOICE

101 Dropback Pass Patterns
Steve Axman, University of Washington
2002 • 124 pp • ISBN 1-58518-591-4 • $16.95

101 Wing-T A to Z Plays
Dennis Creehan, Duke University
2002 • 116 pp • ISBN 1-58518-594-9 • $16.95

101 Zone Offense Plays
Stan Zweifel, University of Wisconsin-Whitewater
2002 • 128 pp • ISBN 1-58518-404-7 • $16.95

101 Offensive Line Drills
Steve Loney, Minnesota Vikings
2001 • 124 pp • ISBN 1-58518-258-3 • $16.95

101 Defensive Line Drills
Mark Snyder, Ohio State University
1999 • 117 pp • ISBN 1-58518-235-4 • $16.95

TO PLACE YOUR ORDER:
CALL TOLL FREE: 888-229-5745
MAIL: COACHES CHOICE
P.O. BOX 1828, Monterey, CA 93942
FAX: 831-372-6075
ONLINE: www.coacheschoice.com